Anti-Oppressive Education in "Elite" Schools

Anti-Oppressive Education in "Elite" Schools

Promising Practices and Cautionary Tales from the Field

EDITED BY

Katy Swalwell
Daniel Spikes

Afterword by Paul C. Gorski

TEACHERS COLLEGE PRESS

TEACHERS COLLEGE | COLUMBIA UNIVERSITY
NEW YORK AND LONDON

Published by Teachers College Press,® 1234 Amsterdam Avenue, New York, NY 10027

Library of Congress Cataloging-in-Publication Data

Names: Swalwell, Katy M., editor.
Title: Anti-oppressive education in "elite" schools : promising practices and cautionary tales from the field / edited by Katy Swalwell, Daniel Spikes ; afterword by Paul C. Gorski.
Description: New York : Teachers College Press, [2021] | Includes bibliographical references and index.
Identifiers: LCCN 2021018659 (print) | LCCN 2021018660 (ebook) | ISBN 9780807765890 (Paperback : acid-free paper) | ISBN 9780807765906 (Hardcover : acid-free paper) | ISBN 9780807779842 (eBook)
Subjects: LCSH: Upper class—Education—United States. | Private schools—United States. | Social justice—Study and teaching—United States. | Critical pedagogy—United States. | Teachers—Training of.
Classification: LCC LC4941 .A58 2021 (print) | LCC LC4941 (ebook) | DDC 371.826/210973—dc23
LC record available at https://lccn.loc.gov/2021018659
LC ebook record available at https://lccn.loc.gov/2021018660

ISBN 978-0-8077-6589-0 (paper)
ISBN 978-0-8077-6590-6 (hardcover)
ISBN 978-0-8077-7984-2 (ebook)

Printed on acid-free paper
Manufactured in the United States of America

For Beau and Thea Henderson
and
Gabby, Hannah, and Maddy Spikes

Contents

Acknowledgments

First and foremost, we are overwhelmed by the quality of contributions each author made to this volume and are beyond grateful to each of them. They demonstrated incredible grace through Katy's maternity leave, Daniel's cross-country move, a pandemic, a last-minute request to shorten their pieces to make room for additional voices, and a slew of delays to see this project through to the end. We thank our partners, Heath and Garisa; our mentors; and our dear colleague-friends who supported us throughout this process in ways big and small. Our gratitude extends to Brian Ellerbeck and Lori Tate at Teachers College Press, as well as Mona Tiwary and Preeti Saini of Westchester Publishing Services, whose support, patience, thoughtfulness, creativity, and expertise made what you're about to read possible. Last, but not least, we would be remiss if we did not acknowledge the influence of Rubén A. Gaztambide Fernández and Adam Howard on this book. Years ago, they envisioned a sequel to their edited volume, *Educating Elites: Class Privilege and Educational Advantage* (2010), and invited Katy to join them. With their gracious support, we have moved this volume forward and are indebted to their groundbreaking work that has influenced a generation of educators. Thank you!

Introduction

One Way to Make Change?

Katy Swalwell

Thank you for picking up *Anti-Oppressive Education in "Elite" Schools: Promising Practices and Cautionary Tales from the Field*. Before diving into the thoughtful essays assembled here, my co-editor Daniel and I wanted to give a bit of backstory about the title. As anyone who has ever written something knows, coming up with the perfect precious few words that make up a title can consume as much time and intellectual energy as the body of the text that follows. In particular, we want to unpack the terms "elite" and "anti-oppressive education" before you dive into the rest of this book.

DEFINITIONS AND CONNOTATIONS

In my past work, and in the contributions to this volume, "elite" has served as a synonym for people who seemingly benefit from unjust power relations—those who engage in opportunity hoarding and leveraging whatever privilege they can to ensure that systems built on white supremacy, colonialism, capitalism, ableism, and heteropatriarchy continue to work for them, even as they may espouse nominal support for a more just world (Kendi, 2019). In this framing, an "elite school" connotes an educational institution aiding and abetting in the production of "elite status"—not a school that is *actually* better than others, even when we may admire the practices within them.

But we know that other understandings and uses of "elite" exist, threatening to be counterproductive in our efforts to disrupt those unjust power relations. For example, check out this tweet that my dear friend, the brilliant scholar Noreen Naseem Rodríguez, shared with me. It was written by Akil Bello, senior director of advocacy and advancement at FairTest.

Electric Summer Slide
@akilbello

elite schools = rich
elite families = rich
elite colleges = rich

stop equating rich with smarter, better, etc

stop saying elite.

7:21 PM · Aug 19, 2020 · Twitter Web App

Point taken.

As someone who taught in a summer program at a swanky boarding school in Connecticut while spending the academic year at a public school in rural Minnesota, I can attest to the fact that a school's national reputation has very little to do with actual quality (i.e., students' intellectual curiosity and well-being, teachers' creativity and competence, and so forth) and more to do with its ability to confer social capital via networks of wealth and institutional power. Switching to the term "elit*ist*" was no better, as that term conveys a belief that one's elevated status justifies greater power. The "truth" of some higher quality goes unquestioned, reinforcing the powerful myth of meritocracy.

As we struggled to come up with a title, I half-jokingly suggested to my co-editor, Daniel, that we should call the book *How to Help Rich, White Kids Not Become Dangerous Assholes*. Something about that seemed unnecessarily cheeky. Of course, it's not just rich, white kids who attend schools of wealth and whiteness—or who are at risk of becoming dangerous assholes. We also wanted our title to convey our mix of optimism and cynicism about what kind of anti-oppressive teaching and learning are even possible in such schools. Even using "elite" in quotes with this introduction explaining our definition makes me a bit nervous, but I was ultimately convinced that Internet algorithms filtering the search terms of our title will help get the book into the hands of the people we want to read it: those who learn and work in schools that are pipelines of institutionalized power.

Which brings me to the other term I want to quickly define: "anti-oppressive education." Anti-oppressive education, in both the content of curriculum and the mode of instruction, works to disrupt systemic white supremacy interwoven with capitalism embedded within heteronormative, ableist, and patriarchal structures continuing to produce distinct paths of opportunities and protections for dominant (i.e., white, wealthy) groups (Ayers et al., 2009). If this is new information to you, the rest of this book will not make any sense. Put it down and start listening to one of the wonderful history podcasts out there focused on counternarratives like *Asian American History 101, All My Relations, Teaching Hard Histories, Our Dirty Laundry,* or *Making Gay History.* Pick up books like *An African American and Latinx History of the United States* (Ortiz, 2018); *Stamped from the Beginning* (Kendi, 2017); *For All the People: Uncovering the Hidden History of Cooperation, Cooperative Movements, and Communalism in America* (Curl, 2012); *How to Hide an Empire* (Immerwahr, 2019); *An Indigenous People's History of the United States* (Dunbar Ortiz, 2014); *The Making of Asian America* (Lee, 2015); *A Black Women's History of the United States* (Berry & Gross, 2020); *A Queer History of the United States* (Bronski, 2011); or *A Disability History of the United States* (Nielsen, 2012). And then come back to this book, of course.

A CONTEXT OF CHAOS

While attempting anti-oppressive education in "elite" schools has always been fraught, it was especially so this past year. The dumpster fire of 2020 was one frustrating, scary mess after another, demanding an urgent reconsideration of what happens in "elite" schools—including whether they ought to exist at all. For example, political leaders' inability and unwillingness to "flatten the curve" of the coronavirus pandemic led to a devastating economic fallout and hundreds of thousands of deaths, exacerbating existing inequalities like racial disparities in health care, saddling working-class parents with impossible childcare dilemmas, escalating anti-Asian racism, and complicating responses to increasingly devastating climate disasters. Unsurprisingly, many well-resourced families and schools found ways to avoid the worst of it. For example, some parents paid thousands of dollars a month for "learning pod" tutors (Berman, 2020), and some private schools actively recruited disaffected wealthy parents away from public schools (Blad, 2020) with perks like an epidemiologist on staff and thermal scanners in the hallway (Miller, 2020). While teachers in *all* settings risked mental and physical health as they juggled between hybrid and virtual offerings, educators at many well-resourced schools did not have to contend with additional layers of frustration facing their under-resourced colleagues like inadequate technology for staff and students and high-stakes testing pressures.

All of this unfolded amidst a uniquely polarizing U.S. presidential administration and a racial reckoning unseen in decades. In April, people trapped inside by quarantine helped video of George Floyd's murder at the hands of police go viral, sparking worldwide protests in support of the Black Lives Matter movement. Black students launched #BlackAt social media campaigns sharing stories of racial trauma at school, revealing the superficiality of their prestigious educational institution's mission statements and diversity initiatives (Nguyen, 2020). Meanwhile, President Trump called celebrated anti-oppressive curriculum like *The 1619 Project* "child abuse"[1] and banned federal agencies from requiring anti-bias trainings focused on white privilege or Critical Race Theory.[2]

In the flurry of handwringing from "liberal" white-centered institutions and individuals, scholars and activists cautioned against performativity rather than the deep and dangerous work necessary for dismantling long-standing systems of oppression. For example, journalist Erin Logan (2020) quoted historian Hasan Kwame Jeffries about the "distinction between the motivations of white and Black protesters"—the former driven by the "fierce urgency of the future" and the latter responding to "intolerable and immediate injustice." According to Dr. Jeffries, "What you're willing to sacrifice, demand and compromise is going to be different. . . . There is a shared sense of the problem but your immediate objective is fundamentally different." Dr. Jeffries's insight has special meaning for anti-oppressive educators teaching in affluent, majority white schools. The pacing and objectives of efforts to dismantle the tangled systems of oppression must center the needs and voices of those most immediately and negatively affected if we have any hope of using young people's education to redirect their formation as "elites" and to influence the distribution of resources in more just and humane ways. Full stop.

QUESTIONS WITH NO EASY ANSWERS

Let's circle back to the word "elite." What would *actually* constitute an elite school in the truest sense of the word as "best,"[3] one that is *genuinely* anti-oppressive and excels at working toward equity and justice, doing right by the most vulnerable kids and communities through a network of interdependence? What structures, policies, and practices would need to be imagined in order to bring this kind of education to life? What would help it survive in a context of hyper-individualism, unsustainable consumerism, and capitalism invested in racism, heterosexism, ableism, and colonialism? At the end of the day, is there any way to leverage conventionally "elite" educational spaces for justice?

These are the questions this book seeks to engage, in all their complications and tensions.[4] They have dogged me for years as I have sifted through advice for anti-oppressive educators, most of which presumes working with oppressed youth. In the "elite" contexts where I grew up, taught, and researched, I noticed students assuming their voices mattered to people in power, easily opining at length on just about any topic, enjoying all sorts of opportunities to demonstrate their "leadership potential," and performing wokeness by expressing outrage about oppression long ago or far away with no attention to their own complicity. In *Pedagogy of the Oppressed*, critical pedagogue Paolo Freire (1970) could have been talking about my own experiences as a straight, cis, affluent, currently able-bodied, settler white woman as he cautioned against the "false generosity" of oppressors, "nourished by an unjust order, which must be maintained in order to justify that generosity" (p. 60). Because oppressors are unable to liberate themselves—as "only power that springs from the weakness of the oppressed will be sufficiently strong to free both" (p. 44)—Freire stresses we cannot be leaders in this struggle given our self-inflicted dehumanization. Instead, he hints at the ways we might serve as revolutionary co-conspirators.

Here was a sliver of hope that anti-oppressive efforts in "elite" educational spaces have a shot at being one way to help disrupt cycles of oppression. It must be different than a pedagogy of the oppressed, but it might just be possible. My own research bolstered my optimism, as I spent a year with two accomplished educators trying to engage in anti-oppressive education at a public and private high school serving predominantly white, wealthy kids (Swalwell, 2013, 2015). While I witnessed many examples of the "false generosity" Freire warns against, something changed for these students when they had to listen deeply to painful truths from the perspectives of people experiencing oppression, make emotional connections to their learning, and confront local historical and contemporary injustices that directly implicated their own families. It seemed like youth who were otherwise being groomed for domination were being rerouted toward joining in efforts of liberation.

To be honest, that sliver of hope from my research and reflection comes and goes. Isn't even this "better" teaching and learning still complicit in oppression if it exists within institutions that rely on racism and capitalism for their existence? In a thoughtful response to my scholarship, Rubén Gaztambide-Fernández and Adam Howard (2013) rightly urged me not to be too optimistic.[5] They noted that the projection of one's self as "justice-oriented" has "considerable ideological value" in that it can easily divert attention away from the power of dominant groups by convincing subordinates that they are "compassionate, kind, and giving." They question "whether and how individuals with economic privilege can ever be effectively involved in social justice efforts and what their role should be." They continue:

> On the one hand, it may be that providing access to the economic resources necessary to support social justice efforts is reason enough to persist in instilling justice-oriented values. . . . On the other hand, if providing such resources only serves to reinforce the hierarchical positioning of wealthy elites as morally superior and as capable of enacting the ultimate form of good citizenship by becoming allies with the poor, fundamental social change is highly unlikely. (p. 3)

Here's what really got me:

> Unless economically privileged individuals are willing to examine their sense
> of entitlement and challenge their own privileged ways of knowing and do-
> ing, being in solidarity with less fortunate others will remain about improving
> themselves. At an institutional level, this means that [elite schools] would have
> to put their very reputations—along with their economic privilege—on the line
> by becoming not just more diverse . . . but by shifting the very fabric of privilege
> that clothes their elite reputations. (p. 4)

Their advice has profoundly shaped my thinking as I seek out others attempting anti-oppressive education in "elite" schools. What are people trying? What is working? And what does it even mean to work? In the words
of Gaztambide-Fernández and Howard, how can we shift the "very fabric
of privilege that clothes [our] elite reputations"?

Sometimes, it's easier to see what obviously *isn't* working. Take Sadhana
Bery's (2014) example of white teachers at a predominantly white private elementary school facilitating a student play about slavery. Red flags already,
right? At a meeting with understandably concerned Black parents, the head
of school explained that the play had come about because some students,
all white, had expressed a desire to experience what it was like to have been
enslaved. Unsurprisingly,

> Black parents questioned why the white students' desires to "experience be-
> ing a slave" was a sufficient reason for the teachers to produce the play. They
> asked why the teachers had not consulted them, since their children, the "de-
> scendants" of the enslaved represented in the play, would be impacted in ways
> that white teachers could not know or fully understand. The Head responded
> that no student was pressured into playing a particular role in the play. The
> teachers had cast the skit by telling all students, Whites, Blacks, and non-black
> non-Whites, to choose their roles, saying, "anyone can be anyone" and "if you
> don't want to be a slave, you can be a slave master." (p. 339)

Education professor Stephanie Jones calls this "curricular violence" (2020),
and it is all too common as a form of trauma for kids with minoritized and
marginalized identities within majority white, wealthy schools engaging in a
facsimile of the anti-oppressive education we're calling for here.

At the end of the day, we can't say with certainty that it's possible for
schools founded on cultivating distinction to *ever* become sites for radical
disruptions. Let's not forget the founding of many "elite" schools is *directly*
related to white, wealthy families resisting desegregation efforts through
the creation of "segregation academies" (Carr, 2012), vouchers (Ford et al.,
2017), magnet public schools (Buery, 2020), and white flight (e.g., Schneider,

2008).⁶ Even some progressive independent schools are tainted with this legacy. For example, the outstanding *New York Times*' podcast *Nice White Parents* reported by Chana Joffe-Wolt documents how white parents wrote letters to New York City school leaders in the 1960s pledging their support for integration but nevertheless sent their children to a majority white private school founded on "progressive values." Margaret A. Hagerman (2018) explains how progressive, white, wealthy parents still get caught in this "conundrum of privilege." In her research, Hagerman heard parents express a desire to align their ideals with their parenting choices, but "when it came to their own children," found them saying, "'I care about social justice, *but*—I don't want my kid to be a guinea pig.'" As a well-off white parent who hears the siren calls to hoard opportunity for my own children, that "but" doesn't surprise me. It does, however, sharpens my commitment to action and these questions with no easy answers.

Whatever brought them into being, schools of wealth and whiteness are unlikely to disappear any time soon. Yet within their walls are educators willing to fight the good fight with children who are soaking up all sorts of lessons informing their civic, financial, professional, and social decisions—decisions made more consequential given the institutionalized power many of them are about to literally and figuratively inherit (Bhalla & Barclay, 2020). When it comes to anti-oppressive education in "elite" schools, I have come to the conclusion that we have to at least *try*.

BUCKLE UP

The authors of the chapters in this book are among those trying hard to figure all of this out. To be sure, none of them offer easy solutions or trite answers to any of the questions raised here. Their wide range of identities and backgrounds brings unique perspective, expertise, and experience to help them address each section's guiding question as frankly as possible. Similarly, while Daniel and I hold different identities and work in different places—I'm a white teacher educator in Iowa and he's a Black assistant superintendent in Texas, for example—I invited him to join me as co-editor because we both value the space for dreaming facilitated by the academy as much as the nitty-gritty realities of the field. Our hope is that the best of both worlds is represented here.

Part I of this volume ("What's the Point? Justifying and Framing Anti-Oppressive Education in 'Elite' Schools") wrestles with the ultimate aims of anti-oppressive education in schools of wealth and whiteness. In "Combating the Pathology of Class Privilege: A Critical Education for the 'Elites,'" Quentin Wheeler-Bell explores which model of justice-oriented education for privileged youth is most justified. Adam Howard outlines the

"Intrinsic Aspects of Class Privilege," using examples from his own teaching to illuminate the development of a "privileged" self-understanding. In "Is Becoming an Oppressor Ever a Privilege? 'Elite' Schools and Social Justice as Mutual Aid," Nicolas Tanchuk, Tomas Rocha, and Marc Kruse draw on Indigenous and Black feminist thought to move beyond the discourse of "privilege" toward one of "mutual aid" using excerpts from *The Hate U Give* to exemplify their theory in action.

Part II ("Cautionary Tales: Problematic Models of Anti-Oppressive Education in 'Elite' Schools") explores the many ways that equity, diversity, and inclusion efforts at affluent, segregated schools (especially those claiming to be "progressive") can go very wrong, very fast. In "Beyond Wokeness: How White Educators Can Work Toward Dismantling Whiteness and White Supremacy in Suburban Schools," Gabriel Rodriguez shares vignettes pointing to ways schools can better serve Latinx students. Petra Lange and Callie Kane use personal narrative in "Dead Ends and Paths Forward: White Teachers Committed to Anti-Racist Teaching in White Spaces" to expose how the binary of "good" and "bad" is unproductive for white teachers working toward anti-racism. Ayo Magwood reviews the research on Black and Brown educators' experiences in independent schools, weaving in candid remembrances to expose "Unspoken Rules, White Communication Styles, and White Blinders: Why 'Elite' Independent Schools Can't Retain Black and Brown Faculty." Tania D. Mitchell takes conventional service-learning models to task in "Critical Service Learning: Moving from Transactional Experiences of Service Towards a Social Justice Praxis." Kristin Sinclair, Ashley Akerberg, and Brady Wheatley expose the reproduction of privilege of a high school study-abroad program called the Island School in "The 'Duality of Life' in 'Elite' Sustainability Education: Tensions, Pitfalls, and Possibilities." Lastly, Cori Jakubiak explores the problematics of English-language voluntourism in "The Possibility of Critical Language Awareness Through Volunteer English Teaching Abroad."

Part III ("Promising Practices? Ideas for Enacting Anti-Oppressive Education in 'Elite' Schools") taps into the expertise of practitioners attempting to avoid the pitfalls outlined in Part II. The question mark is intentional, as they offer honest assessments of how challenging and uncertain this work can be. In "Living Up to Our Legacy: One School's Effort to Build Momentum, Capacity, and Commitment to Social Justice," Christiane M. Connors, Steven Lee, Stacy Smith, and Damian R. Jones provide a step-by-step account of shifting the organizational culture at Edmund Burke School. Robin Moten reflects on the evolution of her social justice class in a predominantly white, wealthy, politically conservative community in "Opening the Proverbial Can O' Worms: Teaching Social Justice to Educated 'Elites' in Suburban Detroit." In "Facilitating Socially Just Discussions in 'Elite' Schools," Lisa Sibbett analyzes a class discussion enacting and exploring social justice to provide ideas for disrupting the "testimonial quieting and smothering" of students with non-dominant identities. In "Mobilizing Privileged Youth and Teachers for Justice-Oriented Work in Science and Education," Alexa Schindel, Brandon Grossman, and Sara Tolbert explore how the science curriculum can help decenter privilege. In "Intersectional Feminist and Political Education with Privileged Girls," Beth Cooper Benjamin, Amira Proweller, Beth Catlett, Andrea Jacobs, and Sonya Crabtree-Nelson reflect on their facilitation of the Research Training Internship, a program to help Jewish teen girls with racial and class privilege develop an emerging critical consciousness through youth participatory action research. Lastly, Diane Goodman and Rebecca Drago provide proactive suggestions for practitioners in "'Not Me!' Anticipating, Preventing, and Working with Pushback to Social Justice Education."

In Part IV, "Conversations with Colleagues," edited transcripts of conversations with practitioners complement their personal narratives. The full dialogues and discussion prompts for the book are available at our website: www.onewaytomakechange.org. Middle school teacher Allen Cross navigates the unresolved tensions and joys of his job in "Out of This Chaos, Beauty Comes: Democratic Schooling in a Progressive Independent Middle School." Gabby Arca and Nina Sethi contextualize a 3rd-grade simulation on wealth inequality and explain their teaching philosophy as women of color in "We Are Afraid They Won't Feel Bad: Using Simulations to Teach for Social Justice at the Elementary Level." Alethea Tyner Paradis, founder of Peace Works Travel, shares how she makes sense of opportunities for "Harnessing the Curiosity of Rich People's Children: International Travel as a Tool of Anti-Oppressive Education." Former admissions counselor Sherry Smith gives frank advice in "Building a Class: The Role of Admissions in Anti-Oppressive Education." And in "'It Shouldn't Be That Hard': Student Activists' Frustrations and Demands," high schoolers Julia Chen, Haley Hamilton, Vidya Iyer, Alfreda Jarue, Catalina Samaniego, Catreena Wang, and Jenna Woodsmall explain how and why they fight for an anti-racist education in two predominantly white, wealthy suburbs.

Is there any way to leverage "elite" educational spaces for justice? Daniel and I wrestle with this uncertainty, and I'm guessing most readers do, too. Educating young people in spaces designed to protect and reproduce unjust hierarchies *may* be one way to make change—and, if it is, it's going to take all of our creativity and savviness to make sure it's not a co-opted, hollowed-out version of what we intended it to be. Our hope as a collective is not to have all the answers, but to start conversations and to spark experiments. As I tell my 4-year-old daughter when she's about to dive into something challenging but exciting: buckle up, buttercup. Thank you for reading, and please keep us posted on your efforts—both the cautionary tales and promising practices of anti-oppressive education in "elite" schools. Good luck!

NOTES

1. https://www.whitehouse.gov/briefings-statements/remarks-president-trump
-white-house-conference-american-history/

2. https://www.whitehouse.gov/wp-content/uploads/2020/09/M-20–34.pdf

3. See Neema Avashia's (2020) essay "Why Landing on the 'Best Schools' List Is Not Something to Celebrate" for a thoughtful examination of these questions.

4. For another take on these questions, see Bellafante's (2017) article "Can Prep Schools Fight the Class War?" which quotes New York City's Trinity Head of School John Allman's fascinating letter to families expressing concern that the school produces a "cognitive elite that is self-serving, callous and spiritually barren."

5. Both scholars have made invaluable contributions to the small but mighty research base of elite education alongside other wonderful scholars like Leila Angod, Claire Maxwell, and Jane Kenway (e.g., Gaztambide-Fernández, 2011; Gaztambide-Fernández & Angod, 2019; Howard, 2013; Howard & Gaztambide-Fernández, 2010; Howard & Kenway, 2015; Howard & Maxwell, 2018).

6. For attention to the ways in which rich, white parents currently work the public schools in their favor, see Nikole Hannah-Jones's fantastic journalism, including the two-part *This American Life* episode entitled "The Problem We All Live With" (2015).

REFERENCES

Avashia, N. (2020, September 4). Why landing on the 'best schools' list is not something to celebrate. *Cognoscenti* from WBUR. https://www.wbur.org/cognoscenti/2020/09/04/boston-magazine-best-high-schools-greater-boston-neema-avashia

Ayers, W., Quinn, T. M., & Stovall, D. (Eds.). (2009). *Handbook of social justice in education*. Routledge.

Bellafante, G. (2017, September 22). Can prep schools fight the class war? *New York Times*. https://www.nytimes.com/2017/09/22/nyregion/trinity-school-letter-to-parents.html

Berman, J. (2020, July 28). From nanny services to 'private educators,' wealthy parents are paying up to $100 an hour for 'teaching pods' during the pandemic. *MarketWatch*. https://www.marketwatch.com/story/affluent-parents-are-setting-up-their-own-schools-as-remote-learning-continues-its-the-failure-of-our-institutions-to-adequately-provide-for-our-students-11595450980

Berry, D. R., & Gross, K. N. (2020). *A black women's history of the United States*. Beacon Press.

Bery, S. (2014). Multiculturalism, teaching slavery, and white supremacy. *Equity & Excellence in Education*, 47(3), 334–352.

Bhalla, J. & Barclay, E. (2020, October 12). How affluent people can end their mindless overconsumption. *VOX*. https://www.vox.com/21450911/climate-change-coronavirus-greta-thunberg-flying-degrowth

Blad, E. (2020, August 6). Private schools catch parents' eye as public school build-ings stay shut. *EdWeek*. https://www.edweek.org/ew/articles/2020/08/06/private-schools-catch-parents-eye-as-public.html

Bronski, M. (2011). *A queer history of the United States*. Beacon Press.

Buery, Jr., R. R. (2020). Public school admissions and the myth of meritocracy: How and why screened public school admissions promote segregation. *NYUL Review Online*, 95, 101.

Carr, S. (2012, December 13). In Southern towns, 'segregation academies' still going strong. *The Atlantic*. https://www.theatlantic.com/national/archive/2012/12/in-southern-towns-segregation-academies-are-still-going-strong/266207

Curl, J. (2012). *For all the people: Uncovering the hidden history of cooperation, cooperative movements, and communalism in America*. PM Press.

Dunbar Ortiz, R. (2014). *An indigenous peoples' history of the United States*. Beacon Press.

Ford, C., Johnson, S., & Partelow, L. (2017). The racist origins of private school vouch-ers. *Center for American Progress*. https://www.americanprogress.org/issues/education-k-12/reports/2017/07/12/435629/racist-origins-private-school-vouchers/

Freire, P. (1970). *Pedagogy of the oppressed* (M. Bergman Ramos, Trans.). Continuum.

Gaztambide-Fernández, R. (2011). Bullshit as resistance: Justifying unearned privi-lege among students at an elite boarding school. *International Journal of Quali-tative Studies in Education*, 24(5), 581–586.

Gaztambide-Fernández, R., & Angod, L. (2019). Approximating Whiteness: Race, class, and empire in the making of modern elite/White subjects. *Educational Theory*, 69(6), 719–743.

Gaztambide-Fernández, R. A., & Howard, A. (2013). Social justice, deferred complicity, and the moral plight of the wealthy. *Democracy and Education*, 21(1), 7.

Hagerman, M. A. (2018, September 30). White progressive parents and the conun-drum of privilege. *Los Angeles Times*. https://www.latimes.com/opinion/op-ed/la-oe-hagerman-white-parents-20180930-story.html

Hannah-Jones, N. (2015). The problem we all live with. *This American Life*. https://www.thisamericanlife.org/562/the-problem-we-all-live-with-part-one

Howard, A. (2013). *Learning privilege: Lessons of power and identity in affluent schooling*. Routledge.

Howard, A., & Gaztambide-Fernandez, R. A. (Eds.). (2010). *Educating elites: Class privilege and educational advantage*. R&L Education.

Howard, A. & Kenway, J. (2015). Canvassing conversations: obstinate issues in studies of elites and elite education. *International Journal of Qualitative Studies in Education*, 28(9), 1005–1032.

Howard, A., & Maxwell, C. (2018). From conscientization to imagining redistribu-tive strategies: Social justice collaborations in elite schools. *Globalisation, Soci-eties and Education*, 16(4), 526–540.

Immerwahr, D. (2019). *How to hide an empire: A short history of the greater United States*. Random House.

Jones, S. P. (2020). Ending curriculum violence. *Teaching Tolerance, 64*, 47–50.

Kendi, I. X. (2017). *Stamped from the beginning: The definitive history of racist ideas in America*. Random House.

Kendi, I. X. (2019). *How to be an antiracist*. One World.

Lee, E. (2015). *The making of Asian America: A history*. Simon and Schuster.

Logan, E. B. (2020, September 4). White people have gentrified Black Lives Matter. It's a problem. *LA Times*. https://www.latimes.com/opinion/story/2020-09-04/black-lives-matter-white-people-portland-protests-nfl

Miller, C. C. (2020, July 16). In the same towns, private schools are reopening while public schools are not. *New York Times*. https://www.nytimes.com/2020/07/16/upshot/coronavirus-school-reopening-private-public-gap.html

Nguyen, T. (2020, July 15). Students are using Instagram to reveal racism on campus. *VOX*. https://www.vox.com/the-goods/2020/7/15/21322794/students-instagram-black-at-accounts-campus-racism

Nielsen, K. E. (2012). *A disability history of the United States*. Beacon Press.

Ortiz, P. (2018). *An African American and Latinx history of the United States*. Beacon Press.

San Pedro, T. (2018). Abby as ally: An argument for culturally disruptive pedagogy. *American Educational Research Journal, 55*(6), 1193–1232.

Schneider, J. (2008). Escape from Los Angeles: White flight from Los Angeles and its schools, 1960–1980. *Journal of Urban History, 34*(6), 995–1012.

Swalwell, K. (2013). *Educating activist allies: Social justice pedagogy with the suburban and urban elite*. Routledge.

Swalwell, K. (2015). Mind the civic empowerment gap: Elite students & critical civic education. *Curriculum Inquiry, 45*(5), 491–512.

Part I

WHAT'S THE POINT?

JUSTIFYING AND FRAMING
ANTI-OPPRESSIVE EDUCATION
IN "ELITE" SCHOOLS

CHAPTER 1

Combating the Pathology of Class Privilege

A Critical Education for the Elites

Quentin Wheeler-Bell

Since the 1970s, inequality in wealth and income has soared and social mobility has stalled (Bartels, 2010; Piketty, 2014; Saez & Zucman, 2016).[1] Disturbingly, persistent racial gaps in wealth, income, and mobility both reflect and reproduce structural inequalities, compounding the impacts of discrimination over generations (Thomas et al., 2020).[2] This chapter examines what kind of education justice demands, and what is justifiable, for children born into the privileged class of this increasing inequality.

THE PRIVILEGED CLASS

First, what makes those privileged by inequality a "class"? As Wright and Rogers (2010) explain, "class" is a way to describe "the connection between individual attributes and material life conditions" (p. 196). Analytically speaking, class has two intersecting components: one *structural* and one *cultural*. The structural component of class is the institutional factors that shape opportunities available to individuals. For example, the increase in inequality over the last 50 years is partly due to the weakening of labor unions, the dismantling of social welfare programs, and skewed tax policies benefiting the upper class (Bartels, 2010). These structural factors create a cultural context in which privileged individuals and their children develop certain habits, skills, dispositions, and perspectives about the world. Individuals within the upper class, for instance, tend to have a higher sense of entitlement than those in other classes and are more likely to feel comfortable challenging authority (Lareau, 2003).

The "privileged class" thus refers to the combination of the cultural and structural advantages that increase individuals' well-being and opportunities across the civic, political, economic, and private spheres (Bourdieu,

1984). It consists of people whose social position (e.g., wealth, social connections) provides them with the capabilities to distance themselves from others when they choose (Chetty et al., 2016; Sayer, 2005) and engage in *opportunity hoarding*—the leveraging of unequal access to resources, goods, and social institutions to ensure reproduction of their class status (Bishop, 2009; Gaztambide-Fernández, 2009; Khan, 2010; Lareau, 2003; Lindsey, 2013). For example, the privileged class tends to live in hypersegregated neighborhoods and send their children to hypersegregated schools where they have little exposure to students from other racial groups, political ideologies, or economic backgrounds (Bishop, 2009; Massey, 2008). The world of the privileged class is also reproduced through *class exclusion*, using its capital (e.g., cultural, economic, and social) to unjustifiably influence the democratic process in ways that secure or better their class position at the expense of others. For example, on almost every possible measure, the affluent are more likely to influence the political process than the poor (see Levinson, 2012; Schlozman et al., 2012). As a result, the least advantaged face a civic oligarchy wherein the wealthy use their arbitrary power (political and economic) to ensure that it is reproduced (Winters, 2011).

THE PATHOLOGY OF PRIVILEGE

Within this context of class domination, the privileged class also develops an ideological world-picture (Bishop, 2009; Chetty et al., 2014): a perspective of the world that assists in stabilizing and legitimating the cultural and structural practices that reproduce their class privilege (Sherman, 2007). This is the *pathology of privilege*. As an ideology (in the pejorative sense), the pathology of privilege creates a form of consciousness that legitimates social institutions and practices reproducing class domination. For instance, those within the privileged class are more likely to see their privilege as rightfully earned or detached from structural problems (Howard, 2007). In addition, members of the privileged class are less likely to recognize how the suffering of others relates to their own class privilege (see Khan, 2010).

In sum, the pathology of privilege systematically incentivizes the formation and performance of a privileged identity wherein affluent individuals receive a cluster of advantages that are corrosive to democracy and fail to meet the standard of public justification. By this I mean that the structure of the economy and the distribution of wealth are *not democratically determined*, and the result provides the privileged class greater opportunities to influence policies and institutional arrangements that reproduce or better their class status. In addition, the pathology of privilege corrodes democratic sensibilities by creating an ideological worldview that negatively affects the credibility of the least advantaged (Sayer, 2005). This means the privileged class fails to recognize or refuses to take seriously the demands put forward by the least advantaged to make structures more just (see Allen, 2007; Bohman, 2000; Fricker, 2009).

PUBLIC AND PRIVATE AUTONOMY

Challenging the pathology of privilege to advance justice means expanding economic democracy and reducing economic domination. Thus, it would seem logical for an education rooted in social justice to teach privileged children to do just that. This is not education's *sole* purpose, however (Brighouse, 1998). As such, a social justice education must recognize the moral tension between the demands of justice and other educational aims. To do so, I examine the aims of *private autonomy* and *public autonomy*.

Public Autonomy

An education for *public autonomy* intends to teach children the skills, habits, and dispositions to effectively transform society in a manner that deepens democracy and expands justice. Public autonomy is the process by which an individual, together with others, ensures that social practices meet the standards of public justification (Habermas, 1998; Rostboll, 2009)—and to make a change when they don't. For example, our current economic system is undemocratically structured, which unreasonably limits the public autonomy of all citizens—especially the poor and working class. Thus, expanding public autonomy would entail dismantling the mechanisms of economic domination that prevent new democratic processes from being constructed, enabling individuals to collectively deliberate and determine how to structure the economy in a manner that meets the standards of public justification (Cunningham, 1987; Fung, 2003).

Because public autonomy is an intersubjective process, it depends upon two civic virtues: *political awareness* and *political solidarity*. *Political awareness* requires an understanding of different normative ideas (e.g., justice, equality, and democracy) and the ability to discern how they influence political disagreements (de-Shalit, 2006, pp. 55–56). For instance, individuals will have different conceptions of values like justice, equality, and democracy. These different (even competing) conceptions of normative values impact how individuals interpret particular social problems (Warnke, 1994). Developing children's political awareness means helping them understand how different individuals interpret the world with different moral languages and how these differences affect an individual's political perspectives. *Political solidarity*, on the other hand, is the willingness to respond to a situation in solidarity with the least advantaged. This means being politically aware of the situations of the least advantaged and acting collectively with those who are disadvantaged to bring about change (Brunkhorst, 2005; Pensky, 2009). Furthermore, political solidarity includes acknowledging the ways in which privilege functions and being willing to *refuse* certain privileges or to *use* one's privileges to advance justice (see Scholz, 2003).

Private Autonomy

The other aim of education is the cultivation of *private autonomy*. Private autonomy, as Habermas (1998) argues, refers to the opportunities to personally flourish without having one's actions publicly scrutinized. This includes but is not limited to establishing healthy friendships and family relationships and using leisure time to engage in meaningful social activities such as hobbies that contribute to one's personal well-being. When education promotes private autonomy, the aim is to provide students with opportunities to engage in activities that they find personally fulfilling, even if such activities are unrelated to their political or civil obligations.

While public and private autonomy are different dimensions of autonomy, the configuration of the public and private realms is neither static, ahistorical, nor incontestable. As Kevin Olson (2006) explains,

> [T]hese two forms are interlocking and mutually supporting in the sense that each presupposes the other. A secure status as a private individual is needed to participate in the public political process. . . . At the same time, public autonomy is needed as participatory freedom to spell out the details of private life and protest it. (p. 143)

Because these two forms of autonomy are contextually determined, they can, and often do, conflict. In fact, class privilege is partly reproduced when these forms of autonomy are systematically misaligned. For example, middle-class families often frame school choice in the language of private autonomy, in which they assume they have "the right" to choose schools even if such policies reproduce class domination and adversely affect the least advantaged (Ball, 2003). In this case, middle-class parents mis-frame school choice policies within the language of private autonomy by wrongly assuming they should *not* be held publicly accountable for where they send their children to school. Properly framing school choice would mean that parents should have the right to exercise their private autonomy to choose schools *only after* democratic decisionmaking has publicly determined the types of schools from which parents can choose. The example of school choice is merely an illustration that the line between public and private autonomy must be democratically determined and that misalignment between the two can reproduce domination.

Even though public and private autonomy can conflict, these two different dimensions of autonomy must be respected when educating children:

An education that overemphasizes public autonomy can be equally as problematic as an education that overemphasizes private autonomy (Rostboll, 2009). Thus, we want a social justice education that reasonably respects privileged children's right to private autonomy while also acknowledging education's role in developing their public autonomy that helps them understand their obligation to deepen democracy. Teachers should help children understand the dynamic relationship between public and private, specifically the way in which the pathology of privilege is partly reproduced by overemphasizing private autonomy. Ultimately, the task of a social justice education is to help students understand the importance of public and private autonomy, as well as the ways in which these dimensions of autonomy become misaligned to reproduce class domination.

THREE APPROACHES TO SOCIAL JUSTICE
EDUCATION FOR THE PRIVILEGED CLASS

Which approach to social justice education is best equipped to address the tensions between public and private autonomy, without depoliticizing the education privileged students should receive to advance justice and deepen democracy into the economy?

Class Suicide

The class suicide approach claims that privileged students did not earn their privilege, and thus have no right to enjoy *any* of the benefits attached to their class position. The role of social justice education within this approach is to help children understand why their class privilege is unjust and why they are obligated to renounce *all* privileges—no matter the personal cost—in the interest of liberating the least advantaged. This approach correctly notes the importance of developing privileged children's political awareness of class domination and emphasizes that democratizing the economy is desirable. It also highlights the fact that advancing justice will require a certain degree of sacrifice on the part of privileged people (Cullity, 2004).

That said, it has two significant shortcomings. First, this approach confuses guilt with civic responsibility. Guilt, as Young (2011) argues, is a particular type of moral responsibility wherein an individual is blameworthy for an action they committed or failed to commit that resulted in some harm. Civic responsibility, on the other hand, refers to what we owe others based upon our responsibilities as citizens or as human beings (see Young, 2011, pp. 75–95). While the line between guilt and civic responsibility can be difficult to discern, we can safely say children are not guilty of intentionally reproducing class domination, because they had little, if any, role in influencing the structural factors causing class domination. Thus, the class suicide approach is unjustified in requiring or advocating that children give away *all* their advantages, because they are not guilty of any moral wrong. However, children are still civically responsible for advancing justice, which requires giving up some (but not all) of their privileges.

Second, class suicide causes privileged students undue alienation because it demands children take on a level of civic responsibility that unreasonably limits their right to exercise private autonomy. For instance, privileged children have developed meaningful bonds with their family and friends that are tied to their class privilege. Thus, requiring privileged students to give up all their advantages would mean renouncing these loved ones. This would cause them undue alienation because it takes away their right to private autonomy (i.e., the right to enjoy meaningful commitments that are separate from their civic responsibilities). This is not to say privileged individuals should not sacrifice certain advantages to advance justice—indeed, they *should*. The point is to help students understand how the line between the public and private sphere gets distorted to reproduce class domination and to help them understand what are *justifiable sacrifices* that must be made to deepen democracy into the economy. In general, a social justice education should help students develop a framework of values that will assist them in making morally justified future decisions on how to reasonably balance public and private autonomy.

Civic Volunteerism

Generally speaking, the civic volunteerism approach focuses on short-term issues where there is little political disagreement or discussion of structural injustices (Levinson, 2012, pp. 169–210). Teachers choose this approach for several reasons. First, civic volunteerism allows them to avoid controversial issues, making it easier to garner support from some parents and administrators (Kahne & Westheimer, 1996). Second, because civic organizations cover a plurality of political perspectives, teachers can encourage participation while appearing "neutral" or "nonpartisan" (Kahne & Westheimer, 1996; Westheimer & Kahne, 2004).

While civic volunteerism is essential to democracy, social justice education should be wary of using civic volunteerism to develop privileged students' public autonomy for two reasons. First, civic volunteerism tends to reproduce the pathology of privilege because many civic organizations do not deal with structural issues, nor do they promote democratic deliberation. As Eliasoph (2011) explains, civic volunteerism can be demeaning and belittling to those it seeks to serve by reproducing the stigma that individuals are "disadvantaged" and in need of help. These initiatives are often designed and run by the affluent and tend to place democratic deliberation at the margins of the organizational structure. As a result, they tend to inaccurately speak for others by assuming they know what is in the best interest of the least advantaged. In addition, they do not optimize spaces for those who are disadvantaged to gain the capabilities needed to represent themselves within the deliberative process (Eliasoph, 2013).

The second problem with civic volunteerism is that many civic organizations are focused more on civic engagement rather than social transformation; as a result, they tend to promote "thin" forms of public autonomy rather than "thicker" forms aimed at expanding democracy. For example, public autonomy is "thickened" the more opportunities individuals have to engage in public deliberation and cooperate to solve particular social problems. Civic volunteerism insufficiently expands public autonomy because it typically focuses on short-term volunteering. Furthermore, many civic organizations are not structured to promote learning across class differences, nor are they structured to directly challenge and eliminate the social conditions that cause class injustices (Eliasoph, 2013). As a result, they are not optimal sites for helping privileged children understand and challenge class domination.

My criticism of civic volunteerism is not a denouncement of civic organizations, nor am I saying teachers who encourage civic volunteerism intentionally reproduce the pathology of privilege. I note the weakness of civic volunteerism to bring into focus the problems faced when assuming civic engagement is an end in and of itself. When this happens, teachers can overlook the ways in which certain sites of civic engagement reproduce the pathology of privilege and class domination. If a social justice education is to expand privileged children's public autonomy, then students must also evaluate the sites of civic engagement and understand which civic organizations are more or less likely to advance justice.

Educating Activist Allies

The activist ally approach, as developed by Katy Swalwell (2013), aims to teach privileged students the skills, dispositions, and willingness to act in a manner that deepens democracy and reduces class domination. An "activist ally," Swalwell argues, is a privileged individual who acts in political solidarity with the least advantaged by participating within social movements aimed at advancing economic democracy. The aim of the ally approach is to expand privileged children's public autonomy by helping students understand the importance of re-networking their advantages within social movements, by which I mean helping privileged students use their bundle of privileges (e.g., cultural, financial, social capital) to advance justice within social movements that deepen democracy.

The ally approach cultivates the two interconnected virtues associated with public autonomy—*political solidarity* and *political awareness*—in the following manner. First, it increases children's *political awareness* by teaching children how to analyze the ways different social institutions, including civic organizations, do or do not advance democracy. More specifically, political awareness must teach children how to understand the different normative ideas within a society (e.g., different conceptions of justice, equality, and democracy), how different normative ideas affect political disagreements, how class domination operates, and how to engage in reasonable deliberation across class lines.

The ally approach aligns with the "deliberative turn" in civic education, which focuses on ensuring children can listen to and learn from perspectives different from their own. However, it moves beyond mere deliberation insofar as it teaches privileged students about the importance of building a sense of political solidarity—the willingness to respond to a particular situation in solidarity with the least advantaged, being aware of the injustices they face, and collectively acting with others to bring about change. Building political solidarity requires linking privileged students with social movements that deepen democracy into the economy.

Building upon Melucci's (1996) definition of a social movement, a democratic social movement has four features: It "(i) *invokes solidarity,* (ii) makes *manifests a conflict,* and (iii) *entails a breach of the limits of compatibility of the system within which the action takes place*" (p. 28), which serves to increase public deliberation and manifest conflicts with the intent to deepen democracy (p. 28). For example, the Occupy movements have sparked larger movements around cooperative businesses and democratizing financial institutions and banks. The basic income grant movement, as well as the social housing movement, are growing internationally. And civic innovation projects are putting pressure on businesses to implement structures of social entrepreneurship in which business decisions are more democratically responsive to the larger community (Malleson, 2014; Nicholls, 2008; Sirianni & Friedland, 2001; Wright, 2010). Social movements are apt spaces for invoking solidarity across divisive lines because they provide spaces for the least advantaged to contribute to the designing and running of said movements and ensure their needs and interests are taken seriously (Hobson, 2004; Porta, 2009, 2013).

The activist ally approach focuses on social movements for several reasons. First, social movements are an effective means for creating radical social transformation and deepening democracy into the economy (Fox Piven & Cloward, 1978). Second, social movements are an effective means for creating radical social transformation because they operate semiautonomously from traditional politics and have greater ability to include voices typically excluded from larger political structures (Giugni et al., 1999; Wheeler-Bell, 2012). By operating slightly outside traditional politics, they open more spaces for discussing issues typically excluded within traditional political organizations and to politically organize in ways that challenge the current political opportunity structure. Finally, social movements are the means by which individuals collectively repair civil society to better ensure they have more democratic control over the major aspects of their lives (Alexander, 2008).

The purpose of the ally approach is to help students critique and analyze social movements that are undermining economic democracy, to educate them about social movements aimed at advancing economic democracy, and to link them to those movements. The ally approach, however, does not require the entire *school* to become a social movement—nor does it force children to participate in a *particular* social movement. The point is to have students learn about different social movements, currently and historically, and engage in different social movements that would expand their public autonomy, specifically in ways that encourage public deliberation across class lines. This is the kind of justifiable, justice-oriented critical education needed to disrupt the pathology of privilege.

NOTES

1. The top 1% of Americans earned 9% of the total income in the 1970s. By 2008, the top 1% earned 21% (Bartels, 2010). As of 2012, the top 1% owned 42% of the country's wealth—and the share of wealth for the top 0.1% grew from 7% to 22%, levels of inequality not seen since the late 1920s (Saez & Zucman, 2016). According to the Pew Charitable Trust (2013), 70% of those raised on the bottom of the wealth ladder and 66% of those raised on the top rungs remain there.

2. This is especially true for Black and Indigenous families (Chetty et al., 2020).

REFERENCES

Alexander, J. C. (2008). *The civil sphere.* Oxford University Press.

Allen, A. (2007). *The politics of our selves: Power, autonomy, and gender in contemporary critical theory.* Columbia University Press.

Ball, S. (2003). *Class strategies and the education market: The middle classes and social advantage.* RoutledgeFalmer.

Bartels, L. M. (2010). *Unequal democracy: The political economy of the New Gilded Age.* Princeton University Press.

Bishop, B. (2009). *The big sort: Why the clustering of like-minded America is tearing us apart.* Mariner Books.

Bohman, J. (2000). *Public deliberation: Pluralism, complexity, and democracy.* The MIT Press.

Bourdieu, P. (1984). *Distinction: A social critique of the judgment of taste.* Harvard University Press.

Brighouse, H. (1998). Civic education and liberal legitimacy. *Ethics, 108*(4), 719–745.

Brunkhorst, H. (2005). *Solidarity: From civic friendship to a global legal community* (J. Flynn, Trans.). The MIT Press.

Chetty, R., Hendren, N., Jones, M. R., & Porter, S. R. (2020). Race and economic opportunity in the United States: An intergenerational perspective. *The Quarterly Journal of Economics, 135*(2), 711–783.

Chetty, R., Hendren, N., Kline, P., & Saez, E. (2014). Where is the land of opportunity? The geography of intergenerational mobility in the United States. *The Quarterly Journal of Economics, 129*(4), 1553–1623.

Chetty, R., Stepner, M., Abraham, S., Lin, S., Scuderi, B., Turner, N., Bergeron, A., & Cutler, D. (2016). The association between income and life expectancy in the United States, 2001–2014. *JAMA, 315*(16), 1750–1766.

Cullity, G. (2004). *The moral demands of affluence.* Oxford University Press.

Cunningham, F. (1987). *Democratic theory and socialism.* Cambridge University Press.

de-Shalit, A. (2006). *Power to the people: Teaching political philosophy in skeptical times.* Lexington Books.

Eliasoph, N. (2011). *Making volunteers: Civic life after welfare's end.* Princeton University Press.

Eliasoph, N. (2013). *The politics of volunteering.* Polity.

Fox Piven, F., & Cloward, R. (1978). *Poor people's movements: Why they succeed, how they fail.* Vintage.

Fricker, M. (2009). *Epistemic injustice: Power and the ethics of knowing.* Oxford University Press.

Fung, A. (2003). *Deepening democracy: Institutional innovations in empowered participatory governance (Real Utopias Project).* Verso.

Gaztambide-Fernández, R. A. (2009). *The best of the best: Becoming elite at an American boarding school.* Harvard University Press.

Giugni, M., McAdam, D., & Tilly, C. (1999). *How social movements matter.* University of Minnesota Press.

Habermas, J. (1998). *Between facts and norms: Contributions to a discourse theory of law and democracy.* The MIT Press.

Hobson, B. (2004). *Recognition struggles and social movements: Contested identities, agency and power.* Cambridge University Press.

Howard, A. (2007). *Learning privilege: Lessons of power and identity in affluent schooling.* Routledge.

Kahne, J., & Westheimer, J. (1996). In the service of what? The politics of service learning. *Phi Delta Kappan, 77*(9), 592–599.

Khan, S. R. (2010). *Privilege: The making of an adolescent elite at St. Paul's School.* Princeton University Press.

Lareau, A. (2003). *Unequal childhoods: Class, race, and family life.* University of California Press.

Levinson, M. (2012). *No citizen left behind.* Harvard University Press.

Lindsey, B. (2013). *Human capitalism: How economic growth has made us smarter—and more unequal.* Princeton University Press.

Malleson, T. (2014). *After Occupy: Economic democracy for the 21st century*. Oxford University Press.

Massey, D. S. (2008). *Categorically unequal: The American stratification system*. Russell Sage Foundation.

Melucci, A. (1996). *Challenging codes: Collective action in the Information Age*. Cambridge University Press.

Nicholls, A. (Ed.). (2008). *Social entrepreneurship: New models of sustainable social change*. Oxford University Press.

Olson, K. (2006). *Reflexive democracy: Political equality and the welfare state*. The MIT Press.

Pensky, M. (2009). *The ends of solidarity: Discourse theory in ethics and politics*. State University of New York Press.

Pew Charitable Trust. (2013). *Moving on up: Why some Americans leave the bottom of the economic ladder, but not others?* http://www.pewtrusts.org/uploadedFiles/wwwpewtrustsorg/Reports/Economic_Mobility/Moving_On_Up.pdf

Piketty, T. (2014). *Capital in the twenty-first century* (A. Goldhammer, Trans.). Belknap Press: An Imprint of Harvard University Press.

Porta, D. D. (Ed.). (2009). *Democracy in social movements*. Palgrave Macmillan.

Porta, D. D. (2013). *Can democracy be saved: Participation, deliberation and social movements*. Polity.

Rostboll, C. F. (2009). *Deliberative freedom: Deliberative democracy as critical theory*. State University of New York Press.

Saez, E., & Zucman, G. (2016). Wealth inequality in the United States since 1913: Evidence from capitalized income tax data. *The Quarterly Journal of Economics*, *131*(2), 519–578.

Sayer, A. (2005). *The moral significance of class*. Cambridge University Press.

Schlozman, K. L., Verba, S., & Brady, H. E. (2012). *The unheavenly chorus: Unequal political voice and the broken promise of American democracy*. Princeton University Press.

Scholz, S. J. (2008). *Political solidarity*. Penn State University Press.

Sherman, R. (2007). *Class acts: Service and inequality in luxury hotels*. University of California Press.

Sirianni, C., & Friedland, L. (2001). *Civic innovation in America: Community empowerment, public policy, and the movement for civic renewal*. University of California Press.

Swalwell, K. (2013). *Educating activist allies: Social justice pedagogy with the suburban and urban elite*. Routledge.

Thomas, M., Herring, C., Horton, H. D., Semyonov, M., Henderson, L., & Mason, P. L. (2020). Race and the accumulation of wealth: Racial differences in net worth over the life course, 1989–2009. *Social Problems*, *67*(1), 20–39.

Warnke, G. (1994). *Justice and interpretation*. The MIT Press.

Westheimer, J., & Kahne, J. (2004). What kind of citizen? The politics of educating for democracy. *American Educational Research Journal*, *41*(2), 237–269.

Wheeler-Bell, Q. (2012). Educating the spirit of activism: A "critical" civic educa-
  tion. *Educational Policy*, 28(3), 463–486.
Winters, J. A. (2011). *Oligarchy*. Cambridge University Press.
Wright, E. O. (2010). *Envisioning real utopias*. Verso.
Wright, E. O., & Rogers, J. (2010). *American society: How it really works*. W. W.
  Norton & Company.
Young, I. M. (2011). *Responsibility for justice*. Oxford University Press.

CHAPTER 2

Intrinsic Aspects of Class Privilege

Adam Howard

Situated on the top of a hill overlooking a river valley and a small town, the college where I teach, Colby College, enjoys a geographical prominence equal to its magnificent campus. Neo-Georgian–style buildings are positioned around expansive, terraced quadrangles. At the highest elevation, the library stands with a sailing-ship weathervane perched on a white tower, conveying a part of the college's history and representing the many directions students can take in life. In the evenings, the tower is illuminated in blue, making it visible to most of the surrounding areas. Although town residents have this constant visible reminder of our presence, the college community mostly remains at a distance. The town's once-thriving mill and factories are no longer sources of employment; nearly 23% of residents live below the poverty line, and many others are barely making ends meet. Our wealthy community on top of the hill has little contact with the drastically different life circumstances of so many who live within this small town.

The incredible beauty and abundance of Colby allow these forms of human suffering, such as poverty, homelessness, and hunger, to remain invisible within this isolated campus. We also rarely give thoughtful attention to the fabric of privilege that clothes our own community. As with most "elite" educational communities, we keep privilege invisible by ignoring and, at times, avoiding it. Collectively, we have not had the kinds of educational experiences that would enable us to work toward a critical understanding of our privilege.

Within this "elite" community, I teach a course each year titled "Social Class and Schooling" that attempts to engage students in a critical exploration of various social class issues both within and outside educational contexts. Not surprising, given the social class makeup of the student body (for example, Colby has more students from the top 1% of the income scale than the bottom 60%), most who take this course are from affluent families. To make the content more relevant to students' lives, we spend a fair amount of time focusing on issues related to class privilege. Of the hundreds of courses offered at Colby, this is one of two courses primarily focused on social class; in fact, only a very few other courses even surface the topic. Since students also have had limited opportunity to learn about social class issues before college, they typically enter the class with little to no prior learning experiences relevant to the exploration of social class and especially class privilege. Even though students usually select the course not just to fulfill a major requirement but because they are genuinely interested in learning more about social class and privilege, they rarely know what to expect in exploring these topics because of their lack of prior experiences.

TEACHING ABOUT CLASS PRIVILEGE

Teaching wealthy students about class privilege requires pointing out, on a fairly regular basis, "the elephant in the room." Students who willingly wrestle with race, gender, sexuality, and religion often balk at exploring class privilege. For many of my students, they find the topics related to social class taboo—not something one talks about in public—and the more specific subject of class privilege a threat to their taken-for-granted assumptions about themselves and others. The concept of class privilege often makes them enormously uncomfortable and invokes such strong emotions as anxiety, fear, confusion, anger, guilt, and resentment. Consistent with Diane Goodman's (2011) observations about privileged people, they typically find it easier to deny that privilege exists than to experience this discomfort.

Realizing class privilege is a troubling concept for students both personally and theoretically, I am guided by particular pedagogical principles as I lead students to uncomfortable places: balance the emotional and cognitive components of the teaching and learning process; support students individually and collectively; build and maintain respectful relationships with students; attend to social relations between students; emphasize student-centered learning through reflection and experience; and value awareness, personal growth, and change as learning outcomes (Adams, 2016). For the most part, my efforts to put these established principles of effective teaching at the college level into practice allow me to create a supportive learning environment for students to engage in discussion about class privilege.

For over 20 years, I have been teaching different versions of my course on social class. When I first taught this class, I used Peggy McIntosh's (1988) work on white privilege and male privilege for several years to encourage my students' reflection on and conversation about privilege. In her popular essay on what she calls the "invisible knapsack" of privilege, McIntosh argues that one way of understanding how privilege works—and how it is kept invisible—is to examine the way we think about inequality. She claims that we typically think of inequality from the perspective of the one who suffers the consequences of the subordination or oppression, not the one who receives the benefits; hence those who receive privilege are not in our focus. As she questions this common way of thinking about inequality,

McIntosh challenges individuals who have privilege to "open their invisible knapsacks," which contain all of the benefits that come to them from their social, cultural, and economic positions. She urges privileged people to take a critical look at all the various (and often unconscious) ways they enjoy benefits and advantages that others do not.

McIntosh identifies two types of privilege. The first is *unearned entitlements*, which are rights that all people should have, such as feeling safe, being respected, and having access to all the opportunities that life offers. Unearned entitlements become a form of privilege—what McIntosh calls *unearned advantages*—when they are restricted to certain groups of people. These unearned advantages give members of dominant groups a competitive edge that they are reluctant to acknowledge or give up; they are often thought of as outcomes brought about by hard work, good choices, and great effort. The other form of privilege is *conferred dominance*, which occurs when one group has power over another. Cultural assumptions related to people's social positions help to determine assumptions about which group is meant to dominate another group. Conferred dominance is entrenched in cultural assumptions that establish patterns of control and maintain societal hierarchies.

We begin to confront privilege, according to this framework, by becoming aware of unearned advantage and conferred dominance—and by understanding how social locations (e.g., schools, workplaces, and communities) create and maintain privilege for certain groups (e.g., white, heterosexual, male, and affluent). McIntosh argues that the more aware people are of their privilege, the more they can contribute to changing themselves and the privileged locations that they occupy. Because privilege is rooted primarily in social systems, change does not happen only when individuals change; locations such as schools and workplaces that support privilege must change as well. Certain people, of course, need to change in order to do the work necessary to bring about change, but it is insufficient for individuals simply to change (see also Bishop, 2002; Goodman, 2011).

Although McIntosh wrote specifically about male privilege and white privilege, I adapted her list to generate examples of the ways in which class privilege is enacted. My list of 40 items included: *I do not fear being hungry. I have access to good medical and mental health care. I bought books for this and other classes without worrying about the costs. I will not need to think about being in debt after college.* Having students go through this list and identify some of their advantages in life was successful, to a certain extent, in making class privilege more visible. However, as students increased their awareness and knowledge of their class advantages, they felt overwhelmed by that awareness and knowledge rather than empowered to find meaningful ways to apply it. They became immobilized, uncertain about what actions they could take to interrupt the role that privilege plays in their everyday lives. Inevitably, students asked by the end of this activity, "What can we do? Are we supposed to give up our privilege? How can we do that? Is that the best approach? Can't we use our class privilege for the betterment of everyone? Why is privilege something *bad*?"

To help them overcome their sense of immobilization, I offered suggestions for how they could use their new awareness and knowledge to take action. We spent a significant amount of time studying models for identifying action steps and planning ways they could take action beyond the course. I encouraged them to further develop and draw upon the relationships they established with each other and me during the course to support their efforts. Despite my multiple attempts, most students never saw themselves as agents of change, capable of changing the world around them to address the problems associated with privilege. And, as a professor, I ended up moving to the next lesson without fully addressing their questions. I began asking similar questions as my students posed to me: After privileged individuals identify and become more aware of their advantages, then what? What do privileged individuals do with that knowledge and awareness? How can educators create the kinds of educational experiences that provoke in privileged students not only a sense of awareness but also a commitment to justice-oriented action? I found the concept of class privilege—or at least, how it is commonly understood—very limiting.

Privilege is a contested concept and, as Koh and Kenway (2016) point out, "a slippery term often mobilised to speak to all sorts of individual and group advantage" (p. 1). Researchers and educators writing about privilege established a critical foundation for making systems of privilege visible and for revealing the ways individuals and institutions work to reinforce and regenerate privilege. This body of work demonstrated the ways in which individuals from dominant groups tend to have little awareness "of their own dominant identity, of the privileges it affords them, of the oppression suffered by the corresponding disadvantaged group, and of how they perpetuate it" (Goodman, 2011, p. 22). In fact, as scholars argue (e.g., Case, 2013), one of the functions of privilege is to structure the world in ways that conceal how privilege works, so that advantages remain invisible to those who benefit from them. These scholars have argued that individuals' lack of awareness of their advantages, what Allan Johnson (2001) calls "the luxury of obliviousness" (p. 24), is an important part of understanding how privilege works.

While this work has generated useful understandings, limitations exist in the ways privilege is commonly conceptualized. By and large, scholars have constructed *commodified* notions of privilege. Privilege, in other words, has been understood extrinsically, as something individuals *have* or *possess,* rather than as something more intrinsic, something that reveals who they *are* or who they have *become* in a fundamental sense. Although some have acknowledged intrinsic aspects of privilege—in particular, the influence of advantages on people's identities (e.g., Seider, 2010)—the prominent views on privilege have ultimately fallen short in providing a framework for exploring those aspects.

PRIVILEGE AS IDENTITY

Through my experiences as a teacher and researcher (e.g., Howard, 2008, 2010; Howard et al., 2014), I came to understand the need for constructing a more useful framework for class privilege. In developing this framework, we must move beyond the conception of privilege as a commodity toward an understanding of privilege as identity—as something more intrinsic. As an identity or an aspect of identity, privilege is a lens through which individuals with advantages understand themselves, others, and the world around them. Their perceptions, interpretations, feelings, and actions are shaped, created, re-created, and maintained through this lens of privilege. Through this lens, self-understandings are constructed in relation to, and in coordination with, the ideologies and emotions privileged individuals absorb and that give their lives meaning.

This view of privilege is more concerned with people's self-understandings and the ideologies and emotions connected to those understandings than their advantages. To think about privilege in this way is not to deny or diminish the importance of advantages that certain individuals and groups have over others, but it is, in fact, to underline the relationship between advantages and identity formation and thus to understand the ways individuals actively construct and cultivate privilege. Class privilege is more than what individuals with economic advantages have; it is a crucial part of themselves and their self-understandings, which they renew, re-create, defend, and modify *ideologically* (that is, making use of ideas to provide guidance for thought and action) and *affectively* (that is, producing emotions to provide guidance for thought and action).

SELF-UNDERSTANDINGS

In establishing this framing of privilege, identities are understood as developing within social and cultural groups and out of the socially and culturally marked differences and commonalities that permeate interactions within and between groups. According to this perspective, identities are marked by many categories: gender, race, ethnicity, sexuality, nationality, class, religion, and ability, to name the ones most commonly discussed. These different categories have meaning in the material and symbolic structures that organize social and cultural groups in societies. Groups are positioned in particular ways to put some groups at an advantage (and therefore others at a disadvantage) in the "accumulation of power, resources, legitimacy, dignity and recognition" (Stoudt et al., 2012, p. 179). But larger structures in societies are constantly in flux; therefore, identities are not fixed. What may be meaningful about identity at a particular moment or in a certain context may not be so meaningful at another moment or in another context.

Because of this continuous placement and displacement of who people are, identities are viewed as multiple, contextual, and contingent.

This view of identities as not fixed and as being constantly influenced by various contexts, structures, and interactions establishes a more useful framing for exploring the intrinsic aspects of class privilege. From this perspective, identities are understood as forms of *self-understanding*: "People tell others who they are, but even more important, they tell themselves and then try to act as though they are who they say they are" (Holland et al., 1998, p. 3). These self-understandings are not, however, simply individual, internal, psychological qualities or subjective understandings that emerge solely from self-reflection. Identities, instead, link the personal and the social—they are constituted relationally, they entail action and interaction in a sociocultural context, they are social products that live in and through activity and practice, and they are always performed and enacted.

With a primary focus on the intrinsic aspects, this conception of class privilege redirects attention toward the agency of individuals. Even though human agency exists within the contradiction between people as social producers and as social products, self-understandings are neither imposed nor stable. Individuals mediate cultural meanings and have the capacity to transform these understandings in order to interrupt the cultural processes that validate and support unequal relations. With the agency to form their own self-understandings, privilege, therefore, is not something one is passively given or possesses, but, instead, something one actively constructs and cultivates. In this process, particular ideologies are employed to uphold privileged ways of knowing and doing.

IDEOLOGIES

To begin our conversation on class privilege in the course previously mentioned, I pose the question, "Do you deserve to be at Colby more than the students who weren't admitted?" Initially, students usually sit in silence with facial expressions that let me know that they are wondering whether I really want an answer. I continue, "Colby has a less than 10% acceptance rate. Are you better than the 90% who weren't admitted?" The silence continues and I notice students squirming in their seats, nervously looking away from me as I glance across the room. In an attempt to break this silence, I connect my questions to the readings just enough to make it less personal at that moment. Making the questions more academic usually initiates responses.

Students begin making the case for why they deserve to be here—*I've worked hard to be here. I didn't let obstacles prevent me from being successful. My privilege didn't play a big factor in me being accepted. I did what I needed to do to get in.* I challenge their responses with additional questions, "So you've worked harder than those who didn't get in? What about those who don't have the advantages as you've had in life? Wouldn't they have to work even harder to get into a place like here to overcome their disadvantages?" They often avoid talking directly about individuals with disadvantages to refrain from expressing certain views—such as they work harder than individuals with disadvantages in life. This allows them to continue projecting a politically correct image. When they do talk about others who do not have their advantages, they do so in ways that uphold the meritocratic belief that anyone can achieve what he or she wants in life through hard work, to explain their own successes in life, and indirectly explain others' lack of success. Using various ideologies—mainly, individual merit leads to success—they establish worthiness of their advantages.

Ideology plays a critical role in maintaining and advancing the dynamics of power and oppression through the production of ideas and principles that support class inequities. Dominant ideologies of the larger society often work like blueprints through which actions, experiences, and understandings of individuals are expressed and constituted. As familiar and respected narratives, ideologies mediate people's self-understandings in profoundly influential and often unconscious ways. However, the meanings embedded in these ideologies take on different values and forms as individuals mediate these cultural meanings in constructing their self-understandings. Ideology and self-understandings meet at the boundary between individuals' inner and outer worlds. Their self-understandings are produced in relation to and in coordination with the ideologies that they adopt and to which they give meaning.

EMOTIONS

Although ideology is a crucial component of the processes involved in creating the lens of privilege that shapes self-understandings, emotions are equally important. Emotions are structured by people's forms of understanding and, specifically, by their self-understandings. In an extension of this idea, Catherine Lutz (1988) argues that although most emotions are predominantly viewed as universal experiences and natural human phenomena, emotions are anything but natural or universal. Although people may experience similar emotions, meanings for those emotions are implicated by one's self-understandings. However, just as self-understandings link the personal and the social, emotions are more than individual responses; instead, they are constituted relationally in sociocultural contexts. Emotions, Lutz contends, "can be viewed as cultural and interpersonal products of naming, justifying, and persuading by people in relationship to each other. Emotional meaning is then a social rather than an individual achievement— an emergent product of social life" (p. 5).

In a previous study exploring the self-understandings of wealthy adolescents (Howard et al., 2014), we identify three emotions—*worthiness, integrity,* and *happiness*—that interact with ideologies to reinforce and regenerate privilege. These emotions play an important role for these young people in upholding a necessary framing of self to feel more at ease with their privileged status, reducing negative feelings associated with their advantages, providing a stabilizing force in their lives, and giving meaning and direction to their actions and plans. Although the meanings that form and support their self-understandings involve an amalgam of emotions, these three positive emotions, in particular, play important roles in affectively negotiating their advantages. Establishing and sustaining a sense of worthiness, integrity, and happiness provide a framing of self, enabling these adolescents to feel more at ease with their privileged status, to reduce negative feelings associated with their advantages, to provide a stabilizing force in their lives, and to give meaning and direction to their actions and plans. These emotions interface with their ideologies in constructing and maintaining privilege as a central aspect of their self-understandings.

CONCLUSION

Scholars are increasingly offering conceptual and pedagogical frameworks for creating opportunities for privileged individuals to increase awareness of their advantages and to engage in justice-oriented action. Some propose a pedagogy for the privileged (e.g., Curry-Stevens, 2007) and a pedagogy of the oppressor (e.g., Breault, 2003; Kimmel, 2010). Others are outlining approaches of a social justice pedagogy specifically designed for developing the critical consciousness of privileged students (e.g., Seider, 2009; Swalwell, 2013) and for engaging privileged individuals at all ages in social justice efforts (Goodman, 2011). These scholars join others in proposing ways for privileged people to become allies with oppressed individuals and groups (e.g., Case, 2013). Although each of these works offers different approaches and frameworks, there is a fair amount of agreement that transforming the understandings and actions of privileged individuals is essential for challenging privilege.

In addition to processes aimed at transforming privileged individuals, several scholars emphasize the need for engaging in processes that challenge the institutionalization of privilege within societal systems. As Bob Pease (2010) points out, "Changing people in privileged groups will not itself abolish privilege any more than empowering the oppressed will eliminate oppression" (p. 170). Transforming the understandings of privileged individuals to increase their critical consciousness will not be in and of itself enough to address the processes involved in the production and maintenance of privilege. Since privilege is generated and reinforced at the personal, cultural, and structural levels, privilege is rooted in societies and institutions as much as it is rooted in the understandings of individuals and their relationships (Johnson, 2001). As such, efforts toward transforming privileged individuals' self-understandings must aim to engage them in action that transforms societal structures and institutions creating and perpetuating inequities.

Educators at "elite" schools play an important role in facilitating the kinds of educational experiences that interconnect personal and social transformation. They can engage students, for example, in collaborative, participatory, embodied, and arts-based projects (for examples, see Howard & Maxwell, 2018; Stoudt, 2009; Stoudt et al., 2012) that emphasize both critical awareness and action. Over the years, I have used participatory action research (PAR) projects not only to advance my students' understandings of class privilege but also to engage them in social justice efforts (see, for example, Howard et al., 2014). PAR projects provided my students the necessary instructional settings to reconsider everyday assumptions that keep class privilege hidden, not talked about, and unexamined. Students put their research to use by engaging the Colby community in dialogue about class privilege, locating problems within our community that their research projects brought to light, and developing action plans for addressing those problems. They broadcasted their action plans in multiple ways—public forums; the campus newspaper; campus-wide electronic postings; flyers posted around campus; "table tents" in the dining halls; and meetings with senior administrators, faculty, and staff. These efforts sparked conversations across campus, challenged common understandings of class privilege, increased awareness of topics rarely considered within our community, and established a collective of individuals committed to changing practices and policies that advantaged some at the expense of others.

As students mediate their self-understandings, they can be offered the necessary cultural tools and resources that transform privilege. Students can be taught alternative lessons about themselves, their place in the world, and their relations with others; lessons that offer alternatives to privileged ways of knowing and doing. However, simply sharing new ideas and new ways of knowing and doing with our students does not always bring about change. As Kevin Kumashiro (2002) points out, "Students come to school not as blank slates but as individuals who are already invested in their thoughts, beliefs, and desires" (p. 73). As I have discovered through teaching at "elite" institutions and researching privileged young people, students enter the schooling context with a well-established sense of self that continually influences how they think and understand and what they know and decide to know. Oftentimes, wealthy students are comfortably socialized to accept (and even defend) particular ways of knowing and doing that protect their advantages. They have an acute interest in maintaining these benefits; therefore, their resistance to alternative ways of knowing and doing should be expected. Their acts of resistance, however, are instructive for deepening educators' knowledge of their students' self-understandings. With this knowledge, we are provided with the necessary footing for taking steps toward transforming our students' taken-for-granted assumptions about themselves, others, and the world around them that encourage and enable them to contest and challenge injustices.

REFERENCES

Adams, M. (2016). Pedagogical foundations for social justice education. In M. Adams, L. A. Bell, D. Goodman, & K. Joshi (Eds.), *Teaching for diversity and social justice* (3rd ed.; pp. 27–54). Routledge.

Bishop, A. (2002). *Becoming an ally: Breaking the cycle of oppression—in people.* Zed Books.

Breault, R. (2003). Dewey, Freire, and a pedagogy for the oppressor. *Multicultural Education, 10*(3), 2–7.

Case, K. (Ed.). (2013). *Deconstructing privilege: Teaching and learning as allies in the classroom.* Routledge.

Curry-Stevens, A. (2007). New forms of transformative education: Pedagogy for the privileged. *Journal of Transformative Education, 5*(1), 33–58.

Goodman, D. (2011). *Promoting diversity and social justice: Educating people from privileged groups* (2nd ed.). Sage.

Holland, D., Lachicotte, W., Skinner, D., & Cain, C. (1998). *Identity and agency in cultural worlds.* Harvard University Press.

Howard, A. (2008). *Learning privilege: Lessons of power and identity in affluent schooling.* Routledge.

Howard, A. (2010). Elite visions: Privileged perceptions of self and others. *Teachers College Press, 112*(8), 1971–1992.

Howard, A., & Maxwell, C. (2018). From conscientization to imagining redistributive strategies: Social justice collaborations in elite schools. *Globalisation, Societies, and Education, 16*(4), 526–540.

Howard, A., Polimeno, A., & Wheeler, B. (2014). *Negotiating privilege and identity in educational contexts.* Routledge.

Johnson, A. G. (2001). *Privilege, power, and difference.* Mayfield Publishing Company.

Kimmel, M. (2010). Introduction: Toward a pedagogy of the oppressor. In M. Kimmel & A. Ferber (Eds.), *Privilege: A reader* (2nd ed.; pp. 1–10). Westview Press.

Koh, A., & Kenway, J. (2016). Introduction: Reading the dynamics of educational privilege through a spatial lens. In A. Koh & J. Kenway (Eds.), *Elite schools: Multiple geographies of privilege* (pp. 1–17). Routledge.

Kumashiro, K. (2002). Against repetition: Addressing resistance to anti-oppressive change in the practices of learning, teaching, supervising, and researching. *Harvard Educational Review, 72,* 67–92.

Lutz, C. (1988). *Unnatural emotions: Everyday sentiments on a Micronesia atoll and their challenge to Western theory*. University of Chicago Press.

McIntosh, P. (1988). *White privilege and male privilege: A personal account of coming to see correspondences through work in women's studies* (Working Paper 189). Wellesley College Center for Research on Women.

Pease, B. (2010). *Undoing privilege: Unearned advantage in a divided world*. Zed Books.

Seider, S. (2009). Social justice in the suburbs: Challenges to engaging privileged youth in social action. *Educational Leadership, 66*(8), 54–58.

Seider, S. (2010). The role of privilege as identity in adolescents' beliefs about homelessness, opportunity, and inequality. *Youth & Society, 20*(10), 1–32.

Stoudt, B. G. (2009). The role of language and discourse in the investigation of privilege: Using participatory action research to discuss theory, develop methodology, and interrupt power. *Urban Review, 41*, 7–28.

Stoudt, B. G., Fox, M., & Fine, M. (2012). Contesting privilege with critical participatory action research. *Journal of Social Issues, 68*(1), 178–193.

Swalwell, K. (2013). *Educating activist allies: Social justice pedagogy with the suburban and urban elite*. Routledge.

CHAPTER 3

Is Becoming an Oppressor Ever a Privilege?

"Elite" Schools and Social Justice as Mutual Aid

Nicolas Tanchuk, Tomas Rocha, and Marc Kruse

Many educators teach students to identify various race, class, gender, ability, and religious-based forms of privilege in the hope that this will better equip them to fight against dominating and oppressive relationships (Adams et al., 2016; Adams et al., 2018; Applebaum, 2010; Ayers et al., 2008; Goodman, 2011; Gorski & Pothini, 2018; Johnson, 2018). In this chapter, we argue on conceptual grounds that educators in academically "elite" schools are right to teach students to identify and fight against complicity in oppressive relationships. The decision to frame complicity in oppression as a privilege or advantage enjoyed by dominant groups, however, is separable from and at odds with this goal (Tanchuk et al., in press). Whenever educators in "elite" schools frame oppression as beneficial to dominant groups, we argue that they needlessly make efforts toward justice with these students appear irrational. Far from elite, we characterize schools where this practice proliferates as "schools at risk" of reproducing vice in their students and oppression in the world.

To show how teachers can reveal that complicity in oppression is disadvantageous even for students in dominant groups, we draw on a point of overlap in Black feminism, Indigenous thought, and other recent work in political philosophy. Across these diverse traditions, we argue that the task of forming relationships that facilitate joint flourishing lies at the heart of ethical and political responsibility. We refer to this point of overlap as a commitment to "growing spheres of Mutual Aid." We trace how educators can teach students explicitly and implicitly that being a part of a world in which they grow spheres of Mutual Aid is better than being a part of a world made of oppressive relationships. We interpret two scenes from *The Hate U Give*, a film that depicts students in dominant and subordinated groups in an "elite" school in light of arguments for Mutual Aid. In the process, we sketch how a commitment to Mutual Aid calls into question the very nature of what it means to be "elite" or advantaged.

THE PROBLEM OF PRIVILEGE IN EDUCATING "ELITES" FOR SOCIAL JUSTICE

A White student once told the educator, psychologist of race, and former Spelman College president Beverley Tatum (2017) that, paradoxically, he'd just learned from her that he has no reason to dismantle racist systems. After all, she'd just taught him that these systems were "working in his favor" (p. 93). The student—let's call him "Adam" for ease of reference—did not deny that he had "White privilege," a long list of unearned "advantages" (p. 88) that he had "received simply because [he] was White" (p. 88). He agreed with Tatum that "every social indicator," (p. 88) from health to wealth, reveals the benefits of being white in the America. Nor did Adam claim that he morally deserves these "advantages" that he receives from racist systems. Adam's question is more fundamental. He asks why he should try to give up these "benefits" and "privileges" if, as he learned in Tatum's class, they really are advantages.

This question, as a review of the literature suggests, is not unique to Adam, but has been asked by other students in dominant groups in classes seeking to educate for social justice generally and at "academically elite" institutions in particular (Howard, 2010, p. 1989; Logue, 2005, p. 371; Nurenberg, 2011, p. 56; Swalwell, 2013a, 2013b). While Adam's case shows a student embracing White privilege, the concept of privilege is used across various axes of unjust domination and subordination. To capture this wider range of usage, the definition of privilege offered in Sensoy and DiAngelo's (2017) leading social justice education textbook is helpful:

> privilege is . . . systemically conferred dominance and the institutional processes by which the beliefs and values of the dominant group are "made normal" and universal. While in some cases, the privileged group is also the numerical majority, the key criterion is social and institutional power. (p. 80)

For these theorists, the concept of privilege refers to a *"benefit"* to "members of the dominant *group*" (p. 81, italics added). For Sensoy and DiAngelo, and many others, the power and access that an individual *possesses* is always cast as an advantage.

What we will call "the Problem of Privilege" occurs whenever members of dominant groups embrace the idea that it is to their advantage—a privilege—to be complicit in oppression, as this discourse teaches. The

Problem of Privilege has its roots in the way Peggy McIntosh (1988/1992) introduced the concept of privilege into social justice education and how it has proliferated since (Rothman, 2014). McIntosh claims that we need the concept of privilege to make visible the "advantages that men gain from women's disadvantages" in a sexist society and the way racism begets advantage to white people through "White privilege" (p. 28). Like Sensoy and DiAngelo (2017), McIntosh takes the recognition of one's privilege to be the first step toward criticizing these "advantages" (p. 28). In contrast with McIntosh's approach, we hope to show how educators can teach students to understand and critique oppressive power relations without teaching that it is ever advantageous to be or become an oppressor. We endeavor to accomplish this later, under the banner of Social Justice as Mutual Aid, by teaching students like Adam to see themselves as a mere part of relationships that can be more or less intrinsically valuable depending upon how each embraces responsibilities to others' flourishing, including life in the natural world.

Many students in academically "elite" settings have or are in a position to acquire social and economic power through current social structures. As such, these students are arguably among the most *at risk* of succumbing to the Problem of Privilege and becoming agents of injustice. For social justice educators in "elite" educational settings, Adam poses an important problem: Why should he pursue justice rather than injustice? Adam, here, is aware of the power he possesses, but like Thrasymachus in Plato's *Republic*, is not convinced that justice is in *his* interest. For anyone concerned with social justice, however it is conceived, this matters. If members of dominant groups see justice as to their advantage and actively pursue it, then it is far more likely that justice will be achieved, and achieved far more quickly, than if members of these groups see it to their advantage to resist it (Swalwell, 2015, p. 494).

A small but growing body of research suggests that teachers would do well to stop foregrounding the extent to which students like Adam are "advantaged" or "privileged" by systems of oppression. Instead, this scholarship asks teachers to start foregrounding ways that students who are in (or are positioned to become) members of powerful groups are in some ways disadvantaged by systemic oppression (Swalwell, 2013a, pp. 13–14). Goodman (2011), for example, suggests teachers might move away from portraying Adam as privileged or advantaged by studying the psychological, social, moral, spiritual, and intellectual costs to oppressors, while seeing how "unlearning privilege/oppression" carries with it the promise of better ways of living with others and greater "joy" (pp. 84–120). In line with this strategy, Nurenberg (2011) reports using George Orwell's story "Shooting an Elephant" to facilitate conversations with his socioeconomically powerful students. Drawing on literature in colonial contexts, these conversations help students "begin to see that the parameters of the role as someone in power . . . was what made them act contrary to their perceived values" (p. 58) in various moments of their lives. Similarly, Logue (2005) recommends engaging students in a re-evaluation of "privilege" whereby we come to see "dominant subjects as insecure, alienated, anguished, violently repressed, and/or pathological " (p. 375).

We believe this strategy is promising but that it is limited without a fundamental rethinking of how we teach students to think about advantage and disadvantage. As in the discourse of privilege, these theorists often treat what is advantageous and disadvantageous to pursue as *possessions* of individuals rather than as features of the world to which one is a mere contributing part. Thus, they stop short of suggesting that "elite" students from wealthy households are necessarily worse off overall than they would be were it not for the unjust domination of others. So long as one thinks of advantage as an individual possession, this implication seems difficult to avoid. Perhaps students will not want to become a frontline colonial soldier, but it's not clear how anguished the life of a chief executive officer (CEO) in a gated community really is. If the costs of domination do not automatically disadvantage students like Adam *overall*, then these sorts of limitations (e.g., guilt, shame, lost economic productivity) may simply reflect line-item costs in the service of what, overall, is still portrayed as a "beneficial" outcome for people like them. Problematically, students can still think they are gaining overall through complicity in oppression and the devastation of others' lives.

SOCIAL JUSTICE AS MUTUAL AID

To make it clear that becoming an oppressor is always bad and resolve the Problem of Privilege, members of dominant and subordinated groups alike must be able to see oppressive domination as an obstacle to the way relationships *should* be between groups. At the same time, all must be equipped to recognize important *differences* among members of different groups. It would be wrong, for example, to suggest that dominant group members experience the same threats to life and flourishing as those in subordinated groups, whether those are human groups or entire species wiped out by human consumption. Under the banner of Social Justice as Mutual Aid, we hope to sketch how educators can accomplish these twin goals.

It is standard in cultures shaped by modern Euro-American political philosophy and ethics to think of how well life is going in terms of one's individual possession of goods (e.g., knowledge, power, property, health, pleasure). Doing so, however, is not mandatory (Bilgrami, 2014). A long history of Indigenous and Black feminist thought, for example, contests this individualistic picture of advantage, which is implicit in the discourse of privilege. Instead, what is advantageous to pursue is defined in these traditions by the extent to which a course of action builds a better world with better relationships (Borrows, 2010; Hill Collins, 2000/2009; Johnson, 1976; Simpson, 2011, 2017; Stonechild, 2016). On these alternative holistic and relational pictures of advantage, processes that allow each to *relate* to others—those of joint knowledge-seeking, communication, and action—are properly placed at the center of each person's ethical and political concern (Borrows, 2016; Hill Collins, 2000/2009; Stonechild, 2016). What each possesses is of secondary importance in service of this higher shared focus on building a better *world* in which all more fully flourish.

Patricia Hill Collins (2000/2009) articulates a vision, rooted in the tradition of Black feminism, that exemplifies the sort of reframing we will propose. Black feminist theories of knowledge, according to Hill Collins, are founded on an ethic of care for situated dialogic relationships. "A primary epistemological assumption underlying the use of dialogue in assessing knowledge claims is that connectedness rather than separation is an essential component of the knowledge validation process" (p. 279). She adds that the ethical commitment to supporting dialogic relationships is "[r]ooted in a tradition of African humanism," wherein, "each individual is thought to be a unique expression of a common spirit, power, or energy inherent in all life" (p. 282). In these holistic African humanist traditions, individuals are called to revere the expression of this spirit in all life and the "individual uniqueness" inherent in each particular life's expressions. Similar themes are prominent in Anishinaabe and Saulteaux Indigenous thought, which foreground responsibilities to care for the flourishing of all of one's relations, including those with plants, animals, insects, and the ecological conditions of life (Borrows, 2016; Kruse et al., 2019; Marin & Bang, 2018; Simpson, 2011, 2017; Stonechild, 2016).

Although not always foregrounding ecological concern, contemporary feminist political philosophy (Anderson, 1999; Marion-Young, 1990/2011) and deliberative theories of democratic education have similarly stressed the primacy of creating civic relationships that enable uncoerced seeking and sharing of knowledge to facilitate the "*conscious* social reproduction" (Gutmann, 1987/1999, p. 14) of society, while respecting individuality. At the core of these diverse traditions is a concern for building capacities and institutions that enable each to relate to others through open-ended processes of inquiry and action that are free of coercion, repression, and discrimination (Gutmann, 1987/1999, pp. 44–45; see also: Habermas 1987/1992, 1990; Hansen, 2009; Jaeggi, 2018; Laden, 2013). We augment the commitment to democratic deliberation in these latter theorists, who seek to advance human flourishing, with a commitment to the flourishing of all life, as in Indigenous thought and African humanism noted earlier.

Failing a reason to reject this latter commitment, we will treat all flourish-ing as bearing intrinsic value. We refer to the task of growing relationships that facilitate the flourishing of all life as growing spheres of "Mutual Aid" (Tanchuk et al., in press).

If we teach students to make the growth of spheres of Mutual Aid the center of their conception of what is advantageous to pursue, then the Problem of Privilege is solved, at least conceptually. A relationship where some are needlessly blocked from flourishing jointly with others is, by defi-nition, revealed to be disadvantageous for all looking at the relationship correctly. In Adam's case, his complicity in oppressive relationships with people of color make him a particularly bad part of a world that is itself worse than it needs to be. The good news is that if he can discover that he is a part of something that is needlessly disadvantageous, he can work to become a part of a better world by fighting against systemic oppression and injustice. By removing the claim that oppression is "working" and good for him, we remove part of the force that pulls students like Adam toward oppressive tendencies. We nevertheless retain the ability to see that others face barriers to joint flourishing that Adam does not face. He is not domi-nated, nor does he suffer profoundly; but others' wrongful domination and suffering should appear as a problem for him and to anyone looking at the world clearly.

How might educators teach students like Adam to embrace a commit-ment to growing spheres of Mutual Aid? There's no one-size-fits-all instruc-tional solution for any topic. There are nevertheless two primary ways that we teach students anything. The first is through what is sometimes called the manifest or official curriculum that educators teach explicitly by advancing facts or arguments (Portelli, 1993, p. 343). The second way we teach stu-dents is often implicit and by way of example and habituation, for instance, by treating some ways of thinking or behaving as natural, true, good, or bad, through what teachers say or do (Portelli, 1993, p. 343). We consider each of these two ways of teaching a commitment to Mutual Aid in the next two sections.

EXPLICIT ANTI-ATOMISTIC TEACHING

Against Adam's claim that he can live well through others' oppression, an educator working in Mutual Aid's framework might start by asking him why only his flourishing should matter in determining what to do. With recent work in political philosophy, we doubt that a good argument can be given for the view that only Adam's life *should* matter in guiding his ac-tion, regardless of what he in fact does in practice (Dworkin, 2002, p. 2; Kymlicka, 2002, p. 4). In brief, if Adam's flourishing matters, as he judges in pursuing his "advantage," then how can he coherently deny that others' flourishing has value, too? After all, other people pursue the same type of goal: trying to live a "truly good life," (Dworkin, 2005, p. 244; Kymlicka, 1991, p. 10) that he pursues in his own case. A teacher can point out to Adam that he likely already sees value in *some* others' lives going well. Perhaps he sees intrinsic value in things going well for his friends or family. If Adam denies that he should extend this same consideration and concern to others, then educators can question the rationality of these denials and encourage him to expand his horizons of concern.

If advancing the joint flourishing of all life is our common goal, then it is crucial that each person can share knowledge about the affordances and consequences of various courses of action for their contexts, free of discrimination or repression (Gutmann, 1987/1999, pp. 44–45; Medina, 2013). For without this information, we are unlikely to know if life is or is not going well for all. In a country like the United States with a history of White supremacy, anti-Black racism, and extractive capitalism, eliminating repression and discrimination will require attention to differences in intersecting identities and material barriers across human lives within the deliberative community. To enable the joint flourishing of all through deliberation and action, educators rightly teach that those who face the greatest barriers to participating in this deliberative project as equals have the most significant complaint and warrant the most material support to remove the barriers they face (Schouten, 2012).

IMPLICIT LEARNING AND *THE HATE U GIVE*

How we conceive of advantage will also inform how we implicitly teach students to understand social life when we interpret and frame social phenomena. To illustrate the implicit impact of the reframing of advantage and disadvantage we propose under a commitment to Mutual Aid, we compare and contrast how an educator might interpret two scenes from a work of young adult fiction: the 2018 film adaptation of the eponymous novel *The Hate U Give* by Angie Thomas (2017). In this narrative, Starr Carter is a 16-year-old African American girl who lives in the predominantly Black, low-income neighborhood of Garden Heights, but attends school at the "elite" Williamson Prep in a predominantly white, high-income neighborhood. Adapted and produced in the context of the ongoing Black Lives Matter movement against police brutality, the story follows Starr as she contends with the agony of being the sole witness of the police killing of Khalil Harris, her childhood best friend. A master code-switcher, Starr navigates a racist society in part by eliding her life outside of Williamson Prep, even as her white peers secure cultural capital for themselves by imitating language, lyrics, and mannerisms they pick up from Black artists, activists, and celebrities.

While Starr is courageous in her response to racial injustice, two scenes in the film skillfully depict how a student like Adam, who we introduced earlier, might respond to these same injustices if educators do not intervene. Early in the story, although Starr's identity as a witness to Khalil's killing remains a secret, her psychological distress is quickly recognized by Hailey Grant, one of Starr's wealthy White friends at Williamson Prep. Hailey inquires after Starr's well-being and encourages Starr to join her and other students in a "Justice for Khalil" protest at school. Hailey makes clear, however, that she is motivated in significant part by a selfish desire to skip math class. Injustice is a tool, in this depiction, for Hailey's comfort. When Starr points out the disingenuousness at the protest, Hailey gets offended and responds flippantly, "Who else is gonna speak up for our people, girl?" Starr, in disbelief at Hailey's attempt to casually identify herself with an oppressed group, retorts, "*Our* people?" (Tillman, 2018, 1:05:09).

In the discourse of privilege, a teacher interpreting this scene might portray Hailey as privileged. She benefits, it might be said, through her disingenuous use of the protest to get out of a class. So long as her grades and future opportunities are not harmed, these acts might be portrayed as ways to gain a sense of importance and recognition from her wealthy peers by performing social awareness without any real concern for Black lives. In the discourse of privilege, Hailey's behavior may be a problem for Starr, but it is unclear why it is a problem *for* Hailey. A teacher interpreting this same behavior through Social Justice as Mutual Aid would want students to see instead that Hailey is making herself a worse part of a worse world through her failure to respond appropriately to the value inherent in Black lives. Were she awake to the world in which she lives, Hailey would become a better part of a better world through a sincere commitment to ending the police brutality and systemic racism that blocks African Americans from flourishing jointly with White people. At this point, though, Hailey is acting in ways that are unequivocally disadvantageous.

In a second scene, Starr and Hailey watch a TV news report on Khalil's killing that emphasizes the "gangs and drugs" (Tillman, 2018, 1:18:01) prevalent in Starr's neighborhood. The report includes an interview with the shooter's father, who frames the officer as a "good boy" and mentions the officer's fear of going outside due to threats against his life. The same sympathetic portrayal is not extended to Khalil's family. Hailey sympathizes with the police officer but not with Khalil, asserting that "his life matters too, you know" (Tillman, 2018, 1:18:11). As Starr, upset, moves to leave, Hailey becomes defensive, accuses Starr of having called her a racist, and storms off.

A teacher working with students to interpret this scene through the discourse of privilege might again portray the police officer and Hailey as benefiting from the media narratives that shelter their ability to hoard power and wealth and that erase Black people's experiences. A teacher interpreting this scene through Mutual Aid, by contrast, would see the root cause of this police officer's discomfort as founded in White people's needless and damaging perpetuation of oppressive relationships that make the world worse than it should be. Precisely because no one should be arbitrarily threatened or killed, Hailey and the police officer, were they rational, would see anti-Black racism is a larger threat to joint flourishing in their context and warranting greater attention than the threats to the officer. Far from helping Hailey, the media contributes to her ignorance and reinforces her vice, making her a worse part of a worse world than she might otherwise be, even if she gains power through these institutional supports. Not all power, after all, is good. Once again, an educator would teach that Hailey is making life worse for everybody, including herself.

In emphasizing the importance of ecology in social justice, Mutual Aid challenges educators to also draw out themes not foregrounded in the narrative of *The Hate U Give*. A teacher committed to Mutual Aid would want students, for example, to consider whether there is a connection between Hailey's exploitative attitude toward people of color and her complicity in ecologically destructive forms of capitalist consumption. Hailey, like many in industrialized nations, one might argue, seems to treat *all* other life as mere tools to support her *possession* of comfort and power rather than as a locus of intrinsic value and respect. At no point, for example, does Hailey challenge consumer culture or consider the ecological impact of her lifestyle and social position. In the discourse of privilege, by contrast, so long as Hailey gains power and comfort, her exploitation of ecological life might appear advantageous *for her*. By interpreting texts through a commitment to Mutual Aid, alongside the explicit teaching of why this way of seeing the world is defensible, teachers may, over time, facilitate the transformation of students who see the world atomistically into agents committed to the flourishing of all, removing barriers to our joint flourishing.

CONCLUSION

This chapter has advanced the idea that we rely on a kind of myth whenever our educational discourse reinforces a synonymy between privilege or advantage and complicity in oppression. This myth is dangerous, for it allows powerful "elite" schools—the students, parents, teachers, and leaders in them—to act on the damaging belief that it can be disadvantageous for an individual to work toward social and environmental justice. Students like

Adam and Hailey, who see it as a "privilege" or "advantage" to be a domi-
nator in a system of oppression, we propose, are *at risk* of becoming a needlessly bad part of a needlessly worse world. Schools that fail to resolve the
Problem of Privilege, correspondingly, are in our view, "schools at risk" of
reproducing vice in their students and harm in the world. For those committed to Mutual Aid, the only kind of elite school that could possibly exist—a
school that is superior in terms of its actual properties—is one that cultivates
in students the capacities and desires needed to advance the flourishing of all.

REFERENCES

Adams, M., Bell, L. A., Goodman, D. J., & Joshi, K. (Eds.). (2016). *Teaching for
diversity and social justice* (3rd ed.). Routledge.

Adams, M., Blumenfeld, W. J., Catalano, D. C. J., Dejong, K., Hackman, H., Hopkins, L., Love, B., Peters, M., Shlasko, D., & Zuniga, X. (Eds.). (2018). *Readings for diversity and social justice* (4th ed.). Routledge.

Anderson, E. (1999). What's the point of equality? *Ethics, 109*(2), 287–337.

Applebaum, B. (2010). *Being white, being good: White complicity, white moral
responsibility, and social justice pedagogy.* Lexington Books.

Ayers, W. C., Quinn, T., & Stovall, D. (Eds.). (2008). *Handbook of social justice in
education.* Routledge.

Bilgrami, A. (2014). *Secularism, identity, & enchantment.* Harvard University
Press.

Borrows, J. (2010). *Canada's indigenous constitution.* University of Toronto Press.

Borrows, J. (2016). *Freedom and indigenous constitutionalism.* University of
Toronto Press.

Cubero García, K., & González Stokas, A. (2020, forthcoming). Centros de apoyo
mutual. An emergent decolonial pedagogy of relation? *Lapiz No. 4.* https://
www.lapes.org/publications

Dworkin, R. (2002). *Sovereign virtue: The theory and practice of equality.* Harvard
University Press.

Goodman, D. J. (2011). *Promoting diversity and social justice.* Routledge.

Gorski, P. C., & Pothini, S. G. (2018). *Case studies on diversity and social justice
education* (2nd ed.). Routledge.

Gutmann, A. (1999). *Democratic education.* Princeton University Press.

Habermas, J. (1987/1992). Individuation through socialization: On George Herbert
Mead's theory of subjectivity. In W. M. Hohengarten (Trans.) *Post-metaphysical
thinking: Philosophical essays* (pp. 179–204). MIT Press.

Habermas, J. (1990). *Moral consciousness and communicative action.* MIT Press.

Hansen, D. T. (2009). Dewey and cosmopolitanism. *Education and Culture, 25*(2),
126–140.

Hill Collins, P. (2000/2009). *Black feminist thought.* Routledge.

Howard, A. (2010). Elite visions: Privileged perceptions of self and others. *Teachers College Record*, *112*(8), 1971–1992.

Jaeggi, R. (2018). *Critique of forms of life*. Harvard University Press.

Johnson, A. G. (2018). *Privilege, power, and difference* (3rd ed.). McGraw-Hill.

Johnson, B. (1976). *Ojibwe heritage*. McClelland and Stewart.

Kruse, M., Tanchuk, N., & Hamilton, R. (2019). Educating in the seventh fire: Debwewin, Mino-bimaadiziwin, and Ecological Justice. *Educational Theory*, *69*(5), 587–601.

Kymlicka, W. (2002). *Contemporary political philosophy: An introduction* (2nd ed.). Oxford University Press.

Laden, A. S. (2013). Learning to be equal: Just schools as schools of justice. In D. A. Reich (Ed.), *Education, Justice, & Democracy* (pp. 62–79). University of Chicago Press.

Logue, J. (2005). Deconstructing privilege: A counterpuntal approach. *Philosophy of Education*, 371–379.

Marin, A., & Bang, M. (2018). 'Look it, this is how you know': Family forest walks as a context for knowledge-building about the natural world. *Cognition and Instruction, 36*(2), 89–118.

McIntosh, P. (1988/1992). White privilege: Unpacking the invisible knapsack. In *Multiculturalism* (pp. 30–37). U.S. Department of Education.

Medina, J. (2013). *The epistemology of resistance*. Oxford University Press.

Nurenberg, D. (2011). What does injustice have to do with me? A pedagogy of the privileged. *Harvard Educational Review*, *81*(1), 50–64.

Portelli, J. (1993). Exposing the hidden curriculum. *Journal of Curriculum Studies 25*(4), 343–358.

Rothman, J. (2014, May 12). The origins of "privilege." *The New Yorker*. https://www.newyorker.com/books/page-turner/the-origins-of-privilege

Schouten, G. (2012). Fair educational opportunity and the distribution of natural ability: Toward a prioritarian principle of educational justice. *Journal of Philosophy of Education, 46*(3), 472–491.

Sensoy, Ö., & DiAngelo, R. (2017). *Is everyone really equal? An introduction to key concepts in social justice education*. Teachers College Press.

Simpson, L. (2011). *Dancing on our turtle's back: Stories of Nishnaabeg recreation, resurgence, and a new emergence*. Arbiter Ring Press.

Simpson, L. (2017). *As we have always done: Indigenous freedom through radical resistance*. University of Minnesota Press.

Stonechild, B. (2016). *The knowledge seeker: Embracing indigenous spirituality*. University of Saskatchewan Press.

Swalwell, K. M. (2013a). *Educating activist allies: Social justice pedagogy with the suburban and urban elite*. Routledge.

Swalwell, K. M. (2013b). With great power comes great responsibility: Privileged students' conceptions of justice-oriented citizenship. *Democracy & Education, 21*(1), 1–11.

Swalwell, K. M. (2015). Mind the civic empowerment gap: Economically elite students and critical civic education. *Curriculum Inquiry, 45*(5), 491–512.

Tanchuk, N., Rocha, T., & Kruse, M. (in press). Is complicity in oppression a privilege? Towards social justice education as mutual aid. *Harvard Educational Review.*

Tatum, B. D. (2017). *Why are all the black kids sitting together in the cafeteria? And other conversations about race.* Basic Books.

Thomas, A. (2017). *The hate u give.* HarperCollins.

Tillman, G. (Director) (2018). *The hate u give* [Film]. 20th Century Fox.

Part II

CAUTIONARY TALES

PROBLEMATIC MODELS OF SOCIAL JUSTICE EDUCATION IN "ELITE" SCHOOLS

CHAPTER 4

Beyond Wokeness

How White Educators Can Work Toward Dismantling Whiteness and White Supremacy in Suburban Schools

Gabriel Rodriguez

"If only they'd take advantage of the opportunities the school has to offer." These words, shared by a White[1] educator at a predominately White and well-resourced Midwestern suburban high school, were jarring to hear. As they were uttered, I was reminded of my experiences as a Brown kid growing up in White suburbia. I recalled my apprehensions in telling people where I was from, fearing assumptions they would make about me having had it "good." I do not deny that my education benefited from my attending well-resourced suburban schools. With that said, it also reflected people's misperceptions of suburban schools and communities. Growing up in a blue-collar community that experienced demographic change provided me insights into what Latinx youth in similar contexts must do to survive.

To assume that all is well for Latinx youth in suburban schools, particularly those with resources, is a mistake. There is no guarantee that Latinx youth are being tracked into opportunity or that their social worlds are being considered. Such a reductionist approach masks colonial, classist, and White supremacist practices that systemically oppress Latinx youth and place the burden on them to conform to an educational system never envisioned for them. Therefore, schools with resources, regardless of the context, must look inward if they want to make sustained inroads to combatting the persisting inequalities that plague the educational system in the United States.

This chapter is a reflection of qualitative research I conducted at Shields High School (SHS, pseudonym), a mainly White, academically high-achieving, and affluent suburban school in the Midwest. Although my study was on Latinx youth, the more time I spent learning from participants, the more I reflected on the role Whiteness and White supremacy played in shaping their experiences. This chapter includes ethnographic snapshots that point to opportunities schools should seize if they aim to be more inclusive and move beyond a rhetoric of "wokeness." By "wokeness," I refer to a subscription to social justice ideology and employment of language and actions used to demonstrate knowledge and support. This chapter is an invitation to educators—specifically White educators—to reflect upon their racial identities in relation to the contexts in which they teach.[2]

In a climate that is increasingly anti-teacher, I understand that being asked to reflect on your racial identity may not be something new for those that are reading this chapter. It is my hope that this chapter is not simply viewed as another researcher calling out educators on their shortcomings, but rather calling them into a critical dialogue. In the forthcoming pages, I provide a brief context to SHS, as well as three things for White educators to consider: their need to better understand their racial identity in order to divest from Whiteness, to work toward changing White Eurocentric school practices, and, finally, to work with White youth to rise to the challenge of becoming advocates alongside minoritized populations.

THE RESEARCH CONTEXT

The reflections from this chapter stem from two years (2014–2016) I spent conducting a critical ethnography centered on the high school experiences of Latinx youth, focusing specifically on their identities and sense of belonging at SHS. SHS serves the suburban communities of La Vista and Northwood. La Vista is a majority White middle- and upper-middle-class community. At the time of the study, median household incomes in La Vista were over $115,000. In comparison, its neighbor, Northwood, is a mainly Latinx community, with a sizeable White population. The town is more working-class in nature, with median household incomes around $54,000. During my study, SHS had an enrollment of just over 2,000 students, with over 71% of the students being White and Latinx students constituting just over 22% of the total student population. Additionally, most of the educators at SHS were White (86%). After being granted access to the school to conduct my research, my early interactions with students were facilitated by educators who allowed me into their classrooms and introduced me to Latinx students. During these two years of fieldwork, I shadowed 19 student participants by spending time with them (e.g., classrooms, hallways). I also interviewed each participant and collected artifacts (e.g., school flyers) to gain a deeper understanding of the school culture and how Latinx youth navigated and made sense of SHS. While I was at SHS to learn from Latinx youth, they were interested in me, too, and what I was doing at their school.

As the child of Mexican immigrants who grew up in a suburb, I shared several commonalities with student participants. We were able to come together and share similar cultural practices, and as a native Spanish speaker,

I was able to connect with participants who were comfortable in speaking and understanding Spanish. These commonalities facilitated the rapport I developed with participants. But despite our commonalities, there were also differences—including certain privileges that set me apart from the youth of the study. For example, citizenship status, socioeconomic standing, age, and education level were differentiators. It was therefore important for me to be aware of these differences rather than assume that our commonalities were sufficient to build trusting relationships. I had to work hard to be present in their lives to get to know them.

BEYOND UNDERSTANDING: DIVESTING FROM WHITENESS

Many of the conversations among educators at SHS focused on equity and social justice and supporting marginalized student populations. It was one of the primary reasons I was drawn to the school from the get-go. Yet the more time I spent at this school, the more I saw the nuances of how Whiteness operated, how it was challenged, and how it was not. SHS's piecemeal efforts reflected the school's inability to make sustained inroads into better supporting its Latinx students. There was also a culture of "wokeness" that reflected their knowledge of social justice issues, but seldom did these conversations go beyond Latinx students or other students of color or dive deeply into how Whiteness operated at SHS. When talking about equity, many educators were good at identifying the schools' areas of growth and espoused a commitment to equity. Yet it was as if the school could only have that conversation and nothing further.

As Lipsitz (1998) argues, many educators have a status quo investment in Whiteness. Good intentions, as Castagno (2014) contends, lead to "powerblind-sameness and colorblind-difference" initiatives that ignore systems of oppression. As Lewis and Diamond (2015) document in their research, good intentions are insufficient in combatting inequality in school, particularly if these intentions engage in color-evasive beliefs and discourses and a lack of understanding of historical precedent of how racial inequalities have always been part of schooling in the United States. Moreover, Kohli et al. (2017) go further by arguing that "much of the racism we experience in K-12 schools today is not evaded but actually framed through equity, justice, and antiracist rhetoric" (p. 188).

This viewpoint speaks to schools who take up the call to combat educational inequity but still engage in deficit-driven practices and, in the end, co-opt social justice language as a cover to ultimately place the burden of change on students. I understand why equity initiatives focus on marginalized student populations, but I argue that the spotlight should also be on Whiteness and White supremacy. This path will not be painless. It will require deep introspection and discomfort. As Lyiscott (2019) notes, ". . . you have to be willing to sit in the inevitability of discomfort that accompanies authentic confrontation, to accept that disrupting something as abiding and pervasive as white privilege will have its costs" (p. xiii). This discomfort requires reflection of oneself, but also a keen understanding of how schooling has operated in the United States.

Deficit thinking (Valencia, 2012) has permeated the thoughts of many White educators, informing their views of students, families, and the communities in which they teach when, in fact, they should reflect on their thoughts and actions instead of blaming their students. Much harm can and has been done under the auspices of "good intentions." Rather, the focus should be on understanding the impact of these good intentions and whether they can actually deepen inequality. The student participants of my study all spoke about how grateful and appreciative they were for SHS's opportunities, as well as the support provided by many of their teachers. This put the students in a bind; they felt like they always had to be "grateful," which in turn showed where power ultimately still lies. One of the challenges of engaging in and sustaining social justice work is balancing a needed focus on supporting Latinx youth and the structures, practices, and actors around them.

As Pollock (2001) argues, we should strive to eliminate racial achievement patterns. Still, as she writes, ". . . our quest to eliminate [them] might profit from a more self-conscious look at the moments when Americans talk about achievement—and the moments when we do not" (p. 2). This suggestion is vital in that it allows for an examination of when a color-evasive lens guides things and when it does not. Moreover, it is important to shift away from conversations on the *achievement* gap, which do nothing but reify Whiteness as the norm, to instead focus on the *opportunity* gaps that exist in the lives of students (Carter & Welner, 2013). By focusing on the opportunity gaps, schools can focus on their practices and examine whether and to what degree they may be furthering disproportionalities and upholding White, middle-class values. While being in an environment that is a sea of Whiteness does not define the lives of Latinx youth, it shapes the ways in which they engage in their schooling. These contexts shape the development of their academic and social identities, forcing them to make difficult decisions about how they present themselves to the world. Even in schools engaged in the work of equity and social justice, more is needed to understand the multiplicities of Whiteness and White supremacy.

DiAngelo's (2018) work on White fragility, Matias's (2016) research on the emotionalities of Whiteness, and Cabrera's (2017) concept of White immunity are compelling frameworks by which to examine White educators. The reactions of White educators when they feel challenged not only speaks to their privilege but also to their investment to something that may espouse disdain. White educators should understand their racial identities first before they can begin to engage in meaningful social justice work. By knowing one's racial identity, I do not mean that White teachers must view themselves as fully developed people, as one's identity and consciousness is ever evolving. Rather, what practices White educators are engaged in to learn more about their racial identity, how they are they reflecting on their race vis-à-vis their students and families, how they are approaching a commitment to social justice work, how reflective in general they are of their practices and making connections to their race when relevant, and so forth. At its core, this type of self-awareness requires an investment in reflection and vulnerability with oneself and other White people. By being in conversation with oneself and other White folks, it allows for conversations that lessen the burden on people of color. It allows for a critical safe space for White people to come together and talk about how they can work toward dismantling Whiteness and White supremacy and work toward transformative outcomes.

CHANGING SCHOOL CURRICULA AND PRACTICES

Another factor that contributes to persistent inequalities in U.S. schools is the White, Eurocentric nature of school courses and practices. Because of this, educators in schools need to audit themselves and consider how they can learn from the cultural and linguistic identities of their students to implement more asset-driven approaches. There is no one asset-based approach that has a monopoly; these approaches must be driven by context. What may work in one school may not work in another. Therefore, I believe that the move should be to have curricula be relevant and sustaining. The work on culturally relevant pedagogy (Ladson-Billings, 1995) and culturally sustaining pedagogy (Paris & Alim, 2017) has underscored the importance of schooling practices that affirm students' identities by reflecting them in the classroom, but also actively working to maintain those identities, given the history of schools' erasure of youth of color's identities and cultures. Next, I detail instances of educators' struggles in trying to do good by their students.

In a presentation I led with high school English teachers—most of whom identified as White—a White teacher posed a question about a perception that their freshmen Latinxs did not care for in Sandra Cisneros's *House on Mango Street*. The teacher felt that their students did not connect to the text. In hearing this educator speak, it was clear their desire was to support Latinx students. Yet there was also a subtext; a belief that they were a good, culturally relevant educator by teaching the Cisneros text. Without my being in the classroom, it is hard to say how it was taught or why some Latinx youth did not like the book. With that said, it is important for educators in similar positions to consider thinking beyond their intent and examine whether any assumptions about students are being made. Or to consider embracing the inclusion of students as meaningful stakeholders in the decision-making process when it comes to curriculum development.

Moreover, if these types of conversations with students do take place, it is important to think about how to best incorporate student feedback and to then select texts that are relevant to them. In the end, embracing culturally relevant and sustaining approaches to teaching go beyond merely selecting texts that seemingly reflect the students we are entrusted with. It is important to never lose sight of the fact that not all Latinx students are the same (e.g., interests, ethnicity). What may work with one cohort of students may not work for another. Further, by implementing additive ways of teaching, teachers provide an opportunity for Latinx youth to embrace their cultural and linguistic identities. In so doing, educators could work toward dismantling an educational system that has more often than not told Latinx youth in different forms that who they are does not matter.

In a different instance, I observed a social studies teacher facilitating a conversation with their mainly White class about the benefits of attending community college as way to save money. Again, the teacher meant well, but the outcome missed the intended goal. In a classroom comprising high-achieving seniors who were mainly affluent and White, community college was never a legitimate consideration. Students were then asked by their teacher to share their college plans upon graduating from high school. All of the White students had already made up their mind about where they were going. They spoke about their plans to attend "elite" private liberal arts colleges (e.g., Swarthmore) or well-respected, large public and private universities (e.g., Duke, Michigan). White students not going to college were taking gap years abroad.

The few Latinx students in the class shared the universities they were considering, and while these universities were nothing to be ashamed about, they felt embarrassed by the differences in their plans from those of their White counterparts, given the context they were in. Here you had an educator who spoke about the benefits of going to community college and speaking about their experiences in doing so, but it missed the mark, as these were seniors who had already made up their mind and were put in a position to showcase their racial and class privilege. A reason why this message fell short and alienated the Latinx youth in this class was that the Latinx students at SHS were immersed in a school community with a predominately White, affluent, college-going culture, while Latinx youth in this area are mainly working-class and those opportunities are often not available to them. Moments like these are damaging to Latinx youth in that the unintended consequences were not considered. It is not that Latinx youth do not want to talk about their post–high school ambitions or that they do not want to go to college, but for many Latinx youth, these conversations are not always part of everyday life, as their opportunities are more financially limited and everything does not revolve around talking about college and gap years like it may for many of the White middle-class youth in this school. Educators should consider finding opportunities to interrupt White youth from engaging in actions that further the normalization of Whiteness, and one of the ways to do so is to make them aware of their privilege and its subsequent necessity for them to be advocates for anti-racist outcomes.

WORKING WITH WHITE YOUTH

Latinx youth are in need of interracial solidarity from their White class-mates. There is growing attention to the racial identities of White children and youth (Hagerman, 2018). More work is needed to better understand White youth and how to support the development of their sociopolitical consciousness as well as advocacy. These are initial foundational steps on a path toward interracial solidarity. On one particular day during my field-work, for example, I shadowed Latinx participants in their science class as their White educator struggled to start class. The teacher contended with a rambunctious group of White seniors who had a playfully combative re-lationship their teacher. The teacher decided to distance some of the more rambunctious White youth from one another. These students were not pleased and were pleading their case at the start of class. They finally acqui-esced and class began, only to be interrupted when another White student entered and was surprised to discover the seating change. This reignited the original debate, during which the Latinx youth sat quietly and occasionally whispered to one another as they waited for class to begin again.

Later in the class, students went to the back of the classroom to do lab work; they were setting up their tables and talking to one another. The White student who came in late was also socializing but becoming disrup-tive as she joked around about throwing an object in a fish tank and then made a mess by spraying water over the countertops near the sink. The teacher saw this and threatened the student by asking her if she wanted to be sent to the dean's office. The student was not intimidated by the threat and continued with her disruptive behavior. Despite her continued behav-ior, the White student was not sent away to the dean's office and went on to complete her lab work with her classmates. This incident made me think about the latitude White youth are allowed when it comes to acting out in comparison to Latinx youth who are disproportionately punished by adults in schools (Irby, 2018; Wun, 2018).

After the election of Donald Trump as president, the majority of students and staff at SHS were dismayed by the outcome. The state of the school after election night entailed a variety of negative emotions (e.g., anger, sadness). There was a collective sense that something needed to happen, and students and staff got together to explore the possibilities. Adults played a supportive role as young people took the lead in an after-school meeting a few weeks after Trump's election. Because it was a moment that featured students from different racial identities and different academic tracks, I sensed the possibility for something powerful to occur; the potential for interracial solidarity, and maybe, just maybe, a youth-led movement. In the end, the meetings dissipated. In this meeting and a few others that came after, White youth took the lead and spoke about important issues, but the amount of space they took up silenced Latinx youth and other youth of color present.

Moreover, the ideas students shared were quite different. Many of the White youth saw an opportunity to mobilize and advocate for action through formal channels, using their privilege to advocate for change (e.g., meeting with elected officials). While for Latinx youth, they were seeking a space to process their emotions, and for some it was an opportunity to raise issues happening in their school. To me, this was an opportunity to honor White youth's ideas, but to also challenge and push back to help youth develop a multifaceted approach. I saw it as an opportunity for White youth to not only share their ideas but to also sit back, listen, and learn from Latinx youth and other youth of color.

I was part of these conversations and failed to build capacity to help these camps. I, along with the other adults present, did not want to silence or take over the direction of the conversations and wanted to allow students the space to run their conversations. In retrospect, our role as facilitators was insufficient. Students attending these conversations were in need of more active facilitation and direction for some of the ideas being generated. While the group did launch an awareness campaign sharing statistics and questions regarding social justice issues with flyers posted throughout the school, conversations dissipated and White youth were not active contributors when the awareness campaign took shape. In the end, the broader school community was unable and unwilling to take up more sustained action, yet I wonder how differently things could have turned out if the school had a more formal vision of how to support the sociopolitical development of its students and had emboldened its staff to do this type of work across content areas.

CONCLUSION

Latinx youth across educational contexts are in need of allies, be they school peers or the adults in their lives, who are not only willing to affirm their existence but advocate on their behalf. The sociopolitical moment that we find ourselves in has left little doubt that more needs to be done. Neutral stances are nothing more than equivocation to the status quo. Having good intentions and espousing a rhetoric of wokeness is insufficient, as they work toward maintaining the status quo if they are not coupled with action. As adults, we must take affirmative measures to learn more about ourselves and the power we possess when we collectively mobilize. Interventionist approaches will do little to stem the tide of oppression and inequality. The lengths to which school programming and resources aim to "fix" students rather than focus on systems and the ways in which they reproduce inequality (e.g., Eurocentric curricula, grit, school discipline) merely nibble around the edges of the issue. They ultimately are only Band-Aids on an issue needing more comprehensive structural change. While transformation does not occur overnight, it requires a foundation that requires doing the work of knowing ourselves and the privileges we possess if we are to decolonize our minds and help young people embrace who they are in all of their complexities.

NOTES

1. I capitalize White because it is important that we recognize it as a racial identity. While arguments made in favor of not capitalizing the word are valid in their own right, for the purposes of this chapter it is important to capitalize White so as not to erase it and to highlight the ways Whiteness is enacted to protect and advance White supremacy.

2. While not the focus of the chapter, it is important to note that teachers of color must also interrogate their identities and actions, as they, too, can harm and undermine social justice efforts.

REFERENCES

Cabrera, N. L. (2017). White immunity: Working through some of the pedagogical pitfalls of 'privilege.' *Journal Committed to Social Change on Race and Ethnicity, 3*(1), 77–90.

Carter, P. L., & Welner, K. G. (Eds.). (2013). *Closing the opportunity gap: What America must do to give every child an even chance.* Oxford University Press.

Castagno, A. E. (2014). *Educated in whiteness: Good intentions and diversity in schools.* University of Minnesota Press.

DiAngelo, R. (2018). *White fragility: Why it's so hard for white people to talk about racism.* Beacon Press.

Hagerman, M. A. (2018). *White kids: Growing up with privilege in a racially divided America.* New York University Press.

Irby, D. J. (2018). Mo' data, mo' problems: Making sense of racial discipline disparities in a large diversifying suburban high school. *Educational Administration Quarterly, 54*(5), 693–722.

Kohli, R., Pizarro, M., & Nevárez, A. (2017). The "new racism" of K-12 schools: Centering critical research on racism. *Review of Research in Education, 41*(1), 182–202.

Ladson-Billings, G. (1995). Toward a theory of culturally relevant pedagogy. *American Educational Research Journal, 32*(3), 465–491.

Lewis, A. E., & Diamond, J. B. (2015). *Despite the best intentions: How racial inequality thrives in good schools.* Oxford University Press.

Lipsitz, G. (1998). *The possessive investment in whiteness: How white people profit from identity politics.* Temple University Press.

Lyiscott, J. (2019). *Black appetite, White food: Issues of race, voice, and justice within and beyond the classroom.* Routledge.

Matias, C. E. (2016). *Feeling white: Whiteness, emotionality, and education.* Sense Publishers.

Paris, D., & Alim, H. S. (Eds.). (2017). *Culturally sustaining pedagogies: Teaching and learning for justice in a changing world.* Teachers College Press.

Pollock, M. (2001). How the question we ask most about race in education is the very question we most suppress. *Educational Researcher, 30*(9), 2–12.

Valencia, R. R. (Ed.). (2012). *The evolution of deficit thinking: Educational thought and practice.* Routledge.

Wun, C. (2018). Angered: Black and non-Black girls of color at the intersections of violence and school discipline in the United States. *Race Ethnicity and Education, 21*(4), 423–437.

CHAPTER 5

Dead Ends and Paths Forward

White Teachers Committed to Anti-Racist Teaching in White Spaces

Petra Lange and Callie Kane

> One metaphor for race, and racism, won't do. They are, after all, exceedingly complicated forces. No, we need many metaphors, working in concert.
>
> —Michael Eric Dyson (2018)[1]

The historical and cultural forces shaping predominantly white suburban schools are almost unidentifiable to those of us who gain the most from them. The structures supporting "elite" schools become "rendered invisible" by policies masking disparate outcomes and curriculum reflecting dominant cultures. Beverly Tatum (2003) compares this constant exposure to oppressive systems, specifically racism, to smog. "We don't breathe it because we like it. We don't breathe it because we think it's good for us. We breathe it because it's the only air that's available" (Herbes-Sommers et al., 2003). Schools filled with this smog are inevitably affected in all facets of policy and practice (Tatum, 2017). If we are constantly and pervasively exposed to racial oppression, to the point we are unaware of it, how do we begin to identify and eradicate it? As we try, it becomes imperative to ask: Which things *are made* to be invisible and forgotten? What "maps" can we use to help us navigate and even transform the landscape of education?

This chapter represents two white English teachers' reflections on our time working together in a suburban high school. We know the hallways in our schools are choked with the smog of white supremacy, our classrooms are dense with the opacity of privilege, and voices of resistance are muffled by racism. We are all too familiar with problematic binaries (e.g., two types of educators—"good" ones who are *not* racist or "bad" ones who are) that give the illusion that only two paths forward exist, polarizing teaching staff and limiting our possibilities to create lasting antiracist changes. For this chapter, we've marked the previously invisible barriers we repeatedly encountered and traced our way through labyrinthine recollections of our own interactions with systems of supremacy.

This winding road isn't a straight progression, but loops back in on itself, so we discover similar landmarks of oppression that appear in new settings. The more familiar we are with these tell-tale signs of oppression, the more likely we are to be successful in dismantling them. Rocky terrains of racism that were once unrecognized or insurmountable can now be navigated while tripping fewer and fewer times. Following Black, Indigenous, and people of color (BIPOC) educational theorists and researchers like Bettina Love, Cheryl Matias, Beverly Tatum, and Renee Watson, paths are illuminated, leading to doorways where the smog can be aired out. With the help of these writers, we can trace our way back through our own whiteness and navigate the haze in order to fully remember and understand what brought us to this point and our desire to equip students to "work for a more socially just society themselves" as "activist teachers engaged in challenging and transforming equitable structures and policies" (Chubbuck & Zembylas, 2008, p. 285). In order to do so, we must chart the steps and missteps we as two white educators have taken in our journey with trying to make ourselves and our schools more anti-racist.

BEING GOOD AT BEING BAD: WRESTLING WITH DEFINITIONS

The beauty of anti-racism is that you don't have to pretend to be free of racism to be an anti-racist. Anti-racism is the commitment to fight racism wherever you find it, including in yourself. And it's the only way forward.

—Ijeoma Oluo (2019)[2]

Teachers, students, and community members filled the high school auditorium, creating a warm sense of community that set the stage for a rather uncomfortable evening of learning. I found a spot in the back of the crowd, settling into a viewing of the film *I'm Not Racist, Am I?* (Green, 2014), a documentary exploring the ongoing growth of a group of students as they learned about race and racism. At the time, I was a 3rd-year teacher just beginning my journey into equity work and recently joined my school's newly formed equity team. When I was invited to view the film, I was eager to expand my learning, and it happened through a definition of racism shared in a simple formula: power + prejudice = racism. The film continued, explaining that, based on this definition, Black people could not be racist—and because white people benefit from this oppressive system, all white people *are* racist. It was a controversial part of the film and one that led a man in the audience to push back on this newer definition during a question-and-answer session with the director. He asserted, reading from the dictionary, the *true* definition of racism was hatred or intolerance directed at a person because of racial differences. While he may have thought he came across as rational by quoting a dictionary, his tone dripped with an authoritative incredulity tinged with anger. The film's definition of racism meant he benefited from a racist system, therefore making *him* racist. Clearly, he disagreed. However, the film's definition was a revelatory moment for me. In reflection of that moment, I still struggle with fully knowing what conception I had of racism before I watched that film. What did I ever think it was before? Was I like the man in the audience who only thought of the dictionary definition?

The eagerness with which many white teachers try to move away from participation in white supremacy is important as we work to incorporate anti-racist pedagogies in our practice. The desire to *not* harm students is a powerful motivation, keeping us engaged in learning about the deleterious ways racism has molded our lives. This knowledge and introspective practice hone necessary skills to be able to see how white supremacy hides in plain sight in our curricular content, instructional strategies, and classroom culture. When we consider the ways racism appears in our teaching, however, it can be disconcerting, even horrifying, to reflect on the unintentional but very *real* harm done to students, upending our self-perception based on how we define "good teachers" and "good people." This impedes our ability to face, reflect, and discuss how white supremacy has shaped us; how it has affected our personal growth; and how it reifies white supremacy in our schools. DiAngelo (2018) terms this the "Good/Bad binary," a false dichotomy that makes it impossible for white people to consider themselves "good" while still participating in racism in any way. We white folks would rather vehemently and *inaccurately* deny our participation in racist systems than admit we're not a "good person." This defensiveness, *white fragility*, manifests in myriad ways (e.g., anger, tears, shutting down) (DiAngelo, 2018). It diverts us from learning through the examination of the need to change our teaching.

While these examples of white fragilities have become more widely known, our experiences illuminate other ways our psyches respond to the shame experienced when we consider the ways we support white supremacy in our teaching. It shows up in our faculty breakrooms during rushed lunches with colleagues when we discuss who the "bad/racist" teachers are. Of course, racism *is* bad, and illuminating practices or policies that create racial inequities is essential. Labeling others as bad/racist, though, allows us to fool ourselves into thinking that we are disconnected from the harmful effects of our whiteness (e.g., "It's those teachers over there being racist, not me!"). In creating a hierarchy where we can place ourselves as superior to the "bad/racist" teachers, we're also deceiving ourselves—and in that deception, we keep hidden the ways that racism shows up in our teaching. If we neglect to internally reflect on how racism shows up in us, we remove the possibility of changing the systems of oppression that start with us. The forgetting/failure to recognize beliefs and actions that could fall on the "bad" side of the binary removes us from ever having to perceive ourselves as the "bad guy." While sitting in that break room, it's easy to compare ourselves to these "bad" teachers, who don't attempt to diversify their curriculum because *we've* got the latest young adult books by various authors of color. In addition to having a diverse set of texts, however, we need to critically examine *every* aspect of our practice—*at all times*. It's not about checking boxes in order to fit into a category to rest assured. Anti-racist teaching takes continual reflection, flexible reactions, and recursive curriculum.

The definition of racism that was shared in the film is defined by Ijeoma Oluo (2018) this way: "a prejudice against someone based on race, when those prejudices are reinforced by systems of power" (Oluo, 2018, p. 27). This emphasis on *systems* allows us to see that racism continues in our history not only through personal ideologies but in policies and practices that structure the institutions we inhabit (Tatum, 2017). This definition helps us collapse the good/bad binary because it is not dependent on where we live, which political party we give our votes to, or how educated we are, but it *is* dependent on the systems and institutions we support—*all* of which are founded in racism.

INTRAPERSONAL DEVELOPMENT AND
EQUITABLE ACCESS TO LEARNING

When considering how the good/bad binaries create tension in naming racism in our own lives and practices, it helps to examine definitions that pull us even further from those dichotomies inhibiting growth and action. For example, in his book *How to Be an Antiracist*, Ibram Kendi (2019) defines "racist" as someone who conveys an idea that asserts one racial group is superior or inferior to another or supports a policy that enforces racial dominance of one group over another through action or inaction (p. 22). He constructs the definition of "antiracist" as one who must express an anti-racist idea or act on dismantling racist policies and replace them with anti-racist ones (pp. 22–23). Naturally, he leaves inaction out of his anti-racist definition, acknowledging that to simply go along and do nothing *is supporting racism*. Like Tatum's (2017) analogy of breathing smog, clearing pollution can't be done through inaction. In every moment, a person could either be enacting racism or anti-racism. For Kendi "'racist' and 'anti-racist' are like peelable nametags that are placed and replaced based on what someone is doing or not doing, supporting or expressing in each moment. These are not permanent tattoos" (Kendi, 2019, p. 23); it is what we *do* or *espouse* that is either racist or anti-racist—not who we are.

Kendi's notion of "peelable nametags" further decimates the good teacher/bad teacher binary by forcing us to examine each moment fluidly to consider if we are expressing a racist or anti-racist idea or supporting racist or anti-racist policies. Teachers must engage in a process of reflective praxis to make sure we don't allow a racist moment to go unchecked. We must hold ourselves accountable through constant critical analysis of our thoughts and actions, gathering feedback that will constructively shift how we interact with curriculum, students, and colleagues. The usefulness of applying the metaphor of "peelable labels" became apparent during a lunch break when I was joined by a third friend, processing something troubling. She had just walked by a group of students conversing in the hallway; perceiving them to be agitated and upset, she went to the nearby counseling office and asked someone to check on them, as she was concerned an altercation was about to take place. The students were all Black young women.

This teacher understandably felt weird about her decision. As she finished her story, she admitted being left with several nagging questions: If they had been white students, would she have chosen the same course of action? If they had been white students, would she have even noticed that they seemed agitated? Did she do the right thing? And if she did the right thing, why did she feel so weird? Her questions were good, and I hope that's how I responded in that moment by telling her how important that kind of questioning and reflection is. But all I remember is how exhausted I felt and how much I wanted to tell her, "I'm sure it's nothing. I'm sure you did the right thing." The snag that caught me from these shallow reassurances was that I had passed by those very same girls. They were students who had been working with me during lunches and planning periods to discuss how they had been traumatized by racism in our school's hallways. What I remember in that moment, when I couldn't formulate any coherent response to my colleague, a friend in the room spoke up and said, "I think you feeling that way tells you that there *was* something wrong there." Later that day, the students came to me to tell their story of a teacher policing their emotional responses to (yet another) microaggression they were processing by getting someone from the counseling office to help them "calm down." Something indeed was wrong there.

If we were to create a permanent tattoo of "racist/bad teacher" for our colleague (or myself for that matter), that labeling would have deteriorated our relationship and prevented growth (both personal and professional). Using the "peelable" label of a racist moment that we could rectify gives us a place to move and continue moving toward anti-racist work (not freeze for fear of being labeled "bad"). If we can't recognize our moments of racism, then we cannot grow in our intrapersonal development as teachers or embody the dispositions that value praxis (Chubbuck & Zembylas, 2008). We have to welcome challenge and need to acknowledge moments we've messed up. Honesty, openness, and resilience are needed to critique ourselves and seek guidance from colleagues in the fight against racism. Instead of hiding this moment from us, rendering it invisible from critique, our colleague chose to share it and embrace being challenged, which helped us all grow.

COMMITTING TO ANTI-RACISM

Anti-racism work is not self-improvement work for white people. It doesn't end when white people feel better about what they've done. It ends when black people are staying alive and they have their liberation.

—Rachel Cargle (2020)[3]

At the end of a long week, a persistent worry, circulating for days, was still on my mind. I finally had the words to articulate what it was I was feeling, and as I walked from my classroom down the long, fluorescent-lit hallway to my colleague's classroom, I felt exhausted and annoyed with myself. I had recently joined the efforts of a student-led anti-racist group. Their tireless endeavors to liberate themselves by transforming their educational institution illuminated how crucial this work is in creating systemic change. Their efforts produced results, their focus was unflappable, and the vision for their school was tangible. They inspired me to want to do more, but where would I begin? And more importantly, I had to wonder: What am I doing this equity work for? Was it for the recognition? To feel like I'm a good white person? I needed to know. Reaching my colleague's door, we started to chat as students flowed around us in the hallway to their next class. If they had paid any attention to our conversation, they would have seen me gesticulating wildly as I expressed this disconcerting feeling, trying to exorcise the grossness of the white savior forming inside of me.

When we consider how our white anti-racist work requires a deep and long-term commitment and that superficial understandings of race can be just as detrimental as unexamined racism, teachers (especially white teachers) must continually learn about culturally responsive pedagogies to understand our own racialization and increase our own comfort discussing race. While we personally benefit from that growth, it is our students of color who should be centered in our teaching. The introspective work white teachers do to identify how we have been socialized into white supremacy (Sensoy & DiAngelo, 2012) isn't done for its own sake, but for the sake of following the lead of those anti-racist students of color: to be able to support them and be able to recognize how our own whiteness may interfere with their goals and remove the barriers our whiteness causes. As critical whiteness scholar Cheryl Matias reminds us, "When you're focusing on understanding whiteness and just applying it only to yourself, that is engaging in the narcissism of whiteness" (Equity Literacy Institute, 2020, 44:30).

We must also be able to imagine a way forward to a better world. Helpfully, Bettina Love (2019) describes "Freedom Dreaming" as "dreams grounded in a critique of injustice. These dreams are not whimsical, unattainable daydreams, they are critical and imaginative dreams of collective resistance" (p. 101). Freedom Dreaming is exactly what was witnessed in the student-led anti-racist group during each of their weekly meetings. They inspire, plan, envision, and dream up ways to create change in a system that makes it nearly impossible to do so. Their Freedom Dreaming is no less effective because of those obstacles they face, but is effective because of what their dreaming represents: the beauty of a better future. Envisioning a better future requires a working knowledge of our past and a realistic view of the present—specifically how race and racism have been formed and continue to form our world. As we write this chapter, the Black Lives Matter movement's liberatory demonstrations and resistance efforts are changing policy and perspectives in our state because, after yet another murder of a Black man at the hands of police was caught on video, we see the upsurge of action birthed from their Freedom Dreaming.

On the other hand, for two white teachers, the posts on our social media have become an unending scroll of white responses to the violence of racism (again). Some white people posted "confessional" type videos where they were either shocked by the racism experienced by people of color or were taking responsibility for their own complicity in allowing racism to go unchecked in their own lives. It was as if white people in the United States suddenly became aware of racism and the deaths of Black people for the first time (again) and they wanted the world to know how they felt about it. This inundation of well-intentioned but seemingly meaningless reflection from these white individuals has not yet been followed with any action that would eradicate racist policies and practices in the real world. These performances, without any lasting anti-racist changes, quickly become disingenuous and self-serving.

The same kind of "white narcissism" Matias (2020) describes shows up here again, centering whiteness and framing the revelatory moments of white people into heroic actions. Similar events happen in schools in the form of "white saviorism," when teachers "saw themselves as kindhearted people who were doing right by less fortunate and students who struggled to maintain their culture and identity while being forced to be the type of student their teacher envisioned" (Emdin, 2016, p. 4). Marks of being a "good teacher" show up when we can recite stories of how well we can "relate with Black male students" (Murray & Yuhaniak, 2017, p. 74), for example. But by centering on white teachers, these stories only serve to keep the same racist systems in place that harm our students of color. Like the many individuals posting in social media feeds who were not following up their messages of support with concrete action, teachers who do not take tangible actions create messages of support that feel like empty gestures, signaling a teacher's "virtue" without having any virtuous action to back it up. Along with the virtue signaling, there is a performative ally aspect where these individuals were centering themselves and their own feelings, sharing how the protests made them feel about racism.

When we are considering the difference between performative and authentic responses to racism, we can follow the spotlight to see whether it's pointing at *lasting* anti-racist changes in our policies and schools. This binary of performance and authenticity, however, like many binaries, is a misleading dichotomy: performance does not have to live on the opposite end of the spectrum as authenticity. Those performances are public declarations decrying racism and serve as an opportunity for white folks to be held accountable. It is necessary for white folks to *do* anti-racism work—not to stand on the sidelines and let the brunt of oppression fall on people of color to experience *and* resolve. In other words, white people bear the responsibility of dismantling white supremacy and engaging in the emotional labor to publicly respond to the racism appearing in our workplaces, worship spaces, dining rooms, and board rooms. These public performances of anti-racism *must* be followed up with action; steps must be taken to disrupt racism where it appears in our daily lives. And it takes emotional acuity to know when to step up and when to step back. Unfortunately, many of these performances are left as statements hanging in the air or online or in faculty meetings, and the revelations, confessions, and promises about anti-racism are quickly forgotten. This collective forgetting by white people, who seemed to care so much before, only makes it easier for the changes suggested by some politicians, administrators, businesses, friends, and loved ones to go unfulfilled. Without tangible action, we are only reinforcing the racist structures we inherited.

TEACHERS CHALLENGING AND TRANSFORMING SCHOOLS

One of the ways educators can work toward lasting change in our school is through transforming the inequitable structures and policies we see daily. While manifestations of these efforts are manifold, we've found success in weekly meetings with our independently formed Equity Professional Learning Community (PLC). The creation of this PLC was not one required by administration, but was created organically by a small group of passionate educators. The essential function of this collaboration is to create systemic change by reflecting critically on our professional practice. It began when four teachers serving on the Equity Team at our school started eating lunch together on Wednesdays. We were seeking an outlet, a place for camaraderie in the face of what felt like insurmountable harm being done to the students of color in our school. Our meetings were built on trust and vulnerability that allowed us to vent, but also allowed us to come together to find ways to create change. We're constantly challenged by the ideas brought forth by our colleagues, but we're also provided a comfortable and nonjudgmental space to ruminate on the new ideas presented.

Over time, these weekly lunches morphed into a more intentional meeting where we focused on critical practice and a place where we would expect a hearty critique of each other's complicity in racism and other systems of oppression. Inequitable structures within our school are being challenged very directly through this community building as we work together to reform our practices (e.g., including students in our curricular decisionmaking) and relationships with students (e.g., supporting them in meetings with the administration to influence hiring committees and school- and district-wide anti-racist professional development, advising student activist groups focused on dismantling racism within our school and community). When teachers, administrators, and district officials support the excellence of students advocating for their own liberation through social justice, it supports structural change that upends traditional oppressive hierarchies that place white adults in charge.

CONCLUDING THOUGHTS

> I knew as well as I knew anything that the oppressor must be liberated just as surely as the oppressed. . . . The oppressed and the oppressor alike are robbed of their humanity.
>
> —Nelson Mandela (1995)[4]

Markers of racism will appear in different interactions, institutions, and intrapersonal reflections; when we recognize them, we can make new, better, anti-racist decisions. We must constantly ask ourselves: Which things *are made* to be invisible and forgotten? Where is the racism trying to retain its permanence in our schools? We must mark it in our memories to remember where there has been progress in hopes that we are less likely to repeat past racist ways of thinking and acting. This reflective practice equips us with tools to help in the passing forward of knowledge, knowing where we need to *unlearn* so much, and remembering where we hope to end—in the future our students are dreaming.

NOTES

1. Quote from the foreword to Robin DiAngelo's book *White Fragility*.

2. Tweet retrieved at https://twitter.com/ijeomaoluo/status/1150565193832943617?lang=en

3. Quote from *InStyle* magazine retrieved at https://www.instyle.com/news/rachel-cargle-george-floyd-amy-cooper-racism-in-america

4. Quote from Nelson Mandela's autobiography, *Long Walk to Freedom*.

REFERENCES

DiAngelo, R. (2018). *White fragility: Why it's so hard for white people to talk about racism*. Beacon Press.

Dyson, M. E. (2018). *What truth sounds like*. St. Martin's Press.

Emdin. C. (2016). *For white folks who teach in the hood . . . and the rest of y'all, too: Reality pedagogy and urban education*. Beacon Press.

Equity Literacy Institute. (2020, July 8). Cheryl Matias interviewed by Paul Gorski [Webinar].

Greene, C. W. (Director). (2014). *I'm Not Racist, Am I?* [Film]. Point Made Films.

Herbes-Sommers, C., Strain, T. H., & Smith, L. (Directors). (2003). *Race: The power of an illusion* [Film]. Public Broadcasting Service.

Kendi, I. (2019). *How to be an antiracist*. One World.

Love, B. (2019). *We want to do more than survive: Abolitionist teaching and the pursuit of educational freedom*. Beacon Press.

Murray, A. D., & Yuhaniak, H. E. (2017). Creating equity warriors in the face of white fragility. *Confronting Racism in Teacher Education: Counternarratives of Critical Practice*, 74–80.

Oluo, I. (2018). *So you want to talk about race*. Seal Press.

Sensoy, O., & DiAngelo, R. (2012). *Is everyone really equal? An introduction to key concepts in social justice education*. Teachers College Press.

Tatum, B. (2003). *Why are all the Black kids sitting together in the cafeteria?: Revised edition*. Hachette UK.

Tatum, B. (2017). *Why are all the Black kids sitting together in the cafeteria? And other conversations about race*. Basic Books.

CHAPTER 6

Unspoken Rules, White Communication Styles, and White Blinders

Why "Elite" Independent Schools Can't Retain Black and Brown Faculty

Ayo Magwood

The *retention*—even more so than *recruitment*—of Black and Brown faculty continues to be a pervasive and enduring problem at independent schools (Kane & Orsini, 2003). Faculty of color currently make up 19% of total faculty members in independent schools; limited research has found that experiences with exclusion, bias, and heightened anxiety lead faculty to leave (Edwards, 2020). For example, a 2003 Association of Independent Schools in New England (AISNE) survey of educators of color in New England independent schools noted that teachers of color "tend to leave schools more quickly than Whites, often because the culture and climate do not feel as supportive as they should" (Brosnan, 2003b, p. 6). The report found that about one-third of educators of color expressed frustration with their jobs and schools and were planning on or considering leaving their school in the coming year. Most of the frustration related *specifically* to their identity in relation to their context.

In this chapter, I elaborate on some of the most commonly named factors that lead Black and Brown faculty to leave—or get pushed out of—independent schools and explore the racial, psychological, and sociological dynamics underlying these challenges. Weaving together findings from research with insights from Black and Brown educators from independent schools, I focus on four challenges likely to be denied and resisted by independent schools as they operate on subconscious or structural levels: "talking the talk without walking the walk," vulnerability to privileged parents, double standards, and White blinders.

TALKING THE TALK WITHOUT WALKING THE WALK

Over the last 2 decades, many independent schools have made concerted efforts to increase their numbers of Black and Brown faculty and students; hire diversity, equity, and inclusion (DEI) directors; increase racial awareness training; and increase multicultural and DEI programming (Brosnan, 2001). Yet these efforts do not seem to be having their intended effect. Over the last year, three reputable independent schools received negative national press when White students perpetrated racist acts (Downey, 2019; Shapiro, 2019; Smylie, 2020). This summer's Black@ posts gave voice to a tidal wave of Black alumni, student, and faculty who shared an overwhelming number of anecdotal personal experiences that publicly gave lie to the insistent claims of independent schools that they are characterized by equitable racial climates.

One reason why these efforts at DEI training and programming are not having a notable effect on actual racial attitudes and behavior at independent schools may be that independent schools are "talking the talk" without "walking the walk." This is out of necessity. While independent schools often profess values of diversity and social justice, they are careful to not pursue racial equity goals aggressively enough to ruffle the feathers of wealthy alumni donors or their paying parent customers or to impede their efforts to make sure their privileged students benefit from every possible advantage that money can buy. The way that these wealthy White parents and the schools they attend resolve what Hagerman (2018) calls the "conundrum of privilege" (i.e., the phenomenon of many progressive wealthy White families maximizing their children's advantages more than their commitment to racial and social justice) is through "performative wokeness," a form of politically correct virtue signaling—"talking the talk" without any substantive "walking the walk."

Thus, the racial equity and social justice programming in many independent schools takes the form of learning about diversity-related concepts and issues through "feel-good" awareness-raising assemblies and workshops (Grinage, 2020) or of learning about social injustice in faraway places. Students never need to question their complicity in systems of privilege or how their lives reproduce inequity. In fact, all too often, the racial equity and social justice programming of independent schools paradoxically becomes reduced to a way of allowing wealthy White students to develop cultural competency skills, signal virtue, and "divert attention away from the power of dominant groups by convincing subordinates that they are compassionate, kind, and giving" (Gaztambide-Fernández & Howard, 2013, p. 3). This superficial racial justice programming and "performative wokeness" becomes a way for independent schools to increase their marketability and improve their brand without having to fundamentally interrogate how their systems, policies, and procedures reproduce a hostile racial environment and double standards for Black and Brown faculty and students or how the school itself reproduces economic and racial inequity.

As one sign of how independent schools "talk the talk without walking the walk," many DEI directors at independent schools note that they often do not receive the support, power, or funds necessary to carry out the initiatives they are charged with and that as one observed, "I am supported as long as I make faculty and staff feel good about the many 'isms' prevalent on our campus. But when I ask the tough questions, I'm viewed as that angry black person" (Brosnan, 2003b, p. 8). Many independent schools also resist meting out serious consequences to White students who perpetrate racist acts. For example, the three schools that received negative national press received it not so much for the racist students acts, but rather for their resistance to meting out serious consequences (Downey, 2019; Shapiro, 2019; Smylie, 2020). Perhaps most persuasively, the Black@ Instagram posts demonstrated that even in schools that tout themselves as racially progressive, Black students, alumni, and teachers over decades share a perception that Black faculty and students face a hostile racial climate.

Even when independent schools and parents talk to White students about the importance of equity, these students are "hearing" and learning from much louder actions about their position in social hierarchies and whether rules apply to them (Hagerman, 2018). They notice that they live in predominantly White wealthy communities and attend predominantly White wealthy schools where they observe the double standards faced by faculty and students of different races and classes, the lack of respect afforded Black and Brown faculty and staff by some White parents, the ways in which the school allows or enables higher-socioeconomic status (SES) White parents to "rig the markets" and unfairly hoard opportunities for their children at the expense of less privileged children (Calarco, 2020; Lewis & Diamond, 2015; Reeves, 2017), and more. This "hidden curriculum" is largely responsible for the hostile racial climate reported in the Black@ posts and takes a toll on the professional growth and retention of teachers of color (Kohli, 2018).

An additional layer of psychological stress is added to the stress of navigating a hostile racial climate if Black and Brown teachers also have to deal with gaslighting. Black and Brown educators who raise concerns about double standards or racial bias are sometimes "racially gaslighted" when White administrators and teachers vehemently deny this racial bias. Whether intentional or inadvertent, the result is the same: the perpetuation and normalization of the school's racial bias and the pathologizing of Black and Brown faculty who raise these concerns (Davis & Ernst, 2017). One teacher of color remembers:

> I was once invited to participate in a school-wide focus-group meeting of staff members—both administration and teachers—to discuss school challenges. I felt a little intimidated about speaking up, as two higher-up administrators were participating. However, I spoke up about two school practices I felt strongly about, explaining why I thought they were racially inequitable. The administrator who was running the meeting nonchalantly dismissed my first concern, explaining "Well, that is the way we like to do it, so that's not for discussion. Next issue." However dismissive this was, it was still much kinder than the response to my second concern, raised much later in the meeting. The second administrator yelled at me, saying in a disrespectful, patronizing, and aggressive

tone, "You are wrong! All teachers have the same access to the head of school and get treated equally! There is no in-circle and out-circle of faculty members." I would note that this administrator was widely known as the head of school's favorite teacher. No one else in the room said a word. I knew it would be political suicide to cross a high-ranking staff member who had the head of school's ear and who held significant unofficial power in the school, so I swallowed my pride and kept silent. Shortly afterward, the allotted meeting time ran out and the meeting was ended before we had a chance to discuss the last item on the agenda: the school's poor retention rate of faculty of color. The first administrator shook his head as he snapped his laptop shut, "It's such a mystery why we can't retain Black and Brown faculty of color."

VULNERABILITY TO PRIVILEGED PARENTS

Related to their schools not "walking the walk" is the vulnerability some Black and Brown educators feel in relation to privileged parents. Some Black and Brown educators report that wealthy White students and parents appear to be more comfortable with unjustly challenging them about grades and academic consequences and, in some cases, that their administration does not sufficiently support them when this occurs. Several studies document how higher-SES White parents pressure teachers and schools to win advantages or exemptions for their children (Calarco, 2020; Lewis & Diamond, 2015; Reeves, 2017). In fact, a combination of direct and indirect pressure from wealthy parents at independent schools may be leading to higher levels of grade inflation (Hurwitz & Lee, 2018). Since Black and Brown teachers tend to have less power in independent schools—particularly as they tend to be newer to the school—it stands to reason that they may be particularly vulnerable to the efforts of overprotective, privileged parents who challenge or pressure teachers to maximize their child's position in the world. Speaking to this phenomenon, three Black and Brown teachers share their experiences:

> If I get pushback from students about grades, it is almost always from a White student, more likely a White male student. These conversations have almost always started with a sentiment that the grade was too harsh or that the assignment itself was flawed in some way. In my first year at my current school a boy insisted that he be allowed to re-write an assignment, even though I had announced to the class ahead of time that I was not allowing re-writes of this particular assignment because the semester was ending and I didn't have time to grade them. He emailed me, his parents, his advisor, and my department chair to claim that I had been unfair in denying him a chance to better his grade. While his advisor had my back, I had to have several lengthy and uncomfortable conversations with my department chair about the situation. (Teacher 1)

Parents often believed their adolescent children over me, the adult authority figure. One set of parents believed their teenage son over me when I let them know that he was falling behind in my class because he spent much of the class engaged in off-task activities on his laptop, and recommended they prohibit him from using his laptop for "note-taking" in class. They responded that he had assured them that he was definitely on-task in my class, and that the real cause of his low grades was my "poor teaching style." It took several months before one of his White teachers also reported that he was doing poorly because he spent most of his class time surreptitiously playing video games on his laptop, before his parents finally took his laptop away. (Teacher 2)

I once had a wealthy, connected parent insist that their child did NOT copy-paste a grad student-level passage on their test. They claimed that their child had read the passage a few days earlier, unconsciously memorized the entire thing word-for-word, then later typed it word-for-word from memory on their test, convinced they were their own words. The head of my department asked me if I could prove the student couldn't have done that. (Teacher 3)

DOUBLE STANDARDS

Black and Brown faculty are often held to higher standards by students, parents, and administration and endure closer scrutiny, whereas White faculty are allowed more leniency and understanding. This racial or ethnic double standard is exacerbated by the tendency to be less lenient with newer faculty, as the high turnover of Black and Brown faculty means that most Black and Brown faculty are relatively new to a school. While White employees are allowed to experiment and fail, Black and Brown staff are expected to do "perfect" work, with anything less considered a diminution of their value as a staff member, and even of their race. In addition, faculty of color (especially women) may be expected to abide by policies (e.g., dress codes or lateness policies) that their White peers are not held to.[1]

Most people assume that "double standards" refers to raising standards for members of outgroups. However, research by social psychologists concludes that double standards, discrimination, and bias are often more of a product of *ingroup favoritism*, giving ingroup members the benefit of the doubt rather than of negative attitudes and behavior against members of outgroups (Brewer, 2007). This phenomenon is known as *leniency bias*, or sometimes as *affinity bias* or *similar-to-me bias*. Individuals also attribute less blame for ingroup transgressions compared with those of outgroups (Halabi et al., 2015). A teacher of color remembers:

In my first year as faculty at an independent school I was one of only two Black teachers in the upper school, and the only one teaching a core subject. My department head had already warned me that White students and parents often gave teachers of color a hard time until we "proved ourselves," while White teachers were automatically accorded this respect. Two different parents asked about my education credentials. I felt like I was under a microscope, alone, being scrutinized by students, parents, and administration. And whenever students and parents did have concerns—no matter how slight—they did not address them with me, but rather went to veteran White colleagues or the administration. Imagine the humiliation of having to "answer to" and "explain myself to" White colleagues. It was one of the first times of my life where I felt that race was a major factor in my workplace. (Teacher 4)

WHITE BLINDERS

White school administrators often deny that racial inequality is a problem in their school, even when the same patterns of inequity are repeatedly identified by different Black and Brown faculty over the course of years. Instead, they attribute the struggles and concerns of Black and Brown faculty to personal failings or to "being a bad fit," rather than to racial and ethnic bias on the part of school administration, teachers, students, or parents. This phenomenon is not specific to independent schools. Broadly speaking, White people's misperceptions and underestimation of racism are well-documented (e.g., Carter & Murphy, 2015). Research from the Centre for Community Organizations found that while approximately 30% of Black or Brown survey respondents said they had left a job due to an unwelcoming racial environment, White respondents underestimated how many people of color were leaving their jobs because of discrimination, thinking instead that their colleagues had left their jobs because, for example, "they got a better job" or "they wanted to spend more time with their family."

I use the term "White blinders" to refer to this "inability" of many White Americans to notice racial bias and double standards in predominately White institutions; to justify, explain away, and deny racism and double standards, even after people of color repeatedly identify them. Of the factors described in this chapter, "White blinders" is the crux. Of what use is it to identify examples of racial and ethnic bias that Black and Brown faculty often face if White administrators are unable to recognize them when they occur in their schools? As long as White administrators insist that Black and Brown teachers are leaving for personal reasons or that they are pushing them out because they are "not a good fit," they will not aggressively implement the recommendations made in *The Colors of Excellence* (Kane and Orsini, 2003) and the AISNE report (Brosnan, 2003a). As long as they are convinced that their school is equitable and inclusive, as long as they individualize and explain away the departure of each Black and Brown faculty member, they will not take a good, hard look at the racial environment of their school and understand how racial biases and double standards affect them.

The "White blinder" tendency is the product of a powerful brew of subconscious cognitive biases. First, since White faculty and administration are not Black or Brown, they do not personally experience or witness racial bias. Instead, they are likely to universalize their personal experiences and assume that Black and Brown teachers also experience the school's students, faculty, and administration the same way that they do. Second, because of *intergroup attribution bias*, White administrators tend to attribute the problems of Black and Brown teachers to personal failings rather than to unfair circumstances like racial bias or double standards. *Intergroup attribution bias* is the tendency for individuals to attribute the problems of ingroup members to outside circumstances such as bad luck or unfair circumstances, while attributing the problems of outgroup members to personal failings (Halabi et al., 2015; Van Assche et al., 2020). And lastly, many Whites assume that racial bias is something that only a "Racist with a Capital 'R'"—a "bad" person—has. So, while they might have no trouble recognizing examples of racism and double standards in a race-awareness workshop or in reports on teachers of color, many Whites struggle to recognize similar examples of bias when they are perpetrated by beloved colleagues, students, and families. These White blinders are so rigid that many White individuals will disparage Black and Brown individuals who raise even well-substantiated concerns about racial bias or discrimination (Kaiser & Miller, 2001).

This tendency to see members of an ingroup in a favorable manner—*self-serving bias*—makes it difficult to believe that people who are ingroup members (both as colleagues and as fellow White people) would act in a biased manner. In fact, researchers have found that this need for Whites to avoid acknowledging racism among fellow Whites is so strong that they tend to use "higher thresholds when detecting racism, applying the 'racist' label only to ingroup members who behave in blatantly racist ways" (Carter & Murphy, 2015, p. 270). Thus, they are much less likely than Blacks to perceive anti-Black bias. It should also be noted that researchers have found that Blacks tend to be more accurate than Whites in their perceptions of racism (Nelson et al., 2013).

It is the combined product of these subconscious cognitive biases ("White blinders) that results in the tendency for White administrators to deny, deflect, justify, and explain away the microaggressions, double standards, and marginalization that Black and Brown faculty at their schools face: "they weren't a good fit" or "they left for personal reasons." As one teacher of color remembers:

At my last school, I had several experiences that I perceived as racist, or at the very least as double standards for Black vs. White teachers. I confided in a White colleague who was a member of our school's "White Anti-Racist Allies" (WARA) faculty group. But each time I told her about another racially suspect situation, she reassured me that they were just coincidences, or could be explained by another, extremely improbable reason. She said we should "assume the best intentions" of people, and "not jump to conclusions." Some months after I left the school, I ran into a Black teacher who had left the year before I started working there. As we shared experiences at our school, I learned that she and many other Black colleagues had experienced almost identical experiences with racism and double standards that few, if any, White teachers had encountered. I then realized that I had indeed experienced racism and double standards, but my "White ally" had denied and explained them away because she was unable to acknowledge racism when they were being done by colleagues she knew. Apparently, racism was much easier to recognize when it occurs in anecdotal scenarios in training materials and when they were perpetrated by distant strangers.

CONCLUSION

The problem of low retention of Black and Brown teachers at independent schools will not be resolved until independent schools push past superficial racial equity programming and introduce structural, systemic reforms—until they actually start "walking the walk" of racial equity. Here, I offer specific recommendations for schools to take if they are genuinely concerned with the retention of Black and Brown faculty:

1. The school contracts an independent inquiry into long-term patterns of low retention rates of Black and Brown teachers. The quick departure of a handful of Black or Brown teachers may very well be due to personal failings or to them not being a good fit. However, long-term patterns of rapid turnover or repeated concerns being raised by Black and Brown teachers suggest that the problem lies in the school itself.
2. The school administration takes aggressive steps to hold all students equally accountable to school rules and expectations.
3. The school administration takes aggressive steps to hold all faculty equally accountable to school rules and expectations and to protect Black and Brown faculty from undue pressure from privileged parents.
4. The school curriculum—particularly the U.S. History curriculum—is revised to include the histories of significant American Black and Brown communities, including a robust history of systemic racism in the United States. Opportunities for education about the history of systemic racism in the United States are extended to school alumni, parents, faculty, and administration.

5. Opportunities are systematically created in the curriculum for students to interrogate the ways in which their family, school, and community contribute to systems of economic and racial inequity and for them to learn about ways to disrupt these. Many of the chapters in this book provide examples and strategies for doing this.

I hope this chapter is of assistance to independent schools that attempt to reduce their hostile racial climates and increase retention of Black and Brown faculty. But I also hope this research serves as further validation, vindication, and confirmation for my fellow Black and Brown faculty who have, like me, faced years of gaslighting by White administrators and colleagues who are stubbornly blind to inequity, insist that we are "complainers" and "troublemakers," and push us out of schools "for personal reasons" or because we "are not a good fit." The research in this chapter further confirms what we were insisting all along—that, despite the vehement claims by White administrators, our concerns are real. This chapter is my modest attempt at making what Representative John Lewis (2018) called "good, necessary trouble."

NOTE

1. See the Centre for Community Organizations' report "Diversité d'Abord: Race and Colonialism in the Nonprofit Sector in Quebec" available at https://coco-net.org/diversite-dabord/ for more information.

REFERENCES

Brewer, M. B. (2007). The social psychology of intergroup relations: Social categorization, ingroup bias, and outgroup prejudice. In A. W. Kruglanski & E. T. Higgins (Eds.), *Social psychology: Handbook of basic principles* (pp. 695–715). The Guilford Press.

Brosnan, M. (2001). Diversity efforts in independent schools. *Fordham Urban Law Journal, 29*, 467–487.

Brosnan, M. (2003a). *The AISNE guide to hiring and retaining teachers of color.* AISNE.

Brosnan, M. (2003b). *Thriving in independent schools: An AISNE guide for educators of color.* AISNE.

Calarco, J. M. (2020). Avoiding us versus them: How schools' dependence on privileged "Helicopter" parents influences enforcement of Rules. *American Sociological Review, 85*(2), 223–246.

Carter, E. R., & Murphy, M. C. (2015). Group-based differences in perceptions of racism: What counts, to whom, and why? *Social and Personality Psychology Compass, 9,* 269–280.

Davis, A., & Ernst, R. (2017). Racial gaslighting. *Politics, Groups, and Identities, 7*(4), 761–774.

Downey, M. (2019, November 21). A reflection and prayer at Marist leads to teacher on leave and students on edge. *Atlanta Journal-Constitution.* https://www.ajc.com/blog/get-schooled/reflection-and-prayer-marist-leads-teacher-leave-and-students-edge/sOJwRDu1JBDTV5sJSitalN

Edwards, S. (2020, March 2). Teachers of Color support each other by developing community networks. *DiversityIs.* https://diversityis.com/teachers-of-color-support-each-other-by-developing-community-networks

Gaztambide-Fernández, R. A., & Howard, A. (2013). Social justice, deferred complicity, and the moral plight of the wealthy. *Democracy and Education, 21*(1), 7.

Grinage, J. (2020). Singing and dancing for diversity: Neoliberal multiculturalism and white epistemological ignorance in teacher professional development. *Curriculum Inquiry, 50*(1), 7–27.

Hagerman, M. A. (2018). *White kids: Growing up with privilege in a racially divided America.* NYU Press.

Halabi, S., Statman, Y., & Dovidio, J. F. (2015). Attributions of responsibility and punishment for ingroup and outgroup members: The role of just world beliefs. *Group Processes & Intergroup Relations, 18*(1), 104–115.

Hurwitz, M., & Lee, J. (2018). Grade inflation and the role of standardized testing. In Buckley, J., Letukas, L., & Wildavsky, B. (Eds.), *Measuring success: Testing, grades, and the future of college admissions* (pp. 64–93). Johns Hopkins University Press.

Kaiser, C. R., & Miller, C. T. (2001). Stop complaining! The social costs of making attributions to discrimination. *Personality and Social Psychology Bulletin, 27*(2), 254–263.

Kane, P. R., & Orsini, A. J. (Eds.). (2003). *The colors of excellence: Hiring and keeping teachers of color in independent schools.* Teachers College Press.

Kohli, R. (2018). Behind school doors: The impact of hostile racial climates on urban teachers of color. *Urban Education, 53*(3), 307–333.

Lewis, A. E., & Diamond, J. B. (2015). *Despite the best intentions: How racial inequality thrives in good schools.* Oxford University Press.

Lewis, J. [@repjohnlewis]. (2018, June 27). Do not get lost in a sea of despair. Be hopeful, be optimistic. Our struggle is not the struggle of a day, a week, a month, or a year, it is the struggle of a lifetime. Never, ever be afraid to make some noise and get in good trouble, necessary trouble. #goodtrouble [Tweet]. Twitter.

Nelson, J. C., Adams, G., & Salter, P. S. (2013). The Marley hypothesis: Denial of racism reflects ignorance of history. *Psychological Science, 24*(2), 213–218.

Reeves, R. (2017). *Dream hoarders: The dangerous separation of the American upper middle class.* The Brookings Institution.

Shapiro, E. (2019, March 12). After racist video surface, private school students protest with overnight lock-in. *The New York Times.* https://www.nytimes.com /2019/03/12/nyregion/fieldston-racist-video-student-protest.html

Smylie, S. (2020, January 23). Black student group at Lab School speaks out against racism and bias. *Hyde Park Herald.* https://www.hpherald.com/news /black-student-group-at-lab-school-speaks-out-against-racism-and-bias/article _bdab4516-3e11-11ea-972a-9f8d009e5d4d.html

Van Assche, J., Politi, E., Van Dessel, P., & Phalet, K. (2020). To punish or to assist? Divergent reactions to ingroup and outgroup members disobeying social distancing. *The British Journal of Social Psychology, 59*(3), 594–606.

CHAPTER 7

Critical Service Learning

Moving from Transactional Experiences of Service Toward a Social Justice Praxis

Tania D. Mitchell

Service learning is broadly understood as a pedagogical strategy that combines a community experience—generally, service-oriented activities to understand concepts or issues (i.e., learning something)—with a reflective process that integrates the service and learning. Students, through this practice, enhance their understanding of the concepts because of the opportunity for (1) meaningful engagement in a service experience that illuminates that concept and (2) focused time to reflect on themselves as a participant in that process, what was achieved during their time in the community, and how they understand that concept better (or differently) as a result. The "concept" that may be the focus of a service learning project can vary widely depending on the context in which a service learning experience is offered. I have participated in service learning where the concept was service itself, and I have supported instructors teaching service learning to advance students' understanding of accounting. Service learning may be issue specific (e.g., poverty), community specific (e.g., Chinatown), or focused on an academic discipline (e.g., chemistry).

Despite these three components—service, learning, and reflection—that make service learning what it is, the way that service learning is traditionally communicated, centers on service. Institutions or individuals identify the partnerships they've developed, the numbers of students participating, and the number of hours contributed to the community. The efforts of the students are highlighted—explaining their work and sacrifice or how far they traveled—and students are generally lauded for putting their energy toward this work as opposed to almost anything else they could have been doing. (Sometimes this is even true when the service learning experience is required.) Rarely is energy spent explaining why the work the students did was needed or who benefited from their labor. Often unacknowledged is the work of the community partners who organized the space, time, and activity. Or that this work is ongoing and would benefit from more volunteers. Or that this project was specifically designed for this class/project/moment and took valuable staff time away from other critical projects.

TRADITIONAL SERVICE LEARNING

Traditionally, in a service learning experience, the orientation to service is minimal. Little is done to prepare students for who they will meet, why those people will be there, and what work they will do. Students are too frequently unprepared to do basic tasks (e.g., knowing to put cans on the bottom when packing food boxes, knowing how to tape off baseboards and other casework before painting, having some training in literacy education before tutoring young people to read, and so forth). Unfortunately, they have not usually had space or time to consider and unpack deficit notions and stereotypes they may hold about the communities where they are engaged in these tasks.

The service learning experience may introduce students to critical issues facing the community, but too often these issues are presented as resulting from individual deficiencies and hardships without taking time to look at structural barriers and systemic inequalities. The histories of the communities service learning often targets are barely explored, and minimal attention is given to current representations in the media that may unfairly position a community as "dangerous" or "in need."

A traditional service learning experience intensifies the hierarchies already experienced. Students (typically from privileged backgrounds) are placed in positions where they have power, authority, or control (e.g., tutoring, distributing food or supplies, coaching) over those who already experience powerlessness in one or multiple areas of their lives (e.g., people whose first language is not English, those who experience food insecurity, kids). These power dynamics are usually not named or explored, and the students in service learning are not encouraged to question or challenge them. They enter the experience told that they are people with skills and resources to "help," but generally do not question how they came to acquire those skills, how much proficiency they have (or should have) in order to do the work they have been tasked with, or why they would (or should) be trusted to do this work instead of others equally or more skilled. Research suggests that service learning can support students in developing their interests, collaborating with others, and developing their capacity for leadership (Furco, 2001), but it also has been shown to exacerbate feelings of pity, reproduce deficit thinking, and lead people to become defensive about their privilege (Espino & Lee, 2011). Yet community service and service learning are becoming central practices in private schools.

SERVICE LEARNING IN PRIVATE SCHOOLS

Gaztambide-Fernández and Howard (2010) suggest, with concern, that service learning has become "an area of distinction for elite students" (p. 203), and Swalwell (2013) cautions that the ethos that guides service learning is often more charitable than justice-oriented and "frequently descends into a platitudinous helperism (Hernandez-Sheets, 2000)" (p. 3). The practice of service learning has flourished in educational settings for dozens of years because of the opportunities it provides to engage important issues of inequality and social responsibility and has become important to signaling (for institutions, educators, and students themselves) a commitment to social justice. This social justice expectation persists through the ways that "elite" private schools position their pedagogical stance and the goals higher education institutions may articulate for their undergraduates, fulfilling the aim of "encouraging students to develop a sense of social justice and to become responsible citizens" (Hurtado, 2007, p. 191). It is important that a civic education moves beyond self-interest and toward an embrace of the public good; it is, perhaps erroneously, often assumed to be linked to issues and concerns of social justice.

UNDERSTANDING SOCIAL JUSTICE

In my experience, we make a lot of assumptions about what social justice means and what a commitment to social justice looks like. Many of us see social justice as a progressive movement for positive change. "A more just community" is a euphemism for a better community, a fair community, or an equal community. At least, we think that is what we mean when we say it. In my experience, we spend very little time considering what is meant by social justice, what it means to enact a commitment to social justice, and how seeing our work as social justice matters in the ways we engage in the community and other aspects of our life.

There is a significant amount of theorizing and some research that links service learning and social justice (Butin, 2007; Cipolle, 2010; Mitchell 2007, 2008; Mitchell & Soria, 2016; Warren, 1998). The idea is that we are out in the community actively contributing to issues in our community that are concerns—but should not be. Homelessness. Unequal education. Kids without a safe place to play. Elders without companionship. People without enough food. The idea is that these are efforts that we are contributing to that illuminate concerns of inequity and injustice. The idea is that community engagement practice creates space and opportunity to think about and participate in efforts to make a better world. The idea is that this kind of engagement may develop our understanding of and commitment to social justice.

Mitchell and Soria (2016) demonstrate through the use of the Student Experience at the Research University survey that students involved in community service who characterized that work as social justice were significantly more likely than their peers to participate in social change factors like social perspective taking, engagement in social action, and reflecting on social problems. This research also showed, unfortunately, that less than 4% of the sample (n = 3,093) characterized their service as social justice. This analysis also includes the nearly 52% of the same sample who characterized their service as charity and were significantly more likely than their peers to report never participating in any of the social change factors that frequently define democratic and civic education. So, the way that students think about and characterize their service *matters*. It affects, significantly, whether or not they are willing to engage in any of the factors that are seen as important to developing a sense of social justice and becoming responsible citizens. And this has extremely important implications for those who develop and plan community engagement experiences for those students. How do we organize experiences in ways that ensure that students can recognize, engage with, and learn from the social justice intentions that inspire, if not inform, our practice?

CRITICAL SERVICE LEARNING

Critical service learning is a framework that I hope moves community engagement toward a social justice praxis (Mitchell 2007, 2008) (see Figure 7.1). It is a way to approach service learning that may support a practice where students are able to recognize, name, and work to dismantle structural inequality through acknowledgment of and reckoning with the privileges and resources they hold and can access, as well as deep consideration for how their actions can perpetuate or disrupt unjust conditions.[1]

I've come to define service as "full and active engagement with the people, problems, and promises of the community where you live" as a generative, collaborative partnership with others that works for and moves toward a more just world (Mitchell, 2018, p. ix). Critical service learning is an orientation toward service learning that emphasizes social justice outcomes; names problems and strategizes to address them; honors the promise, agency, and beauty already present in the community; and works to build and strengthen the capacity of that community and its members.

Nadinne Cruz (1994), a pioneer in service learning, defined the work as "aligning intention and action in a movement towards just relationships." In seeking to operationalize that definition, I offer three key responsibilities that critical service learning practitioners must emphasize: (1) an attention to social change, (2) work to redistribute power, and (3) developing authentic relationships (Mitchell, 2008).

Figure 7.1. Traditional vs. Critical Service Learning

Traditional Service Learning

Community Component

reflection

Learning to Serve ⟷ Serving to Learn

reflection

Classroom Component

Critical Service Learning

Community Component

reflection

A Social Change Orientation ➕ Working to Redistribute Power ➕ Developing Authentic Relationships

reflection

Classroom Component

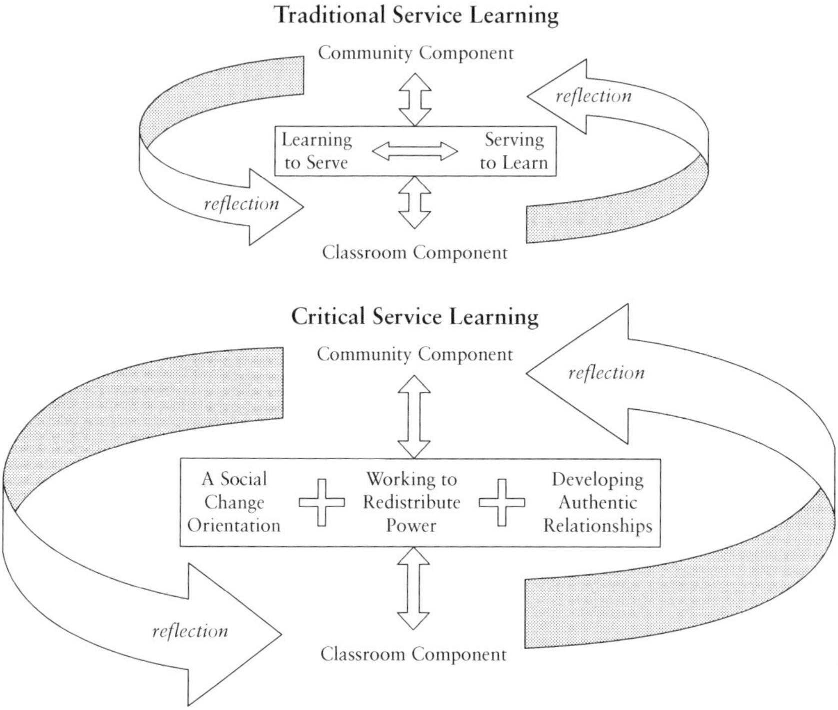

Source: Mitchell, T. D. (2008). Traditional vs. critical service-learning: Engaging the literature to differentiate two models. *Michigan Journal of Community Service Learning, 14*(2), 50.

The first effort, bringing attention to social change, is about challenging Robinson's (2000) concern that the charitable, one-shot, student-focused emphases of most service learning practice are more aligned with welfare than with social change. Bringing attention to social change in community engagement work ensures that we are educating ourselves and our students about the issues and concerns undergirding the service work we are asking or requiring of them. It means that we ask why the soup kitchen is needed and why it is needed *here*—in this space, in particular. It means we critique and question actions happening in the community that are limited in their attention to root causes. It means we explore policies past and present that shape the circumstances facing the community we are in. It means that we reckon with systems and structures of injustice and advantage so that we understand the ways that we are all implicated in the issues we are confronting. It means that we listen to the desires of a community—its elders and its youth—to understand how we got to now. What are the ways the community has already tried or wants to try to respond to this issue? What is the vision for the community we want to work toward? Critical service learning chooses work *in* and *with* community that advances that vision.

The second effort in a critical service learning practice is working to redistribute power. The first step of that effort is recognizing who has power and the ways that service learning reifies that power structure. In case you were unsure, schools and those of us who represent schools often hold (too) much of the power in a service learning relationship. We are so often in the position of identifying that our students need to do X kind of service in order to meet Y outcome in a specific time frame that many nonprofit organizations are now in the business of making sure that they create "service" experiences that meet school parameters rather than partnerships that support meaningful and effective engagement in a number of different ways where the work done advances the vision of that community.

To redistribute power, I am seeking opportunities to disrupt, in as many ways as possible, the traditional hierarchies that define relationships of service and relationships of learning. This can include simple shifts in practice like not standing at the front of the classroom or having students facilitate reflection sessions for their peers. I love experiences that are co-led with a leader from the community organization anchoring the service learning project. I love it even more when the resources to compensate that leader as a co-instructor in both title and dollar are available and offered willingly. Redistributing power in service learning means we are responsive to the requests of the community in terms of the work that we do. Rather than focusing on service experiences that prioritize giving students something to do over ensuring that the work happening in communities builds community capacity, community organizations identify and prioritize the work that needs to happen. I ask students what they did in service but also to articulate how the work done supports efforts toward advancing the vision that the community has established. If a student is tasked by an organization to research voting records of the city council so that we might better understand how to pitch a potential initiative to them, how does that work build capacity? If they are asked to offer accompaniment to an elder who needs to get their prescriptions, where do you see justice in that work? If they are tasked to clean toilets, what did your time doing that task allow someone else to do? Working to redistribute power reminds us of the myriad tasks absolutely necessary for a social change initiative to sustain momentum and succeed and that we can (and should) contribute at all levels to work alongside a community.

The third effort in a critical service learning approach is developing authentic relationships, and to develop authentic relationships, it is imperative that we work on building alliances and developing accomplices and co-conspirators. This requires that we do the work of learning names and histories, as well as seek to understand the bridges and pathways that bring us to the same table. It encourages the co-creative agency that Coles (2011) insists that service learning lacks.

Developing authentic relationships in critical service learning is more than a move from "doing for to doing with" (Ward & Wolf-Wendel, 2000); it is a recognition that if the work is not community led, then it is unlikely to serve the community well. Therefore, it is important that we interrogate the organizations with whom we partner in these efforts: How does the community feel about the work of this organization? What have they accomplished? Who "runs" things and what is their connection to this place or issue? Is the work of this organization viewed as authentic and meaningful by this community? If we don't know or understand that, then our efforts to be seen as authentic participants in a community change initiative may be fraught from the beginning.

What becomes essential in developing authentic relationships is connection. To see myself as belonging, to see myself as implicated, to see myself as harmed (perhaps differently, but still inevitably) by the injustice that persists, to see myself as benefiting (again differently, but inevitably) from the changes that happen. Connection inspires commitment; advocacy; and action that builds desire, will, and capacity.

These efforts bring us toward experiences of service learning that do not supplant "student outcomes" for community impact. These efforts recognize service as a tool and an opportunity for making progress real and tangible in our communities—not merely fulfilling a requirement for graduation or building a resume. With intention, as Nadinne Cruz articulates, service learning can be a transformative experience that moves all of us—ourselves, our students, the communities where we center our practice—toward just relationships.

A critical service learning experience asks students to engage in service while contemplating their responsibilities to create justice in the world. Throughout the experience, students may be introduced to different strategies for change, asked to look at concepts of privilege and oppression and how they manifest in society, and be required to engage in community-centered projects they see as contributing to meaningful social change (and students need to be able to articulate how they understand social change as a possibility through these projects). While some assume the connections between service learning and social justice are inherent, plenty of research demonstrates that students sometimes leave service learning experiences with stereotypes reinforced and with little understanding of the systemic nature of social problems. Service learning experiences must be developed with an intentional commitment to social justice and social change in order to promote and develop commitments to social justice for students and in order to work for sustainable change that may realize more just conditions for the communities where service learning happens.

INTENTIONS AND ACTIONS MATTER

My research requires that I spend a lot of time thinking about what happens in service learning classrooms. I am interested in how students participate in service learning and what they learn from those experiences, but I am also interested in how educators develop these experiences (e.g., their motivations and actions to bring service learning to students), the ways they facilitate these experiences (e.g., what texts they rely on, what assignments are required, how they introduce concepts and ideas to their students), and how they work with community organizations and community members to organize service projects and community experiences for students.

What I have learned is that the educators' intentions and actions are critically important to realizing a service learning practice that might lead to more just relationships. Educators who are invested in the communities where they develop service learning experiences, who have deep relationships with community organizations, who have worked in the community and therefore have the trust of community members tend to organize service learning experiences that truly respond to the critical approach I described earlier. Educators who blend history and current events to demonstrate the systemic nature of oppression, who encourage students to think about how they are implicated in the social concerns centered in the service learning project, who uplift community voices so they are recognized for their expertise and their lived experience bring critical service learning from an imagined practice to a real one. Educators who step back from community projects to let partnering agencies identify what work should be done, why, and on what timeline create service learning experiences where students understand the complexity of a social change project and the myriad kinds of work necessary in order for meaningful change to happen. Educators who stay in and with community members to ensure these service learning projects are not one-shot or temporary are able to support the kinds of longitudinal work necessary to sustain movements toward a more just community.

LEARNING FROM SERVICE LEARNING ALUMNI

More recently, I have been thinking about what happens after students leave service learning experiences. What happens after students leave the safety of the campus environments that facilitated their entry into a community? What happens after those students graduate and have jobs and kids? What happens when they are tasked with living commitments to social justice in the real world when it is not guided by the assignments or requirements essential to service learning?

To answer these questions, I have been interviewing university alumni 5 to 15 years after graduation. In this case, I am focusing on alumni from a private, very high research university, as I believe these alumni are best positioned to represent the adults we imagine might emerge from the "elite" educations that are the focus of this text. Alumni were able to retrospectively offer specific moments from their service learning experiences that shaped their sense of self and their sense of social justice. Through these alumni, we learn that the influence of critical service learning experiences—those that emphasize social justice as a central concern—are enduring and persist well after graduation.

These alumni reported continued engagement in community service and working alongside others to respond to community concerns. They had strong perceptions of their political self-efficacy and demonstrated that by being active and informed community members. They discussed social and political concerns with friends, stayed up to date on political issues, and voted in local and national elections. They saw themselves as informed political actors who could make a difference. Many reported boycotting a company or product as an expression of their values and contacting their public officials to express an opinion. When Hurtado (2007) suggested that higher education should prioritize developing responsible citizens, I think these are the kinds of actions she would hope to see from university alumni.

The alumni all expressed commitments to social justice and credited their service learning experiences with helping them to understand the possibilities for actualizing that commitment. Each of them pointed to a moment in their service learning experiences when they were first challenged to articulate their vision of social justice that has continued to challenge them to live a life aligned with their values. These understandings continue to be deconstructed and reconstructed as new experiences are encountered, different interactions and conversations are had, and updated information is consumed. So, the doctor prioritizes access to medical care in her current conception of justice. The teacher is trying to make sure he is teaching to all of the learning styles in his classroom to respond to his commitment to social justice. The mother is seeking to raise children who are kind to others and grow up respecting the planet and views that as an important contribution to making a more just world.

These alumni reflections demonstrate the ways critical service learning experiences can challenge students to vision a better world and act toward it in their lives beyond (and after) school. I do not, however, want to suggest that the process to shift toward a critical service learning practice is a simple one. It requires a re-education about how we engage with communities and how we ask students to enter into and think about their work in these community experiences. As educators committed to social justice who hope to encourage these same commitments in our students, we must be intentional about the motivations for our community engaged work and make that clear to students. It is sharing with them our recognition of their ability and opportunity to create a more just world, as well as our hope that these efforts toward critical service learning are experiences that do just that.

NOTE

1. One response to the criticisms levied against service learning has been to remove the language of service from the practice. Because of the inherent inequality in the nature of service, some have eschewed this terminology for broader conceptions like community engagement or community-based learning. The shift in language, however, is inconsequential if the practice does not also shift. Others have exchanged service projects—many of them charitable and transactional in their best iterations and harmful and exploitative in their worst—for site visits and neighborhood excursions. These can be beneficial actions to bring resources to a community (especially when participants are encouraged to spend their dollars locally) and to provide students important history and context to better understand the community and the issues community members may be facing. I think these visits can be valuable, though I do worry about the appearance (or real experience) of poverty tourism. I think these kinds of site visits can be powerful orientations to a community and its concerns and may best position students to enter a community thoughtfully and better prepared to contribute in ways that may benefit a community.

REFERENCES

Butin, D. W. (2007). Justice-learning: Service-learning as justice-oriented education. *Equity and Excellence in Education, 40*(2), 177–183.

Cipolle, S. B. (2010). *Service-learning and social justice: Engaging students in social change*. Rowman & Littlefield Publishers.

Coles, R. (2011). *Cultivating pedagogies for civic engagement and political agency: Reflections for discussion of the theory and practice of democratic transformations in higher education*. Kettering Foundation.

Cruz, N. (1994, November). *Reexamining service-learning in an international context*. Paper presented at the Annual Conference of the National Society for Experiential Education. Washington, DC.

Espino, M. M., & Lee, J. A. (2011). Understanding resistance: Reflections on race and privilege through service-learning. *Equity and Excellence in Education, 44*(2), 136–152.

Furco, A. (2001). Is service learning really better than community service? A study of high school service program outcomes. In A. Furco, & S. H. Billig (Eds.), *Service-learning: The essence of the pedagogy* (pp. 23–50). Information Age Publishing.

Gaztambide-Fernández, R. A., & Howard, A. (2010). Conclusion: Outlining a research agenda on elite education. In A. Howard, & R. A. Gaztambide-Fernández (Eds.), *Educating elites: Class privilege and educational advantage* (pp. 195–209). Rowman & Littlefield Education.

Hernandez-Sheets, R. (2000). Advancing the field or taking center stage: The White movement in multicultural education. *Educational Researcher, 29*(9), 15–21.

Hurtado, S. (2007). Linking diversity with the educational and civic missions of higher education. *The Review of Higher Education, 30*(2), 185–196.

Mitchell, T. D. (2007). Critical service-learning as social justice education: A case study of the Citizen Scholars Program. *Equity and Excellence in Education, 40*(2), 101–112.

Mitchell, T. D. (2008). Traditional vs. critical service-learning: Engaging the literature to differentiate two models. *Michigan Journal of Community Service Learning, 14*(2), 50–65.

Mitchell, T. D. (2018). Foreword. In D. M. Donahue & S. Plaxton-Moore (Eds.), *The student companion to community-engaged learning: What you need to know for transformative learning and real social change* (pp. ix–xii). Stylus Publishing.

Mitchell, T. D., & Soria, K. M. (2016). Seeking social justice: Undergraduates' engagement in social change and social justice at American research universities. In K. M. Soria & T. D. Mitchell (Eds.), *Civic engagement and community service at research universities* (pp. 241–255). Palgrave Macmillan.

Robinson, T. (2000). Dare the school build a new social order? *Michigan Journal of Community Service Learning, 7*, 142–157.

Swalwell, K. (2013). "With great power comes great responsibility": Privileged students' conceptions of justice-oriented citizenship. *Democracy & Education, 21*(1), 1–11.

Ward, K., & Wolf-Wendel, L. (2000). Community-centered service learning: Moving from doing for to doing with. *American Behavioral Scientist, 43*(5), 767–780.

Warren, K. (1998). Educating students for social justice in service learning. *The Journal of Experiential Education, 21*(3), 134–139.

CHAPTER 8

The "Duality of Life" in "Elite" Sustainability Education

Tensions, Pitfalls, and Possibilities

Kristin Sinclair, Ashley Akerberg, and Brady Wheatley

In 2019, *TIME* magazine named 16-year-old Swedish environmental activist Greta Thunberg their person of the year (Haynes, 2019). Thunberg's activism speaks truth to power, whether "berating billionaires" about their contribution to climate change or calling on governments to decrease carbon emissions (Haynes, 2019). As Thunberg attributes her activism in part to her schooling experiences—she started studying climate change in school around the age of 9 (Goodman, 2018)—her experiences beg the question: How might education motivate an arguably privileged young person to engage in environmental activism?

The purpose of this chapter is to draw upon our experiences as educators at the Island School, a residential, semester-long sustainability education program for high school students, to explore the tensions, pitfalls, and possibilities of environmental and sustainability education for "elite"[1] students. We—three white, college-educated women from working- and middle-class backgrounds—were immersed in the lives of 400 Island School students between fall 2010 and spring 2014 as history, literature, and research teachers; dormitory heads; sea kayaking expedition leaders; advisors; administrators; and curriculum developers. In this chapter, we interrogate publicly available information from the school's website, social media, and curricular materials alongside our recollections of our time at the Island School.[2] We are not above the critiques we put forth; in fact, critical reflection on our own practices at the school has generated the insights we share here.

If the goal is a more liveable future for everyone, sustainability education that fails to center structures of inequality like capitalism and white supremacy while emphasizing individual, "elite"-led change is at best insufficient and at worst problematic and dangerous. How schools navigate these issues has implications for whether environmental and sustainability education with "elite" students can be transformative—for both young people and the environment—or simply brand students as "good elites" while maintaining harmful systems that limit climate change solutions to individual choices and behaviors (Henderson, 2015; Sinclair & Swalwell, 2017).

THE ISLAND SCHOOL[3]

The Island School (IS) is a place-based sustainability education program on Cape Eleuthera on the southwestern tip of the island of Eleuthera about five miles away from Deep Creek, the closest Bahamian settlement. Founded by a former teacher at a New Jersey prep school, IS is a semester-long, 100-day, study-abroad program for high school sophomores and juniors. The program's central question ("How can we live well in a place?") and vision mantra ("leadership effecting change") undergird the "institutional keystones" of its mission: sense of place, sustainability, and community. These noble goals play out through courses in applied research, histories, literature and writing, applied mathematics, land and environmental art, marine ecology, and a capstone course. Students participate in cultural contact programs with local Bahamians, earn their scuba certification, and engage in experiential learning through multiday ocean kayak expeditions and "down-island" trips where students learn about the impact of the tourism industry on Eleuthera. Students build trusting relationships with teachers and form a tight-knit community—cut off from the Internet and cell phones—while practicing a sustainable lifestyle on a campus that strives to operate off the grid and produce little, if any, waste.

While the demographics of IS students are unavailable on its website, in our experience, most students were from the United States, close to 90% were white, and most were wealthy—children of prominent lawyers, politicians, multinational corporate executives, and so forth. As of 2018, only 30% of students received any financial assistance[4] with the $32,800 tuition. Thus, most IS students were "elite" members of "social groups who have attained a degree of financial influence and are able to mobilize economic, social, and cultural resources in order to secure access to particular kinds of educational experiences" (Gaztambide-Fernández & Howard, 2010, p. 196) like the Island School.

FOUR GUIDING QUESTIONS

We organize our exploration of the tensions, pitfalls, and possibilities of "elite" sustainability education around two sets of guiding questions related to the teachers' and curricula's *explanations* for and functions of climate change, as well as possible *solutions*.

Explanations

Researchers argue that climate change is, in part, a consequence of shifts in the economic and political world order under neoliberalism. Understanding climate change thus means understanding its links to racism, sexism, classism, and other forms of oppression (Hursh et al., 2015; Klein, 2014; McKenzie et al., 2015; Schild, 2016) and how the impacts of climate change fall disproportionately on poor people of color (Bullard, 1993). Common environmental and sustainability narratives, however, are often shaped by white voices (Finney, 2014) and can alienate students of color (Miller, 2018), falling short of giving all students the knowledge necessary to effectively tackle climate change.

Early movements in environmental education were rooted in liberal educational philosophies and focused on nature studies, conservation, and knowledge of the biophysical environment (Stevenson, 2007). Over time, much of environmental education has shifted to the three pillars of sustainability: environment, society, and economy (Gough & Gough, 2010). However, the concept of "sustainability," IS's preferred term, has become a fairly meaningless buzzword that dominates conversations about environmentalism (Stevenson et al., 2013). In fact, the term "sustainability" has often provided cover for businesses and corporations to extract profits in the name of environmentalism and education (McKenzie et al., 2015).

These tensions between the ecological dimensions of environmental and sustainability education and the economic, political, and racial dimensions of climate change played out across IS's curriculum. Here, we consider how IS (1) struggled to situate climate change in its relationship to systems of oppression and (2) did not confront how students and their families likely benefited economically from climate change. In doing so, we watched students leave IS understanding the symptoms *but not the root causes* of climate change while embracing narratives of sustainability and identities as "good elites" who care about changing the world (e.g., Sinclair & Swalwell, 2017).

How Do We Situate Climate Change and Ourselves in Systems of Oppression?
While the IS curriculum engaged students in conversations about their worldviews, positionalities, and cultures and engaged a range of local individual perspectives (e.g., scientists, authors, political figures, community leaders, cultural icons, elders, and educators), it generally stopped short of connecting this learning to broader systems of oppression. Notably, the IS curriculum guide mentions race only once, and the words "justice," "racism," and "oppression" never appear. In our experience, when teachers *did* address these concepts, we did so without providing students the conceptual tools or encouragement to critically reflect on their own positionality within U.S. global power structures or even within the Bahamas itself. For

example, students read *The Rediscovery of North America,* a powerful historical critique that illustrates the colonization, genocide, and enslavement that characterize Caribbean history (Lopez, 1990). Inspired by this book, students were encouraged to cultivate "querencia"—a sense of place that, in theory, interrupts the mentality of the colonizer—*without a discussion of colonialism or students' relationship to that history.* As teachers, we asked students to write in response to the prompt: "What is your worldview, how did it come to be, and how has it changed since you came to Island School?" Students rarely included explanations for how those worldviews had been shaped by race or social class. These are just two missed opportunities where IS teachers could have nurtured students' critical consciousness *alongside* an exploration of their identities (Freire, 1970/2000).

By avoiding this critical reflection, IS curated an educational experience that allowed students to accrue power, not share it. For the hefty $32,000 price tag, students collected stories and perspectives about sustainability that bought access to elite, highly competitive universities and exposure to expansive social networks where they could leverage access to future educational and professional opportunities. The school provided students intellectual access to the "right kinds of ideas" without pushing students to critically reflect or take collective action. As such, IS essentially enabled students to further accumulate power while avoiding taking action to shift resource distribution necessary to positively affect climate change (Klein, 2014).

Notably, conversations about racism and capitalism are hard to have if teachers themselves haven't done the work to understand their *own* positionality and worldviews related to race, social class, and other forms of identity. The IS hired all three of us into teaching and leadership roles for which, in many ways, we were ill prepared. While we had experience and training as educators, we lacked the requisite critical consciousness (Freire, 1970/2000) related to our own racial identities as white women and place-based knowledge to teach what and how we argue for in this chapter. We admit to being unprepared to navigate conversations of race and power and how they related to broader issues of sustainability—unintentionally perpetuating the critiques we bring forth in this chapter. At the time, the school provided little to no training to help faculty develop these skills or dispositions and did not prioritize conversations about racism, sexism, or social class. We now recognize how we led students through largely decontextualized analyses of texts like Derek Walcott's (1990) epic poem *Omeros* and provided a limited understanding of colonialism and the relationship between the United States and the Bahamas as we supported students' ethnographic interviews of local Bahamians, failing to connect the dots between systemic racism and climate change. To avoid these pitfalls, schools must provide faculty the resources and support to develop their own critical consciousness and complex understandings of structural oppression.

How Does the "Elite" Class Benefit from and Contribute to Climate Change? The school also largely sidestepped the tensions between economic profit, capitalism, and climate change. By choosing sustainability as a central concept, IS couched its curriculum in terms familiar to the business and wealthy class. Generally speaking, teachers and curricula avoided confronting how our students benefited from climate change. While teachers and curricula often drew inspiration from environmental educators (e.g., Orr, 1994), a recent revision to the curriculum drew, in part, on a list of "survival skills" derived from the business world (e.g., The Island School Curriculum Guide, 2019; Wagner, 2010). The IS curriculum guide reveals a narrow understanding of how the economy impacts sustainability:

> Sustainability involves much more than recycling waste streams or reducing energy consumption. . . . True sustainability begins with individual lifestyles and requires a commitment from every member of the community to embrace the challenge of personal change. (p. 6)

Individual change, while necessary, is insufficient to adequately address climate change (Chawla & Cushing, 2007). By embracing a conception of sustainability that emphasized "personal change" at the exclusion of "systemic change," an IS education reflected a common practice among "elite thought leaders" interested in social change: using the tools of business and the free market to solve social issues (Giridharadas, 2018). Many "elites" push for reforms that fail to address the root of the problem and/or hold themselves accountable for how they garnered their wealth in the first place.[5] By adopting an approach to sustainability education that neglected economic inequality, the IS curriculum tended to emphasize an incomplete, sanitized conception of sustainability.

Generally speaking, IS missed an opportunity to have students confront the structural inequalities that they have benefitted from—work that could potentially lay a foundation for students to challenge destructive economic systems. For example, we remember students excitedly taking an ocean shower (a common practice at the IS to conserve water) in preparation for their families' arrival via a private jet and another student proudly proclaiming their plans to "go home and put biodiesel in my Hummer," without asking them to explore the hypocrisy in these practices. This duality of life, learning about and practicing individual environmental sustainability while ignoring the role of one's own privilege and power in such a system, was prominent across the IS. Notably, a program that is dependent on donations from their students' wealthy white parents may be hesitant to directly challenge the systems and structures that produced these families' advantage.

Solutions

How schools, curricula, and teachers frame explanations for problems such as climate change has implications for how we think about solutions and change agents. For example, if—as in our experience—students are taught to decry ocean plastic without learning about the capitalist history of consumerism and production that has contributed to its existence, students may believe the primary solution lies in one's own choices rather than as allies in collective action led by those most affected by climate change, given what truly consequential solutions require. At IS, the curriculum prioritized solutions such as changes to individual or small-scale behavior with little attention to collective political action. Starting with the school's vision mantra "leadership effecting change," the curriculum centered and celebrated students as potential leaders in the fight against climate change. Particularly in the absence of conversations about systemic oppression, such approaches to teaching socially and economically privileged students how to address climate change may be counterproductive.

What Types of Solutions Should We Consider? In theory, environmental education develops young peoples' ability to take action on environmental and sustainability issues (Stevenson et al, 2013). However, curricula that focuses on "private sphere environmentalism" and "environmental stewardship" solutions to climate change are necessary but far from sufficient (Chawla & Cushing, 2007). We argue that the IS mission, "living well in a place," requires more than just changing consumption habits or individual practices—it requires collective, critical sociopolitical action that challenges systems and structures that created climate change in the first place through explicit critical analysis of the problem alongside collective work and activism (Watts & Flanagan, 2007; Watts & Hipolito-Delgado, 2015).

A curricular focus on individual or hyper-local change was notable across IS. For example, in Human Ecology, students developed and implemented projects to improve environmental sustainability systems on campus. Some projects turned into impactful programs, like the school's biodiesel production. However, students developed these projects *absent* the broader social context of school or the Bahamas. For example, Brady helped a student group develop a proposal to source school uniforms from a sustainable provider. However, the project focused solely on identifying sustainable materials and *not* the means of production or distribution or a discussion of who would benefit from the purchase of the uniforms.

Outside of class, IS expected students to make individual sacrifices and change their daily behaviors in the name of sustainability. To save water, students took 60-second showers. To save energy, the campus had no air conditioning, despite the hot and humid Bahamian climate. To reduce waste, students brought reusable water bottles and were encouraged to give up food in single-use plastic packaging. While these expectations and experiences impressed upon students the importance of making personal sacrifices, we would argue that the biggest benefit of these "sacrifices" was to students' personal growth as opposed to developing their critical consciousness or capacity for collective action, allowing them to position themselves as "better elites" while only marginally influencing environmental outcomes. For example, students routinely used the rigors of IS life to demonstrate their resilience in application essays for "elite" universities. IS teachers and curricula largely missed an opportunity to develop the skills and critical dispositions that students would need to exercise their considerable influence at the structural or political level, instead encouraging students to pursue solutions to climate change at the micro level—their own behaviors and immediate community—at the expense of collective or sociopolitical action (Watts & Flanagan, 2007).

Who Should Lead the Fight Against Climate Change? Recently, elites have begun to position themselves as those best suited to enact social and environmental change efforts (e.g., Giridharadas, 2018), reflecting a sense of superiority that legitimates and naturalizes privilege (Gaztambide-Fernández and Howard, 2013; Goodman, 2011) and creating a distinction between "good elites" and "bad elites" (Swalwell, 2015). These distinctions—and the positioning of "elite" students as the people who should be leading the charge against climate change—played out across the IS curriculum. Its ambitious vision promised that after 3 months of personal growth and empowerment, students would be poised and prepared to be global change-makers.

In their research classes, for example, students worked alongside mostly non-Bahamian, white graduate students and PhD-level scientists to research local ecosystems, food systems, and marine life. They shared their findings at a symposium attended by government officials and representatives from professional organizations. While useful as an assessment tool, the projects at the symposium did little to address real issues of environmental justice—and likely perpetuated inequitable power dynamics by positioning mostly white, wealthy, non-Bahamian high school students as experts in national-level environmentalism and sustainability. More recently, this framing of students as leaders was evident in a June 2020 IS Instagram post. In response to the protests surrounding George Floyd's (and others') death at the hands of police, it stated: "our communities and the world need our leadership." This post, alongside events like the symposium, centers IS students as "saviors" without grappling with how "elite leaders" facilitate climate change and white supremacy.

RECOMMENDATIONS FOR PRACTICE

Here, we offer some suggestions as to how environmental and sustainability educators of "elite" students might navigate the tensions, avoid the pitfalls, and take advantage of the possibilities we outlined earlier. If a school grounds its reputation in and garners accolades from offering sustainability education that claims to prepare students to "change the world," they must also provide teachers with the necessary training and resources to do this work well.

Given the realities of climate change, we encourage teachers to frame their courses around the concepts of ecojustice education and critical pedagogy of place. Ecojustice addresses the reality of race, class, and gender-based environmental injustice within a larger framework of challenging cultural assumptions underlying and undermining local and global ecosystems (Martusewicz et al., 2011). Similarly, critical pedagogy of place calls on educators to engage students in improving the health and well-being of their natural environment and human communities through critical reflection, engagement with places, and social action (Gruenewald, 2003). Both approaches are inherently political, building upon other socioecological traditions that investigate the cultural, political, economic, and ecological dynamics of places and address many of the concerns raised earlier in our interrogation of the IS curriculum.

How Do We Situate Climate Change—and Ourselves—in Systems of Oppression?

Students are ill prepared to address climate change without an adequate understanding of the interaction between social and environmental systems as well as their positions within those systems. Teachers should aim toward developing their students' (and their own) critical consciousness (Freire, 1970/2000) by naming and discussing how white supremacy and capitalism shape our understanding of our places, the environment, and environmentalism (Finney, 2014; Haymes, 1995). Once students can conceptualize how different aspects of their identity position them within an unjust society, they can more meaningfully critique climate change as an outcome of social, political, and environmental systems.

We have argued that environmental and sustainability education focused on personal change is insufficient, so teachers must teach students to be accountable for personal action while situating the individual in the context of policies and systems. An ecojustice-centered education would provide students with opportunities to understand the systems and policies that lead to climate change, grapple with their positionality to them, and require students to research and enact how to dismantle them. Notably, critical place-based pedagogies provide guidance for how to integrate this work into academic classes across the curriculum (e.g., Gruenewald & Smith, 2008).

How Does the "Elite" Class Benefit from and Contribute to Climate Change?

If the goal of sustainability and environmental education is to actually pre-pare students to address environmental problems, then we must establish a framework for the social distribution of power (Gough & Gough, 2010). Students won't be able to offer realistic and appropriate solutions if they don't understand the differential impact of the choices made by individuals with more or less socioeconomic power. Once students with disproportion-ately high levels of socially positioned power become aware of their ability to exert force (through financial wealth, social networks, access to those who make political and business policy decisions, and so forth), they may be more likely to become not only conscious of environmental problems but powerfully active agents in environmental change-making.

What Types of Solutions Should We Consider?

Ecojustice education's guiding question (How shall we live together on this planet?) (Martusewicz et al., 2011, p. 21) differs in important ways from the IS's mantra (How do we live well in a place?). Ecojustice's use of "to-gether" emphasizes interdependence and the need for collectivity, and the use of "planet" pushes our attention toward the global nature of climate change. Given the limited impact of environmental stewardship behaviors, we encourage teachers to ask themselves: What is *really* changing regarding systems and structures as a result of your work? (McKenzie et al., 2015). Moving toward a positive answer to this question likely involves not only building "elite" students' knowledge of systems of oppression but also giv-ing students the opportunity to practice collective action (Gough & Gough, 2010; Watts & Flanagan, 2007). For example, instead of only limiting stu-dents' individual water use, we might have asked students to look for in-dustries and companies that exploit limited water resources and conduct a social media campaign to boycott such corporations. Additionally, teach-ers should provide students with historical examples of privileged allyship through collective action to learn from models that resulted in real structural change. Other important steps include working across disciplines to merge environmentalism with civics, providing students with knowledge about how governments work and practice pressuring politicians (Schild, 2016).

Who Should Lead the Fight Against Climate Change?

Ideally, students in positions of social and economic power will walk away from environmental and sustainability education inspired to use their re-sources and platforms to be partners for change, trusting in the direction, ideas, and activism of communities who have been doing this work for gen-erations. For example, instead of supporting controversial Marine Protected

Areas in local fishing spots, we could have had students amplify the voices of local advocates who prioritized community concerns and solutions. Teachers should emphasize the importance of collaborative decision-making with local stakeholders (Schild, 2016) that de-centers privileged students and centers those most affected by climate change. Given that traditional systems of Indigenous education are "among the oldest continuing expressions of 'environmental' education in the world" (Cajete, 1994, p. 21), one specific way to begin this work would be to learn alongside and from the history and present of local Indigenous communities and cultures (Gilo-Whitaker, 2019; Martuseciwsz et al., 2011; Tuck et al., 2014).

CONCLUSION

As educators who care about environmental justice working with students who benefit immensely from unjust systems, we must help students understand structural inequality and to exert systemic influence that leverages their privilege toward environmental justice. We acknowledge that doing this work with "elite" students can present discomforts and challenges. Some students and parents may be upset by critiques of privilege and capitalism and may push back on the curricular goals we describe here. Similarly, board members and donors to private and charter schools may balk at efforts to challenge the system that contributed to their wealth and status. Quite simply, challenging the economic systems that have created "elite" groups and calling for collective, critical action is risky *but crucially important* work—both for these students and for the health of our planet.

ACKNOWLEDGMENTS

The authors would like to acknowledge and thank Emma Alexander and Kristal Ambrose, former IS teachers, for their insightful feedback and critical comments on earlier drafts of this chapter.

NOTES

1. In keeping with the introduction (Swalwell, this volume), we use "elite" as a "synonym for people who seemingly benefit from unjust power relations," not as an indicator of superiority.

2. We acknowledge that what happens on the ground at IS likely differs from what is found on the program's website and that day-to-day life at IS may have changed since our tenure. Regardless, we hope that educators find our observations a useful guide for their own practice and that researchers will take up the questions we pose.

3. Information in this paragraph was derived from the IS's website (http://www.islandschool.org/) and curriculum guide.

4. http://www.capeeleutherafoundation.org/support-1#sharing-solutions

5. Notably, the top donors to the funding arm of IS include business leaders, investment bankers, and public officials like Dick and Betsy DeVos (http://www.capeeleutherafoundation.org/s/Annual-Report_2019_final.pdf).

REFERENCES

Bullard, R. (Ed.). (1993). *Confronting environmental racism: Voices from the grass-roots*. South End Press.

Cajete, G. (1994). *Look to the mountain: An ecology of indigenous education*. Kivaki Press.

Chawla, L., & Cushing, D. (2007). Education for strategic environmental behavior. *Environmental Education Research, 13*(4), 437–452.

Finney, C. (2014). *Black faces, white spaces: Reimagining the relationship of African Americans to the great outdoors*. University of North Carolina Press.

Freire, P. (1970/2000). *Pedagogy of the oppressed (30th Anniversary Edition)*. Continuum.

Gaztambide-Fernández, R., & Howard, A. (2010). Conclusion: Outlining a research agenda on elite education. In A. Howard & R. A. Gaztambide-Fernández (Eds.), *Educating elites: Class privilege and educational advantage* (pp. 195–209). Rowman and Littlefield Education.

Gilo-Whitaker, D. (2019). *As long as grass grows: The Indigenous fight for environmental justice, from colonization to Standing Rock*. Beacon Press.

Giridharadas, A. (2018). *Winners take all: The elite charade of changing the world*. Vintage Books.

Goodman, A. (2018, December 11). School strike for climate: Meet 15-year-old activist Greta Thunberg, who inspired a global movement. *Democracy Now*. https://www.democracynow.org/2018/12/11/meet_the_15_year_old_swedish

Goodman, D. (2011). *Promoting diversity and social justice: Educating people from privileged groups* (2nd ed.). Routledge.

Gough, N. & Gough, A. (2010). Environmental education. In C. Kridel (Ed.), *Encyclopedia of curriculum studies* (pp. 340–343). SAGE Publications.

Haymes, S. N. (1995). *Race, culture, and the city: A pedagogy for Black urban struggle*. State University of New York Press.

Haynes, S. (2019, May 16). 'Now I am speaking to the whole world:' How teen climate activist Greta Thunberg got everyone to listen. *Time Magazine*. https://time.com/collection-post/5584902/greta-thunberg-next-generation-leaders/

Gruenewald, D. (2003). The best of both worlds: A critical pedagogy of place. *Educational Researcher, 32*(4), 3–12.

Gruenewald, D., & Smith, G. (Eds.) (2008). *Place-based education in the global age: Local diversity*. Routledge.

Henderson, J. (2015). 'Not for everyone, but kind of amazing': Institutional friction and the nature of sustainability education. *Environmental Education Research, 21*(2), 295–296.

Hursh, D., Henderson, J., & Greenwood, D. (2015). Environmental education in a neoliberal climate. *Environmental Education Research, 21*(3), 299–318.

Klein, N. (2014). *This changes everything: Capitalism vs the climate.* Simon & Schuster.

Lopez, B. H. (1990). *The rediscovery of North America.* University Press of Kentucky.

Martusewicz, R. A., Edmundson, J., & Lupinacci, J. (2014). *Ecojustice education: Toward diverse, democratic, and sustainable communities.* Routledge.

McKenzie, M., Bieler, A., & McNeil, R. (2015). Education policy mobility: Reimagining sustainability in neoliberal times. *Environmental Education Research, 21*(3), 319–337.

Miller, H. K. (2018). Developing a critical consciousness of race in place-based environmental education: Franco's story. *Environmental Education Research, 24*(6), 845–858.

Orr, D. W. (1994). *Earth in mind: On education, environment, and the human prospect.* Island Press.

Schild, R. (2016). Environmental citizenship: What can political theory contribute to environmental education practice? *The Journal of Environmental Education, 47*(1), 19–34.

Sinclair, K., & Swalwell, K. (2017). Becoming a "better" elite: The proliferation and discourses of educational travel programmes for elite youth. In H. M. Gunter, D. Hall, & M. W. Apple (Eds), *Corporate elites and the reform of public education* (pp. 89–103). Policy Press.

Stevenson, R. (2007). Schooling and environmental education: Contradictions in purpose and practice. *Environmental Education Research, 13*(2), 139–153.

Stevenson, R., Brody, M., Dillon, J., & Wals, A. (Eds.). (2013). *International handbook of research on environmental education.* Routledge.

Swalwell, K. (2015). Mind the civic empowerment gap: Elite students and critical civic education. *Curriculum Inquiry, 45*(5), 491–512.

The Island School Curriculum Guide. (2019). http://www.islandschool.org/academics

Tuck, E., McKenzie, M., & McCoy, K. (2014). Land education: Indigenous, postcolonial, and decolonizing perspectives on place and environmental education research. *Environmental Education Research, 20*(1), 1–23.

Wagner, T. (2010). *The global achievement gap: Why even our best schools don't teach the new survival skills our children need—and what we can do about it.* Basic Books.

Walcott, D. (1990). *Omeros.* Macmillan.

Watts, R., & Flanagan, C. (2007). Pushing the envelope on youth civic engagement: A developmental and liberation psychology perspective. *Journal of Community Psychology, 35*(6), 779–792.

Watts, R. J., & Hipolito-Delgado, C. P. (2015). Thinking ourselves to liberation? Advancing sociopolitical action in critical consciousness. *Urban Review, 47*(5), 847–867.

CHAPTER 9

The Possibility of Critical Language Awareness Through Volunteer English Teaching Abroad

Cori Jakubiak

In August 2019, the National Public Radio program *All Things Considered* featured a story on Renee Bach, a white, 30-year-old woman from Virginia who ran a "nutrition clinic" in Uganda for 10 years without any prior medical training. The story reported that Bach, a former missionary, consulted YouTube videos for guidance before administering intravenous (IV) fluids to patients and that she regularly gave children blood transfusions based on her own diagnoses. Between 2010 and 2015, 105 Ugandan children died while in Bach's care (Aizeman, 2019). A group of Ugandan mothers, who have since filed a lawsuit against Bach, claim that Bach mispresented herself and her credentials to the local community. The plaintiffs report that Bach consistently wore a white lab coat and stethoscope while examining patients and that she never disclosed her lack of medical expertise to the families who visited her clinic (King, 2019).

The story of Bach's malpractice in Uganda provides a tragic, worst-case example of what can happen when inexperienced outsiders from the Global North[1] intervene in Global South communities. And while teaching English abroad as a volunteer is a far cry from performing invasive medical procedures on sick children without the requisite professional credentials, Bach's story is part of a larger formation that encompasses them both. This formation is international volunteer tourism, or the practice of unskilled, often inexperienced but well-meaning people from the Global North inserting themselves into Global South communities in the names of humanitarianism, development, and civic service (McGehee & Santos, 2005; Wearing, 2001).

In this chapter, I chart some of the ways in which a popular form of volunteer tourism, "English-language voluntourism" (e.g., Jakubiak, 2014), or short-term volunteer English language teaching in the Global South, reflects some of the same problematic assumptions that undergird the Bach case in Uganda. Using the theme of *transformation* as a lens, I make three central claims. First, although many peoples' attitudes toward volunteer tourism have transformed in recent years, moving from celebratory to cautious and even ironic (Schwarz & Richey, 2019), this transformation has not yet extended to the presumed value of English in vulnerable peoples' lives. This oversight is noteworthy, as research suggests that English alone, absent local economic restructuring or increased access to higher or technical education, rarely mitigates peoples' economic vulnerability or increases their access to resources (May, 2014). Instead, English education in many Global South contexts siphons limited resources *away* from other, more substantive, educational programming (Bruthiaux, 2002). Moreover, English does not have consistent exchange value among people in different social structural locations (Park, 2016). In that sense, English-language voluntourism, like Bach's putative nutrition clinic, provides an illusory and thin form of assistance.

The Bach case and English-language voluntourism also cohere in how they devalue professional knowledge and experiences. English-language voluntourism relies on and extends what Robert Phillipson (1992) calls the *native speaker fallacy*: the idea that any monolingual, prestige-variety, dominant-variety English speaker is also a natural and effective language instructor. And although a child is unlikely to suffer bodily harm at the hands of an underprepared English teacher, the practice of people taking on professional identities that they don't possess and practicing those identities on real people (Simpson, 2005) raises ethical questions. English-language voluntourism promotional literature routinely suggests that volunteers need not be familiar with language pedagogy or classroom teaching. Instead, English-language voluntourism is marketed as an opportunity for visiting volunteers to *add* classroom teaching to their list of professional experiences. Like Renee Bach cutting her medical teeth by practicing on vulnerable patients, many English-language voluntourists often try their hands at teaching in the contexts of underresourced Southern classrooms. As the commercial English-language voluntourism sponsor, Projects Abroad (n.d.), puts it: "You'll gain practical teaching work experience in Costa Rica. . . . This is a great addition to your CV and will be a fascinating topic to talk about in future job interviews."

Not all English-language voluntourists, however, take up these programs' dominant discourses uncritically. Drawing upon retrospective interview data, I highlight how some former volunteers became skeptical of English-language voluntourism through their experiences abroad. While few in number,[2] some former volunteers expressed discomfort with how students' community languages were devalued by English-focused educational policies, and they reported being uncomfortable with English-language voluntourism's recommended instructional practices. These data suggest that, while not guaranteed, a possible and unforeseen outcome of participating in English-language voluntourism can be a transformed perspective on educational language policy and the role of language teaching in social change. Similar to how the Bach case in Uganda has brought increased attention to American hubris in the Global South, some former volunteers developed *critical language awareness*

(Alim, 2005) by participating in these programs. Critical language awareness sees "educational institutions as designed to teach citizens about the current sociolinguistic order of things, without challenging that order, which is based largely on the ideology of the dominating group and their desire to maintain social control" (Alim, 2005, p. 28). Demonstrating critical language awareness, some former volunteers came to question English's dominance in global schooling practices. They also expressed discomfort with English-only immersion pedagogies that ignore students' multilingual resources.

(SOME) TRANSFORMATIONS IN PUBLIC PERCEPTIONS OF VOLUNTEER TOURISM

Scholars have noted a recent, dramatic shift in public perceptions of volunteer tourism. Although community leaders, college admissions boards, and even employers have long associated volunteer tourism with active civic engagement and public service (McGehee & Santos, 2005; Wearing, 2001), an increasing number of academics, public intellectuals, and former volunteers now view the practice through a more "cautionary" lens (e.g., Kuo, 2016). Scholars have raised serious doubts, for example, about whether volunteer tourism contributes to equity-oriented material and social change in the Global South (Butcher & Smith, 2015; Palacios, 2010), and many observers have expressed dissatisfaction with these programs' colonialist undertones (e.g., Keyl, 2016; Vrasti, 2013). Other critiques of volunteer tourism have centered on the lack of critical pedagogy within these programs (Simpson, 2004) and the (im)possibility of even teaching short-term volunteers about structural injustice given time and resource constraints (Henry, 2019).

Following this latter line of critique, American journalist Teju Cole (2016) views short-term, one-off humanitarian efforts such as volunteer tourism as part of what he calls "The White Savior Industrial Complex." This complex is an assemblage of aid packages, uneven mobility, sentimentality, racial formations, and volunteerism, all of which aim to "make a difference" in global poverty without analyzing or historicizing its causes. Observing how humanitarian efforts in Africa, for example, rarely require volunteers to think *constellationally*, or about how actions taken in one's home country affect other places, Cole writes: "If Americans want to care about Africa, maybe they should consider evaluating American foreign policy, which they already play a direct role in through elections" (p. 348). Highlighted here is how individual efforts to "make a difference," such as Bach's doctoring or volunteer tourists' English-language teaching, have little long-term impact on the political and economic structures that create and sustain inequality.

Responses to widespread publicity of the White Savior Industrial Complex and negative attention to volunteer tourism more generally have been swift and taken on different forms. For one, there has been a marked uptick among volunteer tourism stakeholders to create a more responsible volunteer tourism. TedTalks and numerous senior theses, for example, urge people to look critically at volunteer tourism marketing materials and to monitor how sponsoring nongovernmental organizations (NGOs) use program fees (e.g., Wood, 2019). Other resources now provide "best practice" guides for being an ethical volunteer (e.g., Rolfe, 2019).

In addition to these efforts among various actors to create a more responsible volunteer tourism, there has been a parallel, largely digital, movement among young people to frame volunteer tourism ironically. Many youth are now using social media platforms to critique volunteer tourism, and their efforts have focused on the self-aggrandizing images that some volunteers post online. Kaylan Schwarz and Lisa Richey's (2019) compelling work in this area details how White volunteer tourists risk social media backlash if they post pictures of themselves surrounded by children of color to sites like Instagram or Tinder. Schwarz and Richey also trace how YouTube and other social media platforms are being used to criticize volunteer tourism's patronizing rhetoric. One of the YouTube productions that they highlight is a mock "Who Wants to Be a Volunteer?" YouTube gameshow, in which a potential White female volunteer tourist is asked, "How many countries are in Africa?" and quizzically responds, "One" (SAIH, n.d.). This game show parody, as Schwarz and Richey (2019) put it, "challenges the callowness of international volunteers who have no conception of the vast African continent, who are underqualified for the roles they play overseas, and who are more concerned with self-image than social justice" (p. 1933).

Thus, public perceptions of volunteer tourism have transformed dramatically in recent years. A decade and a half of academic criticism, more public awareness of volunteer tourism's limitations, public media-shaming, and debacles such as the Bach case in Uganda have brought mounting skepticism toward volunteer tourism and similar, well-intentioned but undertheorized humanitarian efforts. Still, these widespread critiques have done little to dislodge positive perceptions of short-term, volunteer English-language teaching as a Global South development initiative. To better understand why this is so, literature in critical applied linguistics provides a useful point of departure.

ENGLISH, THE SEEMINGLY ALWAYS-USEFUL TOOL

Even a cursory look at English-language voluntourism promotional materials makes it clear: These programs stress an instrumental view of language-in-education in which English is a value-added skill (cf. Urcioli, 2008) for anyone who learns it. Promotional websites and volunteer tourism brochures suggest that if poor people across the world only possessed English-language skills, they would have immediate access to high-paid work in the global economy, more equitable access to higher education, innumerable future opportunities, and even increased self-confidence. By way of illustration, the NGO, New Hope Volunteers, hails prospective English-language voluntourists as follows:

> Would you like to spread the joy of teaching in a developing country? Look no further than in Ghana. English may be the official language of Ghana, but the opportunities for quality English education [are] not provided to students in rural schools. It is essential for the young children to have a good grasp of the language because a solid ability in English means securing seats in good universities, and later on, good jobs. . . . By encouraging constant speech and dialogue, you'll be boosting the self-esteem of the children, allowing them to be more confident and believe in themselves. (n.d.)

The celebratory stance (Pennycook, 2000) taken toward English in this excerpt reflects what Joseph Sun-Yul Park (2016) calls the ideology of *language as pure potential*. In precarious economic and social contexts in which job opportunities are scarce, workers are expected to continually "re-skill" and acquire new competencies, degrees, or proficiencies in order to remain employed (Urcioli, 2008). Within this view, acquiring a dominant language—defined instrumentally, not as a cultural practice—ostensibly adds value to one's professional portfolio and helps one mitigate economic vulnerability.

We can see the ideology of language as pure potential quite literally in English-language voluntourism discourse. Marketing materials offer that no matter where a person currently lives or how they are raced, classed, or gendered, English-language learning with a visiting volunteer will allow them to "reach greater heights and fulfill their *true potential*" (Global Crossroad, n.d., emphasis added). Notably, within English-language voluntourism promotional materials, the solution to underemployment, inequality, and uneven educational opportunity is never to alter broader structures.

English-language voluntourism's adherence to the ideology of language as pure potential does not go unchallenged by all volunteers, however. As I discuss next, some former English-language voluntourists developed critical language awareness by participating in these same programs. These volunteers' views on English-language teaching and learning as development were transformed by their experiences abroad.

TRANSFORMED BY VOLUNTEERING: THE DEVELOPMENT OF CRITICAL LANGUAGE AWARENESS AMONG FORMER ENGLISH-LANGUAGE VOLUNTOURISTS

As part of a larger, multisited ethnography of English-language voluntourism, I interviewed over 60 in-service and former volunteers between 2007 and 2014. Although most of my study participants took a largely uncritical stance toward English and its place in international development (Jakubiak, 2016), a small number of study participants expressed discrepant views. Though difficult to characterize as a group, these outlier participants were often multilingual themselves and conversant in social theory. They often came from homes in which more than one language was spoken, and they had frequently completed academic coursework in education, anthropology, or sociology—fields that theorize structural inequality and examine how identity categories such as race, class, gender, sexual orientation, language use, and dis/ability both create and limit individuals' agency. These dissenting volunteers remarked that seeing English-language voluntourism "on the ground," in practice made them question their previous assumptions about global English-language education and its role in social change.

Peg, a former volunteer in Namibia, underwent such a personal transformation. A U.S. Midwesterner in her early twenties who had worked with refugees prior to attending an Ivy League college, Peg had volunteered in a Namibian high school that had a strict English medium-of-instruction (MOI) policy. This meant that all classes were taught in English and that the students' home language, Oshikwanyama, was never used in classroom instruction. Witnessing how English-only, restrictive educational languages policies worked in a Namibian school made Peg rethink the role of English education in development. When asked whether participating in English-language voluntourism had complicated her worldview, Peg said:

> One other thing that I became more aware of and more sensitive to . . . is language in education and how important it is for kids to be able to express themselves. In Namibia, schools are entirely in English. . . . But my students, outside of school, they all speak Oshikwanyama all the time, even in school, when they're not in class. . . . And, they don't put any formal instruction that says, like, "This in Oshikwanyama means this in English." It's just, they're immersed in an English language medium and they're expected to understand it, and then they're expected to memorize all this information in nine different subjects and regurgitate in on the tests. Totally ineffective! And, like, half of the tenth grade was repeating. Like, that was their second or third or fourth time taking the tenth grade. Because, like, it's useless to try to memorize random words in a language that you barely understand. . . . When I got there and actually saw [this educational language policy] in practice, I was like, "Oh, no! This is a disaster."

Peg's revised, cautious stance on the English MOI policy resonates with equity-oriented research. Scholars note that English MOI practices can lead to dis-citizenship,[3] as students are unable to learn to express their opinions when they don't understand the language of schooling (Bhattacharya, 2016). Students are effectively silenced and learn passivity as an outcome of schooling when they don't have access to their full linguistic repertoires

(Bach, 2020), and restrictive, English-only educational MOI programs often prohibit students from engaging with course material (Brock-Utne, 2002).

Graham, another former English-language voluntourist in his twenties, experienced a similar transformation. Raised by a German mother who had done anthropological fieldwork in American Samoa, Graham identified as a multilingual American who was comfortable in international settings. Reflecting on his volunteer teaching experience in the Marshall Islands, Graham noted that the strict English MOI policy there seemed to stifle students' access to content. Graham said, "It's rote memorization [in the school] and . . . not a lot of understanding, and most seniors in high school couldn't draw you a map of the world." Graham then offered a specific example of how English MOI policies influenced one of his students. He said:

> [This] boy would do his homework and ask for my help. And just the most ridiculous assignments. He was in fourth grade, so he spoke almost no English. And they were doing an astronomy unit—and it's all in English now—and his quiz at the end of this big unit was a series of ten sentences that he had to memorize. . . . So, questions [like], "What is the circumference of the earth?" "The circumference of the earth is X. . . ." "[W]ho was the first person to land on the moon?" . . . "In 1968, Neil Armstrong." . . . [H]e had these verbatim sentences that he was told to memorize, and he just asked me to help practice them. . . . And it turned out he . . . didn't understand a single word in these sentences! . . . He was able to memorize them all phonetically, and then he aced his test. And he's, like, at the top of his class. . . . And that's the school system.

After sharing this troubling narrative, Graham spoke wistfully about the value of local languages and the potential of school language policies to legitimize them. Graham had observed that his Pohnpeian-speaking students had a rich cultural life outside of school, and he lamented that the school's restrictive educational language policy neglected his students' personal lives and interests. Graham reflected:

> It would be nice if [the school] could continue teaching English and the local language side by side. . . . I feel like it gives a language some legitimacy when it's taught in school. I mean . . . education has the stigma of legitimizing things, and maybe teaching Pohnpeiian to the kids all the way through high school would sort of make them feel like [it] is also a legitimate language in the world and not just something that we kind of playfully use with our friends and family.

Graham's observations about the role of schools in legitimizing and promoting nondominant languages align with culturally responsive pedagogical approaches. Studies suggest that when schools adopt promotion-oriented (Wiley, 2013) language policies, emergent bilingual students have more positive experiences in school, achieve more academic success, and feel more pride in their identities (McCarty & Nichols, 2014). Neriko Musha Doerr's (2018) longitudinal work with Maori-English bilingual speakers in New Zealand is also insightful in this regard. Doerr demonstrates that even though heritage language shift may occur over time—particularly in English-dominant contexts like New Zealand—if speakers once participated in a school-endorsed bilingual program, they are more likely to maintain a connection to these community languages and even pass these languages along to their children. Thus, Graham's evolving understanding of the role of schools in community language shift and language loss is an important form of critical language awareness, and it demonstrates that English-language voluntourism programs can help build allies for linguistic pluralism.

Other former English-language voluntourists became wary of the native speaker fallacy by participating in these programs. Although few in number, some former volunteers expressed discomfort with English-language voluntourism's dominant instructional strategies. Joanne, a U.S. undergraduate and former volunteer in Costa Rica who was majoring in anthropology, criticized English-language voluntourism for disrupting students' day-to-day instructional continuity. She said:

> I'm not sure that it's the best strategy [for volunteers] to go to a place for a really short amount of time . . . and take over the English class. I mean, we're completely untrained and we're, like, twenty years old. . . . It's kind of a funny idea to stick a twenty year old who has [had] no teacher training . . . into a school and [make them] responsible for, like, sixty children and their education and then leave at the end of two months, at which point [the students] go back to their old curriculum with their old teachers.

Here, Joanne reveals an ethical struggle with English-language voluntourism's ideological underpinnings. She questions the way in which these programs place large amounts of professional responsibility in the hands of inexperienced and underprepared volunteers, and she expresses dissatisfaction with how English-language voluntourism disrupts broader educational routines. Like Peg and Graham, the dominant discourse of "teach English, help people" was disrupted by Joanne's experiences abroad.

CONCLUDING THOUGHTS

Whether characterized as "life-changing" (Love Volunteers, n.d.), "defining" (Projects Abroad, n.d.), or "one of the most significant experiences of your life" (Global Volunteers, n.d.), participating in volunteer tourism is frequently lauded for its transformational potential. As volunteer tourism scholar Kathie Carpenter (2015) observes, "The quest for a transformative experience is often considered a primary motivation for voluntourism . . . and the expectation of this transformation probably motivates many volunteers" (pp. 19–20). In this chapter, I sought to tease out what *transformation* can mean in the context of English-language voluntourism, as *how*, exactly, volunteer tourists will be transformed is rarely specified or detailed.

My analysis suggests that although dominant attitudes toward volunteer tourism may be in the process of transforming, celebratory stances toward English-language education as a Global South development intervention remain largely intact. Although some volunteer tourism stakeholders have become wise to critiques of "save the world in a week" rhetoric and the White Savior Industrial Complex more generally, the idea that English-language learning and teaching are universally valuable remains a popular belief. Yet as I highlight in this chapter, a small number of volunteer tourists are transformed in unique, unexpected ways by participating in these programs. They develop an appreciation for linguistic pluralism by living in distant host communities, and they become critical of English-only, restrictive educational language policies when they see them in practice in real classrooms. Some former volunteers' perspectives on language pedagogies are also transformed by their experiences abroad. They question the value of temporarily replacing local teachers and wonder about long-term disruptions.

It is difficult to account for what, exactly, might make certain volunteers amenable to re-evaluating English-language voluntourism's claims and recommended practices. In the context of this study, the volunteers who became more critical toward English MOI policies and the native speaker fallacy often identified as multilingual themselves; they may have thus been already included to appreciate linguistic pluralism. All of the volunteers featured in this chapter, moreover, had taken prior coursework in social studies, which may have provided them with theoretical tools for examining structural inequality. This suggests that what volunteers study *before* they participate in these programs influences how they interpret their experiences (see also Palacios, 2010).

The case of Renee Bach and her clinic in Uganda has yet to go to trial. As social justice educators watching on the sidelines, we might do well to metaphorically put ourselves on the stand and ask ourselves a series of questions. What practices do we engage in unreflectively in the name of "help"? What unchecked assumptions and beliefs undergird our best intentions? What are our own roles in causing and sustaining others' pain? As the voices of the former volunteers in this chapter show, we never know when and how we might be transformed and alter our approaches to problem solving. The Renee Bach case and its parallels to English-language voluntourism provide a moment for us to ponder how "making a difference" might mean challenging our own ways of thinking.

NOTES

1. I use the terms Global North and Global South, rather than "developed" and "developing" or "First" and "Third" world, throughout this chapter. My word choice reflects work in human geography and critical anthropology, which highlights how historical and contemporary processes have produced Global North countries' wealth and technologies through the violent extraction of labor and resources from the Global South.

2. My other work highlights how a majority of voluntourists took a celebratory stance toward English-language voluntourism and its development claims (see, for example, Jakubiak, 2016).

3. Rather than seeing citizenship as something merely obtainable (e.g., "to acquire citizenship"), Vaidehi Ramanathan (2013) views citizenship as a flexible process that allows people to participate fully in public life. Following this definition, she claims that dis-citizenship occurs whenever people are excluded from full participation in public life (e.g., in school classrooms), as restrictive language policies literally silence certain students.

REFERENCES

Aizeman, N. (2019, August 9). American with no medical training ran center for malnourished Ugandan kids. 105 died. *All Things Considered*. National Public Radio.

Alim, H. S. (2005). Critical language awareness in the United States: Revisiting issues and revising pedagogies in a resegregated society. *Educational Researcher, 34*(7), 24–31.

Bach, A. J. (2020). Education in citizenship on the U.S./Mexico border: The language and literacy instruction of emergent bilingual *transfronterizx* students. *Anthropology and Education Quarterly, 51*(2), 233–252.

Bhattacharya, U. (2016). The politics of participation: Dis-citizenship through English teaching in a suburban Indian village school. *The Journal of English as an International Language, 11*(1), 71–85.

Brock-Utne, B. (2002). *Language, democracy, and education in Africa.* Nordiska Afrikainstitutet.

Bruthiaux, P. (2002). Hold your courses: Language education, language choice, and economic development. *TESOL Quarterly, 36*(3), 275–296.

Butcher, J., & Smith, P. (2015). *Volunteer tourism: The lifestyle politics of international development.* Routledge.

Carpenter, K. (2015). Childhood studies and orphanage tourism in Cambodia. *Annals of Tourism Research, 55*, 15–27.

Cole, T. (2016). *Known and strange things: Essays.* Random House.

Doerr, N. M. (2018). *Refusals to translate: Politics of resistance in Aotearoa/New Zealand.* Paper presented at the annual meeting of the American Anthropological Association, San Jose, CA.

Global Crossroad. (n.d.). *Volunteer teaching in Cambodia!* https://www.globalcross road.com/cambodia/volunteer-teaching-in-cambodia

Global Volunteers. (2002–Present). *Teach conversational English.* https://global volunteers.org/community-projects/

Henry, J. (2019). Pedagogy, possibility, and pipe dreams: Opportunities and challenges for radicalizing international volunteering. *Journal of Tourism and Cultural Change, 17*(6), 663–675.

Jakubiak, C. (2014). Moral ambivalence in English language voluntourism. In M. Mostafanezhad & K. Hannam (Eds.), *Moral encounters in tourism* (pp. 93–106). Ashgate.

Jakubiak, C. (2016). Ambiguous aims: English-language voluntourism as development. *Journal of Language, Identity and Education, 15*(4), 245–258.

Keyl, S. (2016). Learning English in the margins: Migrant worker knowledge production in Beirut's NGO spaces. In J. A. Álvarez, C. Amanti, S. Keyl, & E. Mackinney (Eds.), *Critical views on teaching and learning English around the globe: Qualitative research approaches* (pp. 157–176). Information Age Publishing.

King, B. (2019, June 25). Virginia missionary accused of impersonating doctor, causing deaths in Uganda. *CBS 6 This Morning.* https://wtvr.com/2019/06/25/virginia -missionary-accused-of-impersonating-doctor-causing-deaths-in-uganda/

Kuo, L. (2016, April 20). Instagram's White Savior Barbie neatly captures what's wrong with "voluntourism" in Africa. *Quartz Africa.* https://qz.com/africa /665764/instagrams-white-savior-barbie-neatly-captures-whats-wrong-with -voluntourism-in-africa/

Love Volunteers. (n.d.). *Love volunteers.* https://www.lovevolunteers.org /destinations/volunteer-moldova/teaching-english-causeni

May, S. (2014). Justifying educational language rights. *Review of Research in Education, 38,* 215–241.

McCarty, T. & Nichols, S. (2014). Reclaiming indigenous languages: A reconsideration of the roles and responsibilities of schools. *Review of Research in Education, 38,* 106–136.

McGehee, N. G., & Santos, C. A. (2005). Social change, discourse and volunteer tourism. *Annals of Tourism Research, 32*(3), 760–779.

New Hope Volunteers. (n.d.). *New Hope Volunteers.* https://www.newhopevolunteers .org/volunteer-in-ghana/teaching-project.php

Palacios, C. M. (2010). Volunteer tourism, development and education in a postcolonial world: Conceiving global connections beyond aid. *Journal of Sustainable Tourism, 18*(7), 861–878.

Park, J. S.-Y. (2016). Language as pure potential. *Journal of Multilingual and Multicultural Development, 37*(5), 453–466.

Pennycook, A. (2000). English, politics, ideology: From colonial celebration to postcolonial performativity. In T. Ricento (Ed.), *Ideology, politics, and language policies: Focus on English* (pp. 107–119). John Benjamins Publishing Company.

Phillipson, R. (1992). *Linguistic imperialism.* Oxford University Press.

Projects Abroad. (n.d.). *Volunteer teaching English in Costa Rica.* https://www .projects-abroad.org/projects/volunteer-teaching-costa-rica/

Ramanathan, V. (Ed.). (2013). *Language policies and (dis)citizenship: Rights, access, pedagogies.* Multilingual Matters.

Rolfe, D. (2019). 12 tips on ethical volunteering and how to avoid the voluntourism trap. http://www.hostelworld.com

SAIH. (n.d.). Norwegian Students' and Academics' International Assistance Fund. http://www.saih.no

Schwarz, K. C., & Richey, L. A. (2019). Humanitarian humor, digilantism, and the dilemmas of representing volunteer tourism on social media. *New Media & Society, 21*(9), 1928–1946.

Simpson, K. (2004). 'Doing development': The gap year, volunteer-tourists and a popular practice of development. *Journal of International Development, 16,* 681–692.

Simpson, K. (2005). Dropping out or signing up? The professionalization of youth travel. *Antipode, 37*(3), 447–469.

Urcioli, B. (2008). Skills and selves in the new workplace. *American Ethnologist, 35*(2), 211–228.

Vrasti, W. (2013). Universal but not truly 'global': Governmentality, economic liberalism, and the international. *Review of International Studies,* 49–69.

Wearing, S. (2001). *Volunteer tourism: Experiences that make a difference.* CABI Publishing.

Wiley, T. G. (2013). A brief history and assessment of language rights in the United States. In J. F. Tollefson (Ed.), *Language policies in education: Critical issues* (2nd ed.; pp. 61–90). Routledge.

Wood, E. (2019). *Voluntourism uncovered: Toward a standard for meaningful work.* Unpublished senior honors project. Laramie, WY: University of Wyoming.

Part III

PROMISING PRACTICES?

IDEAS FOR ENACTING ANTI-OPPRESSIVE
EDUCATION IN "ELITE" SCHOOLS

CHAPTER 10

Living Up to Our Legacy

One School's Effort to Build Momentum, Capacity, and Commitment to Social Justice

Christiane M. Connors, Steven Lee,
Stacy Smith, and Damian R. Jones

In 1968, during a time when many visionary educators critically examined established institutions' ideologies and practices, Edmund Burke School's founders, Dick Roth and Jean Mooskin, sought to build a school that would adopt a more egalitarian, democratic, and participatory approach to learning. They started with the idea that an important goal of education should be to cultivate a sense of civic responsibility and community engagement. For inspiration, they looked to the famous quote often attributed to 18th-century Anglo-Irish statesman, Edmund Burke: "All that is necessary for the triumph of evil is that good men do nothing." Fifty years since its founding, Burke has become an urban elite independent school located in Washington, DC, serving students from different racial, social, and economic backgrounds in grades 6 to 12. With approximately 33% of students receiving some level of financial aid and students of color comprising 40% of the student body, Burke has a reputation among its peer institutions as a community committed to academic excellence and social responsibility.

Over the years, it developed three strong programs (Service, Equity and Inclusion, and Leadership), which aimed to cultivate in students the necessary awareness, knowledge, and skills to be thoughtful and active citizens. While clear connections existed, these three programs often operated independently from one another. Moreover, the programs' activities usually engaged students after school, on weekends, and during the summer with few clear connections to their core curriculum. Not coincidentally, Burke's board of trustees' strategic plan in 2016 mandated that the programs integrate and become more central to students' learning experiences. Given this directive, the directors of each program quickly determined social justice was the common denominator and agreed that learning about social justice should constitute the core of a Burke education. This chapter shares our journey to comprehensively transform Burke into a "social justice school" through its curriculum, instruction, and leadership with the hope of providing ideas and insights for others embarking on the same journey.

SEEDING THE GROUND

We, the authors, came into this work as leaders of the Service, Equity and Inclusion, and Leadership programs alongside Burke's head of school, who assiduously guided the process in its entirety. As director of service, Christiane oversaw the middle school's service-learning program and the high school's community engagement initiatives and partnerships. As director of equity and inclusion, Steven worked to ensure that principles of affirmation and fairness were reflected in everything happening at Burke, from assemblies to course curricula to affinity spaces, and attended all board of trustee meetings. As the director of student leadership, Stacy ran a high school leadership program that she helped to create when she started at Burke over 20 years ago. Finally, as the head of school, Damian brought the vision that made this undertaking possible every step of the way.

When we began this work in 2016, it would have been inaccurate to describe Burke as a "social justice school" despite its founding ethos and progressive roots. The school made an official commitment to equity and inclusion the year prior when the board of trustees ratified a formal statement of equity and inclusion; however, in practice, concern over such priorities was primarily focused inward (i.e., within our school community) rather than outward. This is not to say that teaching social justice was entirely absent. Similar to other progressive schools who purportedly believe in equity education and provide their faculty the autonomy to design their own courses, a number of our colleagues (especially in the humanities) included social justice–related topics in their curricula. However, we did not want any given student's education in social justice to be dependent upon what teachers they happened to be assigned during their academic careers—nor did we want this education to be limited to select disciplines. Thus, to truly become a "social justice school," we decided that our *entire* adult community (faculty, staff, and administrators) needed to be trained in research-based social justice pedagogy and provided both the encouragement and necessary support to innovate in this realm.

In order to financially support this ambitious initiative, we applied for an E. E. Ford Grant at the beginning of the 2016–2017 school year and embarked upon a 9-month application process that required community-wide support. The lengthy application process worked in our favor and provided us time to strategically introduce our vision and engage our colleagues in a democratic process to explore what social justice should mean at Burke. In the next section, we discuss elements that ensured a successful application and a real shift toward becoming a social justice school. First, we identify what ensured impactful collaboration at the start of the process. Second, we outline what strategies were employed to build momentum and capacity. And third, we share transferable lessons we learned that might assist other schools embarking on a similar initiative.

IMPACTFUL COLLABORATION

Leadership from the Head of School

Although Burke's founding was inspired by the social protest movements of 1968, the term "social justice" was rarely explicitly applied to programs and curriculum. This language has become much more common within both independent school and mainstream discourse; several years ago, however, it was necessary for us to carefully consider the risks of declaring a social justice education as the ultimate aim of this initiative. After much deliberation, we determined that this critical step—announcing the intentional incorporation of social justice into our communal understanding of a Burke education—required the authority of the head of school. Subsequently, we had multiple conversations with our head about how and when to introduce this foundational concept and the purpose of our initiative to our fellow faculty, staff, and administrators.

Since our head was both relatively new to Burke and African American, we did not want him to be regarded as a single-issue leader or create significant resistance among our colleagues (especially while he was still in the process of earning the trust and respect of our adult community). Thus, we were grateful that he was willing to utilize a significant amount of his social capital to formally present this initiative during an all faculty and staff meeting. Declaring social justice to be in the DNA of Burke's history and institutional identity, he evoked the school's founding ideals and strategically interpreted the final clause of our mission statement through a social justice lens:

> Burke consciously brings together students who are different from one another in many ways, actively engages them in their own education, holds them to high expectations, gives them power and responsibility, and supports and advances their growth as skilled and independent thinkers *who step forward to make positive contributions to the world in which they live.* (italics added)

We recognized that this declaration was not in itself sufficient to garner the buy-in of our colleagues and speculated that there was a range of attitudes and opinions about "social justice." We also knew that it would be disrespectful to move forward on a grant proposal that would potentially affect so much of the school without more communal input. We thus decided to provide our entire faculty, staff, and administration an opportunity to reflect upon and articulate their understanding of and relationship to social justice.

Democratic Process

Shortly after Damian's declaration, we led a two-hour professional development session aimed at creating a space for our colleagues to reflect on social justice in their personal and professional lives and to seed our collective thinking around where social justice education belongs at Burke. We divided our colleagues into groups of three and provided each group with an iPad. We conscientiously created these groups, drawing upon a matrix we as a leadership team had created where we assigned a code (green, yellow, and red) to every colleague based upon our perception of their understanding and support of social justice pedagogy. Our goal was that, over time, everyone would be "code green." This matrix allowed us to take into consideration which groupings might best ensure colleagues would participate fully and honestly, as well as engage in thoughtful dialogue around two direct questions:

1. What role, if any, does social justice play in your life?
2. What, in your mind, is the relationship between equity, inclusion, and social justice?

The intent of the first question was to encourage reflection upon social justice not as an abstract idea, but as a personal lived experience that might manifest in different ways depending upon the individual. The intent of the second question was to encourage our colleagues to reflect upon the extent to which "social justice" was either a markedly similar or different value/ aim. It was unsurprising that many of our colleagues discovered an interrelationship between these concepts, and it met our hope that engaging in the exercise would foster a level of comfort with this term.

Afterward, we treated the data collected as qualitative researchers would and scrupulously viewed each video, coding common concepts and terms. From the outset of this exercise, we did not anticipate a groundbreaking definition of social justice; however, we wanted a definition that was unique to Burke and derived from a collective endeavor in which each community member had an opportunity to contribute their opinion. At a subsequent faculty and staff meeting, we presented the community's working definition and statement of social justice back to our colleagues, which read:

> Social justice is the commitment to a lifelong pursuit to build a more just world based on the critical understanding that systemic, institutional inequities exist that divest people of their human dignity. Burke seeks to educate students to

think critically about injustice and equip them with the capacity to recognize and value all people and to build a more just, inclusive and equitable world.

Unsurprisingly, these efforts did not completely quell all anxiety, critique, and resistance. A small minority expressed concerns that by adopting social justice pedagogy, Burke would no longer be a school that welcomed all students and allowed them the freedom to pursue anything they desired. These colleagues feared a curriculum and pedagogy that was explicitly political and prescriptive and that it would replace the "free exchange of ideas" with "indoctrination." We responded to these concerns from a Seventh Generation mind-set, believing that our actions today were necessary to laying the foundation for a true social justice school to emerge seven generations from now.

While concerns were certainly valid, these necessary first steps created space for deeper conversations regarding how social justice pedagogy at Burke would produce students and teachers truly committed to building a more equitable society. Ultimately, some of the more critical colleagues became our most pivotal advocates. At a memorable meeting when the department chairs considered a proposal to change the math and science final exams to allow the entire 11th grade to go on an environmental justice trip, a well-respected colleague whose attitude toward our efforts were never clear, tipped the scales in our favor. He made an earnest appeal: "There's no real decision to be made. If we're going to do this work, then we have to really do it and accept the changes it requires." The meeting ended shortly afterward with all the chairs approving the schedule change, thereby giving a green light to a major cross-disciplinary, justice-oriented curriculum for the 11th grade.

Support from the Board of Trustees

Because at Burke, social justice is truly a whole-institution endeavor, we ran a half-day retreat on this topic for our board of trustees, which provided them with a deeper understanding of how we would execute their mandate as stated in their strategic plan. After we were awarded the E. E. Ford grant, a small group of trustees volunteered to read the same articles on social justice pedagogy as our Social Justice Professional Growth Track participants ("With Great Power Comes Great Responsibility: Privileged Students Conception of Justice-Oriented Citizenship" and "Confronting White Privilege" by Katy Swalwell). Subsequently, in the fall of 2018, Christiane and Steven facilitated a discussion of these two articles at a trustee's home and made a short presentation to the entire board during a monthly board meeting.

On the last day of the 2016–2017 school year, Damian announced at the final faculty and staff meeting that he had just gotten off the phone with the president of the E.E. Ford Foundation: We got the grant. The loud applause and cheering following his announcement was significant on many levels. Although only a handful of folks worked on the proposal itself, everyone had been involved at some stage and understood it was enabling the school to move forward in meaningful ways. It also signaled to the school's educational leaders that this work was going to happen regardless of whatever obstacles might emerge.

STRATEGIES TO BUILD MOMENTUM AND CAPACITY

As much as possible, we strove for a bottom-up democratic approach. In hindsight, several particular elements proved critical to our efforts to legitimize the work, fuel momentum, and build capacity.

A (Remote) Scholar in Residence and Professional Development

The E. E. Ford grant funded a key component of our plan: to work with an academic with research expertise and professional clout in social justice teaching and learning in elite secondary school settings. This idea came at the recommendation of Jim Reese at the Washington International School who had already overseen several highly regarded E. E. Ford grants. Rather than christening ourselves as the experts, we contracted with Dr. Katy Swalwell, a leader in the field. Throughout the 2-year grant cycle, Dr. Swalwell provided expert counsel in both the theoretical and practical realms via monthly Zoom calls and four visits to Burke. During calls, we updated Dr. Swalwell on our progress and troubleshooted together, benefiting from her outsider perspective and firm grasp on the bigger picture. During her visits to Burke, Dr. Swalwell met first with the school's educational leaders (department chairs, grade deans, administrators) to familiarize them with her academic work. Next, she addressed all faculty and staff during a day-long professional development day. We also hosted an evening lecture open to parents and practitioners from peer schools. Finally, during the last summer of the grant cycle, leaders of each grade level held video conference meetings with her to discuss further developments of their curriculum themes. "Katy" became a household name on campus and was someone faculty and staff came to trust, relate to, and learn from.

As a result, when Dr. Swalwell addressed the entire faculty and staff for the last time, the visit contrasted noticeably with customary one-off professional development speakers. Dr. Swalwell led off with the question, "Social justice through private schools?" and facilitated a conversation of the inherent contradictions that felt as though we had come full circle from where we had started 2 years ago. Noticeably, a lot of colleagues participated, more than would normally feel comfortable in a large setting. At the same visit, Dr. Swalwell led a similarly robust conversation about theories of re-distribution and recognition that would have had some dissenters at the beginning of the grant—but instead prompted thoughtful smaller group discussions.

Grade-Specific Integrated Frameworks

"The Frameworks" became another household name on campus, referring to the grade-specific, theme-based, year-long integrated experiences all students participate in at Burke. At Damian's request, we began drafting a framework for each grade to guide how our three programs (Service, Equity and Inclusion, Student Leadership) would actually educate "activist allies" and deliver experiences conscientiously anchored in Dr. Swalwell's (2015) definition:

1. Make personal connections to students' lives, histories, and communities to avoid "over there and back then" thinking.
2. Elicit emotional as well as intellectual responses when identifying and questioning power/oppression.
3. Encourage listening to perspectives and experiences of people within struggles in contrast with speaking about them.
4. Construct sustained relationships with shared goals that offer students opportunities to learn with and from established social movements rather than volunteer or charity work.

Through the Frameworks, Burke students in all grades now move through a purposeful learning sequence to cultivate their awareness of injustice in their communities, an understanding of its root causes, a sense of responsibility to dismantle structural inequities, and a capacity to work toward creating a more just and equitable world. Table 10.1 outlines each grade level's theme, some of which are still under construction and being rolled out in phases.

Department chairs were always included in their capacity as advisors to support their grade dean colleagues in realizing the framework, without the burden of having to prematurely alter their own department's curriculum. Nurturing this dynamic gave everyone time to consider what social justice learning might look like beyond the school's core curriculum, as well as created a collaborative space to reimagine how our programs could become more central to students' experiences. While we had each worked closely with grade deans previously, it was usually to implement our agendas; now, grade deans became co-architects of the Frameworks.

Table 10.1. Grade-Specific Integrated Frameworks

Grade and Theme	Description
6th Grade: Citizenship at the Margins	Students focus on what it means to be a citizen, past and present, and the identities that have forced some groups to exist at the margin vs. the center of American life. Students apply these questions to their comparative study of American identity starting with the first interactions of Native communities to today. The year culminates with a capstone experiential learning trip to New York City to trace narratives from immigrant communities and their collective work to create more just spaces.
7th Grade: Sustainable Pathways for a Better Tomorrow	Across the curriculum, students examine how and why certain environmental issues affect some communities differently than others. They practice framing critical questions through disciplinary lenses, including world geography, anthropology, science, ethics, mathematics, and language arts, and identify root causes of our greatest sustainable challenges. Students organize an environmental summit with peers from other schools.
8th Grade: Social Change and the American Civil Rights Movement	Students learn about the cultural, literary, historical, and political lives of citizens of the DC area and the southern United States through an interdisciplinary program in history, music, English, values and ethics, and visual arts that explores the Black Freedom Struggle and culminates with a trip to the Deep South. After the trip, students continue to attend performances and visit places integral to DC's civil rights history, as well as organize and run an all-school assembly program about their learning.
9th Grade: Food Justice in the DMV (District-Maryland-Virginia)	Through a critical lens, 9th-graders explore Food Justice in Washington, DC, by engaging in direct service, learning, and advocacy at several local nonprofits and within the school curriculum and with guest speakers. They also lead a schoolwide food drive, an Empty Bowls fundraiser, and participate in two day-long retreats on leadership, equity, and inclusion.
10th Grade: Action Civics in the DMV	Beginning with the question, "What is an important issue facing my community today?," each student researches, writes, and delivers a soapbox speech on their issue. Students then engage in an oral history project, interviewing individuals directly affected by their issue and analyzing the intersections of power, people, and places. The year culminates with a "listening party" when they share their learning. The curriculum is delivered in partnership with Mikva Challenge DC and DC Humanities oral history project.

Grade and Theme	Description
11th Grade: Environment and Social Justice In West Virginia	A year-long cross-curricular examination of environmental justice, storytelling, and labor history prepares students for a week-long experiential learning trip to West Virginia where they learn to appreciate nuance in communities, arguments, and allyship as they draw connections between their communities in DC and West Virginia. Upon returning, students lead a teach-in for parents on issues explored throughout the year and on the trip.
12th Grade: Effective Allyship and Ethical Leadership Through Scholarship	Each senior enrolls in a senior seminar organized around issues and topics of social justice and global challenges. Students produce a college-level analytical research paper that concludes with policy-based recommendations and actions that address structural inequities. At the time of writing this chapter, design of this graduation requirement is still underway, including considerations of expanding the options for the student product beyond a research paper and requiring an interview component with individuals directly affected by the issue the student is researching.

Professional Development Growth Track

In 2016, Burke's Professional Development Committee (upon which both Christiane and Steven served) decided to discontinue "one-off" single-topic professional development sessions, which were largely regarded as ineffective, to create four distinct "growth tracks" reflecting the school's professional development priorities. The other growth tracks were Adolescent Development, Innovative Teaching and Learning, Leadership—eventually replaced by Cultural Competency—and Social Justice Pedagogy. Every adult is required to complete all four growth tracks over a 4-year period. By meeting five times during the year for an hour and a half with a cohort of 16 to 18 colleagues, the growth track time allowed for sustained exploration of social justice pedagogy with the same facilitators. The inclusion of Social Justice Pedagogy as a growth track was a welcomed gift to further define our work as an institutional priority. Moreover, this restructuring of professional development allowed us to introduce social justice pedagogy over the course of a school year in a more intimate setting rather than a typical in-service day.

The curriculum for these meetings highlighted Dr. Swalwell's research to provide a more intimate and individualized setting for colleagues. It has also featured guest speaker Ayo Magwood, a former U.S. history teacher, who presented a compelling social justice lesson she developed in response to the social unrest in Ferguson, Missouri. Participants in each cohort developed a social justice pedagogy "action plan," with some choosing to work individually while others worked in groups. For instance, four science teachers collaborated on an action plan to incorporate an environmental justice focus into their departments' curriculum. This year, advisors are creating a schoolwide response plan when breaking local, national, or international news affects the school community.

TRANSFERABLE TAKEAWAYS

Our journey is only as useful as the takeaways we can share with peers. Thus, we have synthesized five key lessons we hope others might find transferable.

Bring Gatekeepers to the Table

Consider at the start and throughout the process: Are the right gatekeepers at the table? We had a few false starts that we attribute to lacking the involvement of key administrators—namely, the head of middle school and school operations and the high school academic dean. Once we established consistent pathways of communication with these key school leaders, our agenda progressed, as these administrators were instrumental in bringing grade deans and department chairs on board.

Reflecting on the process that began four school years ago, another key factor related to "gatekeepers" that worked in our favor was the leadership's unwavering support for our work. First, it was not unrelated that Burke's new head of school brought with him a specific vision to expand social justice programming and prioritize securing funding sources to do so. Second, the Board's endorsement of the work via the strategic plan proved to be a critical reminder to us and our colleagues as to why we were integrating and reimagining our programs.

Acknowledge Early Adopters' Influence

Before we received the E. E. Ford grant, we created a task force of carefully selected faculty and staff who we saw as "early adopters," folks who were already developing social justice–themed curricula. During several off-campus, half-day retreats, we brainstormed what social justice looked like at our school. We threw a lot out there and much of it did not stick, but in retrospect, the process was as important as the product. We disbanded the task force once the Frameworks took center stage; nonetheless, these "early adopters" became models for their colleagues of what it might look like. For instance, Burke's theater director, Jim, addressed the lack of racial diversity among students participating in the after-school drama program. While trying to recruit students of color, a student challenged him: "Why do we have to start showing up for you to do a more diverse play? Why can't you pick a diverse show and we'll start showing up?" This question prompted Jim to collaborate with many students and adults of color in the school to provide guidance and context. He settled on *West Side Story* and engaged in color-conscious casting to convey the weight of its story about the destructive power of racism, ultimately assembling the largest cast in Burke Theater history, along with well-attended "talkbacks" where the cast and crew discussed their experiences with audience members. Early in the process, Jim modeled for all of us how to examine whether our institutional values are reflected in our school's programs and how to correct discrepancies.

Collaborate Across Initiatives

As part of a schoolwide initiative on innovative teaching and learning, Burke invited consultant Sam Chastain to campus. His presentation included time for teachers from different disciplines to collectively brainstorm learning experiences. While this visit initially was not focused on social justice, much to our delight, our colleagues embraced this opportunity, and several social justice-themed projects were born in a single morning session. For example, a group of teachers from our departments of art, English, history, and music brainstormed a multifaceted curriculum centered around a local professional theater production called *Nina Simone: Four Women*. Ultimately, this evolved into a fully developed curriculum that included an 8th-grade field trip to see the show, a middle school mural illustrating both the artistic and political life of Nina Simone, an all-school concert featuring Simone's music, and classroom lessons in both English and history that provided necessary cultural and historical context.

Opportunities for cross-school collaboration also emerged as we sought ways to share our work and collect feedback from peers beyond our school. We became members of the Independent Schools Experiential Education Network (ISEEN), National Network for Schools in Partnership (NNSP), and Private Schools with Public Purpose. Subsequently, we presented at each of these annual conferences and led a follow-up webinar. We also regularly connected with our local networks such as the DC independent schools service and diversity directors, which proved especially useful when learning went online due to the coronavirus pandemic.

Respect the School's Culture

Our unofficial motto was "Culture eats strategy for breakfast." Whenever possible, we allowed the process to evolve organically to avoid leaving people with the sense that it was forced. Thus, some of our efforts fell to the wayside as we determined that our attention was better focused on other initiatives. This was a further reflection of the strains Burke faculty and administrators were under, given the school's small size and the likelihood that teachers and staff were wearing many hats.

CONCLUSION

Given the school's history, we never stopped believing that social justice is in the school's DNA. Nonetheless, it was one thing for faculty and staff to conceptually and emotionally support such a change and quite another to put this change into practice. As an entire community—faculty, staff, students, parents, alums, and trustees—we have revisited the founders' vision and have sought new ways to ensure we live it for another 50 more.

CHAPTER 11

Facilitating Socially Just Discussions in Elite Schools

Lisa Sibbett

High-quality discussions are a cornerstone of good education, especially one aiming to build a more socially just world in our multicultural but unequal democracy. And in an era when political polarization is rising and support for democracy declining (Foa & Mounk, 2017), it is more urgent than ever for students to participate well in discussions. One major dilemma teachers face is that when we invite students to discuss, *we cannot know what they will say*. Students may make claims that are factually indefensible, harmful to peers, or both. These issues are especially pronounced in "elite" classrooms, where arguments made by students with dominant identities can have an outsized, negative impact on the classroom climate and the safety of students with nondominant identities. Of course, such outcomes are not fated. In this chapter, I describe how Nancy, a teacher at an elite private school, largely accomplished such aims during a class discussion of a speech by Malcolm X.

SOCIAL JUSTICE DISCUSSIONS
IN ELITE SCHOOLS

Researchers have documented ways classroom conversations about injustice can backfire as privileged people distance themselves from the ways they benefit from others' subjugation (e.g., Hytten & Warren, 2003). Some teachers avoid engaging their students in substantive discussions altogether (Hostetler & Neel, 2018), especially those that pertain to oppression (Howard, 2003; Lo, 2019). Yet if education is to contribute to realizing the promise of our democracy, young people must have access to frequent, robust "social justice discussions" about social issues (Parker, 2003) that help disrupt inequity in their own classroom (Sibbett & Au, 2017). In other words, they both *enact* and *explore* social justice.

Discussions Enacting Social Justice

Discussions *enact* social justice when they function as "sites of belonging" (Butler, 2018) where students with marginalized identities feel comfortable participating frequently and freely. This matters especially in schools where the majority of students have privileged identities. A major part of disrupting inequality during a discussion entails confronting what philosophers call "epistemic injustice"—a term coined by Miranda Fricker (2007) meaning "a wrong done to someone specifically in their capacity as a knower" (p. 1). Dotson (2011) identified two ways epistemic injustice can unfold during discussions: *testimonial quieting*, when an audience fails to identify a speaker as a credible knower, and *testimonial smothering*, when a speaker withholds ideas she believes will not be heard or understood by her audience because of prejudice.

In classroom discussions among participants with unequal power and privilege, epistemic injustice is common. For example, Hess and McAvoy (2015) documented a case where white students in a majority-white classroom told Amanda, a Black student who had carefully researched affirmative action, "we don't want to hear your facts" (p. 104). Amanda experienced testimonial quieting when her white peers discounted her credibility as a knower about affirmative action. Testimonial smothering may have followed if she stopped participating in class discussions as a result. In response to such dilemmas of epistemic injustice, teachers may construct discussion guidelines such as "listen respectfully" and "assume good intentions." Paradoxically, however, such guidelines can serve the interests of elites at the expense of those with marginalized social positions (Sensoy & DiAngelo, 2014).[1]

To combat epistemic injustice, participants with nondominant social positionings may need help recognizing and reclaiming the value of their knowledge (Sensoy & DiAngelo, 2014). Participants with dominant social positionings need to be taught to recognize—in many cases, *defer* to—the knowledge of peers whose life experiences grant them a wider view and to develop the courage to take risks and be vulnerable, even—or perhaps *especially*—when they do not come out "looking good." They should learn to participate well in what Arao and Clemens (2013) have called a "brave space." In contrast with "safe" spaces, brave spaces require participants to remain engaged when confronted with hard truths. Discussions that enact social justice are not about privileged people feeling good or signaling their virtue, but rather about supporting all participants in better understanding and combating injustice (Leonardo & Porter, 2010; Sullivan, 2014).

Discussions Exploring Social Justice

Classroom discussions *explore* social justice by engaging students in examining how inequity is reproduced and disrupted. This work happens frequently in social studies and language arts (e.g., Christensen, 2009) but is not exclusively for the humanities. A mathematics teacher might teach statistics in discussions of racial profiling (Gutstein & Peterson, 2013), or a biology teacher could facilitate discussions on gender diversity as part of a genetics unit (Long, 2019). Regardless of discipline, it is important to note that "resource pedagogies" (Paris, 2012) focused on *affirming* students' experiences and views may not be the best way to inquire with elite students, as they are more likely to ignore or deny how systems have contributed to their privileged positions (Abdullah et al., 2016). In fact, when students in "elite" schools discuss the social world together, they may amplify and spread one another's oppressive worldviews (e.g., Hostetler & Neel, 2018). Students privileged by white supremacy and capitalism may therefore benefit from what San Pedro (2018) has called "culturally disruptive pedagogy"—teaching them not only to *identify* the conditions of their social world but also to *complicate and challenge* their understandings by exploring the resources, resilience, and resistance of communities unlike their own; imagining how they can support these communities' struggles for social justice; and practicing acting on their idea (Sibbett & Au, 2017).

A SOCIALLY JUST DISCUSSION

In spring 2018, I was researching how experienced social justice educators respond to affluent white students' resistance to an anti-oppressive curriculum.[2] One classroom in this study stood out because student resistance seemed so rare. This was Nancy's 8th-grade Global Studies class at Beachview Girls' School (BGS), a small independent middle school for female-identified and gender-creative students. Much of what went right in Nancy's class—as Nancy would be the first to say—arose from the school's genuine, lived commitment to social justice education. While many independent schools center diversity, equity, and inclusion in their mission statements, BGS "walks the walk." They recruit and support a racially diverse faculty and administration, fund teachers to engage in high-quality social justice professional development, provide ample time and resources for teaching teams to align anti-oppressive content across grade levels, offer well-attended monthly affinity groups for staff and students, and participate as a school community in political demonstrations and protests.

At the time of my research, Nancy was in her 25th year in the classroom and her 15th year at BGS. Although Nancy hesitates to claim the mantle of a skilled "social justice educator"—she freely identifies and reflects on the limits of her knowledge, including those imposed by her own positionalities as a white middle-class woman—I see her as highly skilled insofar as her curriculum centers on the voices of historically marginalized groups and supports students in becoming reflective change agents. Classroom discussions are a cornerstone of Nancy's instruction: Students regularly participate in simulations, role plays, structured academic controversies, inquiries, Socratic seminars, and—on the day I will describe—town hall discussions.[3] The class meeting featured in this chapter took place during the spring semester when the class community and routines were well-established. Eighteen students were present, only two of whom self-identified as students of color: Sasha (Black) and Christina (mixed race, Black and white). The discussion I examine here was not perfect. Yet on this day, much went right.

Nancy's 8th-graders had recently begun studying African decolonization. On the day in question, they engaged in a town hall about a speech by Malcolm X, delivered at the 1964 founding rally of the Organization of Afro-American Unity. In his speech, Malcolm X applied the insights of African decolonization to the African American civil rights movement. Students began the day's 80-minute block preparing by watching and reading key excerpts and writing reflections about X's views, including his famous call for Black liberation "by any means necessary" and his remarks on the role of white people in the struggle for racial justice. During the subsequent discussion, 15 of the 18 students in the room made at least one substantive contribution (including both of the two students of color present that day), and most contributed several times.

A Discussion Enacting Social Justice

Responsiveness. Setting up the speakers' queue at the outset of the town hall, Nancy told students: "This is just to speak, and it can be responding to a question someone brought up or building on a point they did, or it can be one of your takeaways or questions." Inviting students to respond to one another paid off. Of the 91 substantive turns of talk in the discussion, students explicitly credited one another's ideas 15 times and built on or responded to each other's ideas without explicitly crediting one another many more. In so doing, they exhibited an awareness—uncommon among elites—that knowledge is built collectively and is not the achievement of individuals in isolation.

Nancy also aimed to affirm students of color's contributions. She told me: "As a white teacher of students of color who are in the minority, affirmation is really critical so they feel comfortable to keep sharing." Affirming their ideas was not just about comfort, however, but also about activating their collective knowledge resources. Students of color "have a perspective I never have [as a white person]," she explained, "so it's really important" that their voices are heard. On the other hand, Nancy recognized the risk, especially at predominantly white BGS, of burdening students of color with the responsibility to educate white peers. "[T]eachers teaching in privileged situations really need to give kids [of color] talking space, but not rely on them and certainly not over-ask, because that really would be burdensome and painful." With these reflections, Nancy named a tension common for teachers: They need to ensure that minoritized students' voices are heard and their perspectives valued while avoiding putting those students on the spot or asking them to speak for their social group.

In practice, Nancy navigated this tension and elevated the voices of students of color by ensuring that their ideas received substantive airtime. For example, in the Malcolm X discussion, Christina (mixed race, Black and white), proposed expanding the school's celebration of Black History Month:

> I noticed that in February when it was Black History Month, it's supposed to be a whole month, and it turned into women's rights month. You [white people] have every other month, and Black History Month is specifically February, and I think that's one thing we could change, is keeping the specific month.

A few turns of talk later, Iris (white) credited Christina's idea: "I like Christina's suggestion about focusing more on Black History Month," she said. As students were seeming to turn to another topic, Nancy chimed in, "I have tended to believe that it's so intertwined yearlong, that to teach it for a month—that feels artificial to me. . . . I have perhaps not highlighted enough that it *is* Black History Month." Here Nancy modeled humility and accountability as she explained her approach to teaching Black history and admitted culpability for not celebrating the month in a more visible way. Once Nancy had weighed in, other students referred to Christina's idea—although no one else credited Christina for originating it.

While Christina spoke only once in this discussion, Sasha, the other student of color, spoke frequently and freely. Indeed, she was the second student to speak and the second-most frequent speaker. Many of her comments elicited specific responses—follow-up questions, affirmations, elaborations—from classmates. Within the culture of responsiveness that Nancy encouraged, Sasha's free and frequent participation suggested a confidence that her ideas would be appreciated and understood.

Cultivating a Brave Space. To cultivate intellectual humility and emotional risk-taking among her students, Nancy modeled listening generously while also being willing to challenge their ways of thinking. She told me, "[I]f we're going to progress . . . especially in a school committed to anti-bias education with a more privileged group, part of my job is to shake things up a little and pose challenges." Creating a brave space for them to rise to those challenges required a delicate balancing act. She went on: "As a teacher there's got to be some affirmation there. . . . You never want to just shut a kid down." In practice, Nancy framed uncertainty not as a problem, but rather as a learning opportunity. Introducing the town hall, she told students: "I'd love it if there's a question you have, instead of having me come up with the questions for discussions." Later she elaborated: "I'm going to try not to talk, because you are all so good at this. You're so wise." It was clear this was not empty praise: During my weeks in her classroom, Nancy consistently voiced appreciation for students' questions and ideas. In such ways, Nancy framed students' uncertainties as opportunities for all to conduct meaningful inquiry into topics of shared concern.

Nancy also modeled wrestling with uncertainty herself. When students were discussing actions for white allyship, Renata (white) suggested asking people of color for their insights: "How do we really know . . . if we don't talk to people [of color] about how to be allies?" Here, Nancy faced a decision point. On the one hand, she wanted to affirm this contribution, noting later that Renata "took a risk to say that" and appreciating her point. On the other hand, Nancy recognized a long history of white people asking people of color to teach them about racism. "[Y]ou don't want to put responsibility on people who are already marginalized to educate you," she told me. In the moment, Nancy responded to Renata's suggestion by telling students about her internal tug-of-war as a white person:

> There's a tension, isn't there, between wanting—it's a white problem, right? . . . It's a hard thing. Because you don't want to put people in the spot of having to have the answers for your group. . . . That's putting the responsibility to take care of our problem back on the People of Color. Like, that feels funky, too. But I completely agree with you . . . about the need to understand other people's experiences.

By naming the tension she wrestled with, Nancy modeled humble inquiry into power and privilege, making visible that uncertainty is okay.

A Discussion Exploring Social Justice

Empathizing. For Nancy, learning to empathize with others' experiences requires getting to know unfamiliar points of view. In addition to highlighting the importance of recognizing others' social groups as internally diverse, Nancy modeled empathizing with unfamiliar perspectives—including giving a fair hearing to perspectives elites may find threatening. At the start of class, she asked students to reflect on X's famous call for racial justice "by any means necessary" and reminded them about Martin Luther King Jr.'s use of nonviolent direct action. She named that these perspectives are "very different" but did not (that I could detect) telegraph an opinion of either as right or wrong. In response, students expressed openness and curiosity about the two leaders' approaches. For example, Jordan (white) compared their competing tactics for racial liberation to what they had learned in an earlier unit about competing perspectives on the Israeli-Palestinian conflict. She observed:

> Dr. King taking the more peaceful route whereas Malcolm X was taking the less peaceful route—it kind of reminded me of . . . the Palestinian-Israeli thing because . . . you could combine both states or make them two different states. I was just thinking that it's kind of similar, and so we could use this as like a—well, which one worked?

Nancy responded not by taking a side, but by highlighting what proponents of each side believe. "I'm so glad you brought up the Israeli-Palestinian issue," she enthused, continuing:

> Some people feel that if Palestinians had adopted more of the Dr. King nonviolent direct-action strategy, they might've gotten more sympathy among Israelis. Others feel that it's like the JFK quote, "if you make peaceful revolution impossible"—which the Israelis sort of have, the more hardline [ones]—"you make violent revolution inevitable."

By highlighting the thinking of both sides, Nancy avoided tacitly endorsing one or the other. She communicated that both perspectives merit our careful attention. As a result, although many students advocated a nonviolence-only approach to racial justice, several empathized with Malcolm X's perspective—despite the fact that "elites" often perceive his views as threatening (Younge, 2007). Olivia (white) expressed her own and classmates' realization succinctly: "You're being hypocritical if you're violent, but if you're peaceful you're not heard." While some advocated nonviolence in all situations, others agreed with Leah (white) that "it depends on the situation." By hesitating to classify nonviolence as right and violence as wrong, these privileged students relinquished signaling their own virtue in favor of trying to better understand X's views.

Conceptualizing Allyship. Allyship[4] also merits students' serious consideration in Nancy's class: She does not leave their understanding to chance, but rather centers the concept of allyship in her curriculum. Year-long guiding questions for the class include "What should the United States' role in the world be?" and, relatedly, "How can we be good allies?" Examining allyship among nations, for Nancy, leads to exploring allyship in students' own lives, and vice versa. She explained:

> Something teachers of privileged kids need to be aware of is the whole savior notion. So, something to probe would be . . . if we do go help in human rights situations—how do we do so in a humble, non-judgmental way that honors and empowers cultures?

Privileged students need models of allyship in their own lives because they face pressure to protect the status quo. She told me: "Whatever the issue is that they want to go after—and hopefully part of it is dismantling oppression—there'll be plenty of their own peer group who would rather not go there."

In the Malcolm X discussion, Nancy focused students' attention on allyship from the outset. Introducing the discussion, she told them:

> I would love your thoughts on what white allyship could look like if it's to empower, as [Malcolm X] is envisioning, not just African Americans living here but anyone of African descent anywhere. . . . What's the best way to be a white ally in this world?

To prepare students to weigh in on this question, Nancy made sure to include X's (1964) ideas about white allies among the excerpts they read. In response, students explored allyship at length during their discussion, referring several times to X's (1964) remarks. For example, X declared, "Now, if white people want to help, they can help . . . in the white community, but they can't join. . . . They don't ever need to come among us and change our attitude." Parker (white) was first to highlight this quotation, observing: "that resonated a lot to me." Lydia (white) noticed how X's argument "switched the perspective around," challenging dominant conceptions that Black people need whites' advice. Jordan (white) made a connection to her life: "For me personally, as a white person, I would take a step back and let [people of color] do their thing and . . . work in my own community."

Acting Locally. Nancy observed that privileged youth need help developing agency when learning about structural injustice because they are otherwise susceptible to debilitating feelings. "Especially with privileged kids who come from liberal backgrounds, there's guilt," she observed. "[T]eachers need to be ready to say 'we have to engage with the mistakes of the past, we have to own them. But they have to help us progress, not be paralyzed.'" She therefore selects materials that show how people have used their privilege to fight for social justice:

> When kids learn about a huge issue that seems really daunting, [I emphasize] finding some kernel of agency in that: What can I do? . . . You learn from examples of other people doing work: mediation kind of work, raising awareness kind of work, seeing each other's point of view kind of work.

Here Nancy conceptualizes the exercise of agency expansively. By throwing a wide net, she creates the conditions for students to feel success with small actions (e.g., "seeing each other's point of view") and prepares them to work their way up to more challenging and complex interventions in an unjust social order.

In practice, Nancy cultivated students' agency by encouraging them to identify racial injustices in their community and taking seriously their proposals for redress. Early in the discussion, Iris (white) referred to her school's role in the gentrification of the city's historically Black Angel Hill neighborhood. "What is BGS's role as a private school in Angel Hill?" she wondered, continuing. "[A]re we contributing to—or being good allies—as part of the gentrification . . . and as a predominantly-white, wealthy, female student base?" Sasha (Black) kicked off the class's responses by sharing that she had done a project on local gentrification and "learned that BGS is a big part of it." She also wondered if BGS could participate in the Black Lives Matter movement. Nancy chimed in: "I love that question. In fact, that'd be a great question for the faculty. We have development time on Friday. . . . I'm going to mention you thought of that," framing Sasha's idea as worthy of follow-up.

Bolstered by Nancy's enthusiasm for their ideas, many students' reflections on BGS's role in racial justice efforts included a call to action. Gabi (white) observed: "For claiming to be such an inclusive school, we need to do more . . . like, *actually* taking action." Lydia (white) advocated using the school's privilege: "As a school, because we have so much freedom, we need to make sure that we—as our mission—stand up and support everybody in our community." Agreeing with Lydia, white students and students of color alike advocated several courses of action collaboratively and at length. These included being aware of the racist pitfalls of what Iris (white) named as "white feminism" and asking teachers to teach about BGS's role in gentrification. Far from expressing resignation or powerlessness, with their teacher's encouragement, they exhibited a strong sense of agency to contribute to local racial justice efforts.

CONCLUSION

Despite the many ways the Malcolm X discussion succeeded, it was not perfect. Christina, one of two students of color in the class, participated only once. Only after Nancy weighed in on the idea did several other students chime in, some even crediting white peers for their ideas about Black History Month but not crediting Christina. Such omissions can be hard for teachers to notice, especially white teachers. That said, a great deal went right with Nancy's 8th-graders. They wrestled with unfamiliar perspectives and seriously considered allyship and activism at length. Facilitating discussions that enact and explore social justice in such contexts is no easy feat. Examining discussion in Nancy's classroom thus offers not a set of prescriptions, but a vision of what is possible.

ACKNOWLEDGMENTS

Thank you to Wayne Au, Emily Donaldson-Walsh, Rebecca Drago, Stephanie Forman, Diane Goodman, Jesslyn Hollar, Kara Jackson, Jessica Masterson, Walter Parker, and Katy Swalwell for valuable feedback on earlier drafts of this chapter. Also, a huge thank you to Nancy and her students for welcoming me into their classroom and demonstrating, lovingly and exuberantly, the possibilities of social justice education in elite schools.

NOTES

1. For suggestions on revising discussion norms to better serve minoritized participants (and facilitators), see Arao and Clemens (2013) or Sensoy and DiAngelo (2014).

2. I am a white, middle-class teacher educator with a longstanding interest in social justice education in elite schools stemming from my years as a high school social studies teacher of an Ethnic Studies course in an affluent, mostly white school. My experience led me to graduate school to research how social justice educators can tailor their practice to privileged communities.

3. In a "town hall," students circle up to discuss a text or issue they have studied in advance. Nancy supplies questions to guide their thinking and gives them time to prepare. During the town hall, students make eye contact with Nancy to indicate a desire to speak and she tracks the queue. Nancy participates, but the bulk of airtime is given to students, who are tasked not only with contributing but also with grounding their comments and questions in the text and responding to their peers' ideas.

4. The term "ally" has been increasingly critiqued for the ways in which it often comes to substitute for meaningful action—or provides cover for unjust action. Activists have thus called for would-be allies to take up the mantle of "accomplices" or "co-conspirators." Anti-racist activist Brittany Packnett (2019) explains, "An ally shows up when it is convenient. An accomplice shows up when there is a risk. A co-conspirator decides to go into the risk proactively because they helped create the pain in the first place." I use "ally" as Swalwell (2013) does in the spirit of an accomplice or co-conspirator.

REFERENCES

Abdullah, C., Karpowitz, C. F., & Raphael, C. (2016). A conversation with Jane J. Mansbridge and Martha McCoy. *Journal of Public Deliberation, 12*(2), 1–19.

Arao, B., & Clemens, K. (2013). From safe spaces to brave spaces: A new way to frame dialogue around diversity and social justice. In L. Landreman (Ed.), *The art of effective facilitation: Reflections from social justice educators* (pp. 135–150). Stylus.

Butler, T. T. (2018). Black girl cartography: Black girlhood and place-making in education research. *Review of Research in Education, 42,* 28–45.

Christensen, L. (2009). *Teaching for joy and justice.* Rethinking Schools.

Dotson, K. (2011). Tracking epistemic violence, tracking practices of silencing. *Hypatia, 26*(2), 236–257.

Foa, R. S., & Mounk, Y. (2017). The signs of deconsolidation. *Journal of Democracy, 28*(1), 5–15.

Fricker, M. (2007). *Epistemic injustice: Power and the ethics of knowing.* Oxford University Press.

Gutstein, E. R., & Peterson, B. (Eds.). (2013). *Rethinking mathematics: Teaching social justice by the numbers* (2nd ed.). Rethinking Schools.

Hess, D. E., & McAvoy, P. (2015). *The political classroom: Evidence and ethics in democratic education.* Routledge.

Hostetler, A. L., & Neel, M. A. (2018). Difficult discourses: How the distances and contours of identities shape challenging moments in political discussions. *Journal of Social Studies Research, 42*(4), 361–373.

Howard, T. (2003). The dis(g)race of the social studies: The need for racial dialogue in the social studies. In G. Ladson-Billings (Ed.), *Critical race theory perspectives on social studies: The profession, policies, and curriculum* (pp. 27–44). Information Age.

Hytten, K., & Warren, J. (2003). Engaging whiteness: How racial power gets reified in education. *International Journal of Qualitative Studies in Education, 16*(1), 65–89.

Leonardo, Z., & Porter, R. K. (2010). Pedagogy of fear: Toward a Fanonian theory of "safety" in race dialogue. *Race Ethnicity & Education, 13*(2), 139–157.

Lo, J. C. (2019). The role of civic debt in democratic education. *Multicultural Perspectives, 21*(2), 112–118.

Long, S. (2019). Diversity is what makes it interesting to study living things: Teaching gender diversity in biology. *Rethinking Schools, 34*(1).

Packnett, B. (2019, June). Visionary voices: A candid conversation with Brittany Packnett. *Ethical Society of St. Louis.* https://www.youtube.com/watch?v=c7yaLgwdGIQ

Paris, D. (2012). Culturally sustaining pedagogy: A needed change in stance, terminology, and practice. *Educational Researcher, 41*(3), 93–97.

Parker, W. C. (2003). *Teaching democracy: Unity & diversity in public life.* Teachers College Press.

San Pedro, T. (2018). Abby as ally: An argument for culturally disruptive pedagogy. *American Educational Research Journal, 55*(6), 1193–1232.

Sensoy, Ö., & DiAngelo, R. (2014). Respect differences? Challenging the common guidelines in social justice education. *Democracy & Education, 22*(2), 1–10.

Sibbett, L., & Au, W. (2017). Critical social studies knowledge and practice: Preparing social justice oriented social studies teachers in the Trump Era. In C. Martell (Ed.), *Research in social studies teacher education: Critical issues and current perspectives* (pp. 17–45). Information Age.

Sullivan, S. (2014). *Good white people: The problem with middle-class white anti-racism*. State University of New York Press.

Swalwell, K. (2013). *Educating activist allies: Social justice pedagogy with the suburban and urban elite*. Routledge.

X, M. (1964). Speech at the founding rally of the Organization for Afro-American Unity. https://www.blackpast.org/african-american-history/speeches-african-american-history/1964-malcolm-x-s-speech-founding-rally-organization-afro-american-unity/

Younge, G. (2007, September). Scaring white America. *The Guardian*. https://www.theguardian.com

Mobilizing Privileged Youth and Teachers for Justice-Oriented Work in Science and Education

Alexa Schindel, Brandon Grossman, and Sara Tolbert

Social justice in science? Isn't that an oxymoron? As science educators, we have found that the process of *envisioning* ways that science can be taught for personal and political transformation is a significant step in the process of developing as a social justice educator. Envisioning teaching science for social justice not only involves rethinking and confronting racial, class, and gender inequities *and* beliefs about the discipline of science, it also involves reshaping understandings of science teaching and learning. What does teaching science for social justice look like? Who is science for? And how does social justice fit with our ideas about objectivity in science?

We center our teaching on our students and their lived experiences and would argue that, because of this, teaching science for social justice will look different in different contexts. We ground our work (and stay grounded ourselves) through developing caring relationships with students, communities, and the land (for an articulation of these, see Tolbert & Schindel, 2017). As science teachers and university-based educators who identify as White and who often work with White preservice teachers, we reflected on the following questions: How do we mobilize White people for justice-oriented work in science teaching and learning spaces? How do we engage in this practice with elite students? What can teaching and learning science for social justice look like within elite schooling environments?

SITUATING OURSELVES IN SCIENCE

Washing one's hands of the conflict between the powerful and the powerless means to side with the powerful, not to be neutral.

(Freire, 1984, p. 524)

As a course instructor for an elementary education program, I (Brandon) often ask students to reflect on Freire's proposition. The quote usually generates rich class discussions around the importance of working to disrupt systems of oppression that mark the learning environments of youth. Yet I often see privileged teacher candidates struggle to make sense of, develop, and apply anti-oppressive pedagogies and frameworks in classrooms—particularly in science classrooms. This observation aligns with research suggesting that science teachers struggle to reason with how social justice issues like racism are relevant to science teaching and learning because of how notions of race evasiveness, objectivity, and meritocracy intersect with common conceptions of science and science teaching (Larkin et al., 2016).

The tendency of science teachers to overlook the importance of race in science classrooms is troubling, given the history of the scientific enterprise. Manali Sheth (2019) points out that science is often (falsely) characterized as an unbiased field that seeks to develop objective knowledge about the natural world, all while simultaneously benefiting from, exploiting, erasing, and excluding the bodies, knowledge, and perspectives of communities of color. Even the word "scientist" itself has a troubling history. In exploring the historical origins of the word, Sydney Ross (1962) notes that while many objected to the use of the word "scientist" for several reasons, no one objected to the notion that it was devised to be an "exclusive title held by a small group of professional men" whose knowledge would be greater than all others' knowledge, which would be "deemed no better than . . . ignorance" (p. 75). It is essential that we continually grapple with the sociopolitical context of science education and the ways in which teachers' and students' racial, cultural, and gendered backgrounds position them in science classrooms. To not do so is equivalent to washing our hands of the conflict between the powerful and the powerless.

One activity that can help surface troubling perceptions of science and scientists is the Draw-A-Scientist Test, originally developed by David Chambers (1983) and later modified by other scholars (Farland-Smith & McComas, 2009). The test prompts students to draw a picture of a scientist at work, then analyze them for "stereotypic" features: an older white man or "mad scientist" with crazy hair wearing glasses and a lab coat, working alone in a laboratory, often holding a beaker with chemicals. While this test has historically been used as a research tool to examine students' perceptions of scientists and measure the impact of various educational interventions, it is being increasingly adapted to serve as an educational activity used by teachers to support students investigating the ways in which they have been socialized around science (e.g., Kirch & Amoroso, 2016). I have used this activity often as a science teacher. No matter the setting, participants always seem surprised by how closely their depictions resemble problematic and exclusive representations of scientists. Discussions that follow the activity are often centered around the following questions: Where did these perceptions come from? How are scientists portrayed in books, movies, and other media and why? What can *we* do to push back on these troubling representations and perceptions? I also sometimes ask participants to anonymously share a list of words that represent the way they feel when they walk into a science classroom or try to learn science. The words most commonly shared are fear, test anxiety, wrong, nervous, bored, and ignored. These feelings are emblematic of the kinds of hurts people experience in science learning spaces as they are elbowed out of a discipline that has historically been reserved for "a small group of [white] professional men."

While surfacing the ways in which power, privilege, and oppression are relevant to teaching and learning science is important—and how white people and other folks are complicit in perpetuating the violence that characterizes many individuals' experiences in science—the focus on examining privilege in science learning spaces is not without pitfalls. Many anti-racist pedagogies take the form of what Levine-Rasky (2000) refers to as white privilege pedagogies, which implore white people to acknowledge or confess their individual white privilege (McIntosh, 2008). Lensmire and colleagues (2013) have argued that these approaches can serve as a stand-in for difficult anti-racist work. For example, the overwhelming focus on privilege can lead some white students to wrongly believe that they can somehow abandon their privileges and that this is equivalent to anti-racism. The Draw-A-Scientist Test and similar activities, when used in elite schooling spaces to help privileged students understand their privilege in science, must move beyond confessing individual privilege toward consequential anti-racist action in science. This work, examples of which are provided later in this chapter, can take a variety of forms across diverse settings.

DECENTERING POWER AND PRIVILEGE
WITH ALTERNATIVE NARRATIVES

As science educators, we continuously grapple with the ways we teach and present science teaching and learning. While the work of situating oneself in relation to science as a discipline is highly personal, it is also deeply political and embedded within broader contexts and systems of power. We build upon the work of situating ourselves in science by critically examining science in relation to common sense or taken-for-granted beliefs by challenging narratives of power and privilege. We do this through learning experiences that are woven throughout the curriculum in order to (1) decenter power and privilege, (2) view power and privilege through scientific lenses, and (3) reconstruct alternative narratives. We begin with topics that decenter humans generally (rather than their own identities or privileges) and which allow students to raise questions about the social and cultural structures that support their common sense understandings. An entry point for students can be found in challenging their sense of humans as dominant beings on the planet. We ask our students: How exceptional are we? Students explore this topic by reflecting on their own ideas about what makes humans special and then investigating whether their ideas have any scientific basis as being uniquely human. They have been surprised to learn that aspects of animal behavior, sex, culture, and migration are not unique to humans, which allows students to rethink their understandings about other animals (Rutherford, 2019). When we challenge narratives of human exceptionalism, we open space for decentering multiple forms of power and privilege.

Another form of challenging narratives lies in exploring science as a discipline, which our students often view as objective and apolitical. Yet science has been constructed through ideological belief systems. In our work with preservice science teachers, we conceptualize justice in science through a process of decentering commonsense beliefs about science and the role of science in belief systems. Decentering here means critically questioning issues of race, power, and privilege and unsettling (Tuck & Yang, 2012) harmful beliefs. Our exploration of scientific objectivity sheds light on the relationships between science and race/racism, sexuality, heteronormativity, gender, poverty, and capitalism (among other topics). An excellent student-friendly resource debunking scientific objectivity is Sophie Wang's illustrated comic "Science Under the Scope: Putting Science in Perspective" (https://freerads.org/science-scope-full/). Wang exposes power and privilege in science by questioning who scientists are, what questions they explore, how science gets funded, and who benefits or gets harmed through science. Students consider scientific objectivity alongside race and racism in science.

Within the United States, scientific knowledge has been invoked as a tool to uphold racism. Perhaps one of the most eye-opening histories that demonstrates this process can be seen in eugenics. We find that a majority of our students have never encountered the horrific history of eugenics or been taught its persistence in modern science. Eugenics was a movement that united people with the desire to use science to create an "improved" society and which advocated for selective mating to breed "desirable" hereditary traits and remove disease and disability (Levine, 2017). Many eugenics proponents infamously claimed that nonwhites, immigrants, people living in poverty, and the "feeble-minded" held undesirable traits. Eugenics is perhaps most known for social campaigns and coercive policies, such as forced sterilization. Scientists and policymakers in the United States wielded the tools and authority of science to enact racist and devastating policies (Washington, 2006); while in Germany Hitler relied on eugenics in his genocidal quest to form an Aryan race. In the early 20th century, eugenics was considered mainstream science (Kevles, 1985); now, most mainstream scientists would consider eugenics "racist pseudoscience" (see Washington, 2006 for an account of medical experimentation on Black Americans without their consent). Horrifically, however, race science continues to influence scientific practice, as Saini (2020) details in her book *Superior: The Return of Race Science*. Examining eugenics with our students provides them with opportunities to decenter their conceptions of science and scientific objectivity and critically evaluate its relationship to racism.

As another example, we examine the Ebola outbreak in 2014 to question: "Is the guise of objectivity being used to present racism or other biases as scientific fact?" (Schindel & Tolbert, 2016, p. 50). Studying the Ebola outbreak, we dive into deeper understandings of viruses and viral disease transmission—specifically comparing the transmission processes of Ebola and measles. With this background knowledge, our students investigate how racism, colonialism, and othering occur through news media. Our students often shift their U.S.-centric perspectives after reading a tweet by Nigerian novelist Elnathan John, who shared: "Our thoughts are also with the measles-ravaged country America. I hope we are screening them before coming to Africa." Ultimately, we explore deficit images of Africa and contrast them with asset-based perspectives seen in a few (non-U.S.) media sources that expose a depth of capacity in Africa through communities working together and individual brilliant actions that save lives and fight the spread of disease. Studying the relationship between media, racism, and the tools of science, our students develop critical perspectives on racism and how the tools of science can be wielded by media.

Science and scientific endeavors are also typically taught through lenses that support Western ideologies, including Western ways of viewing the world and individualistic ideologies that promote capital accumulation at the expense of others, including humans, nonhuman others, and the planet (Tolbert & Schindel, 2017). These ideologies are reinforced in science when we do not provide our students with opportunities to create counternarratives. In our methods courses, we develop counterstories about Western science by examining place and climate change through Native Science (Cajete, 2004; Canipe & Tolbert, 2016). Native Science perspectives teach our students to consider the history of the land and our connections to land and to view the land through our experiences, those of other humans, and those of other species as shared experiences and ways we can come to know the natural world (Cajete, 2004). For example, I (Alexa) ask my students to come to know a landscape through Native Science perspectives by viewing it through the imagined lenses of multiple species (e.g., we lie on the ground to explore an ant's-eye view). Preservice science teachers further engage in Native Science perspectives when examining climate change by studying evidence of bird migration and change shared by Indigenous communities and climate scientists (an activity developed by Canipe & Tolbert, 2016). A majority of our students share that the combined evidence provides a more reliable and complete narrative of reality. One future high school physics teacher shared that she thought the evidence from Indigenous communities was significantly more reliable because it was based on lived experience. She questioned the climate scientists: "They just showed up and took some temperatures and left? They don't know the places the same ways that the Indigenous people know them." The process of creating counternarratives in science provides students with multiple opportunities to decenter Western science and to develop alternative narratives that we hope can be both personally and politically transformative.

WIELDING THE POWER OF SCIENCE IN THE NAME OF JUSTICE

We are committed to interrogating and dismantling the ways that science has historically marginalized people of color, women, and Indigenous ways of knowing. At the same time, we view scientific practice and knowledge as "power-ful" tools for asking and answering critical questions and examining inequalities. Karen Zacor, an elementary school teacher in Chicago, for example, used the Flint water crisis to help her students understand "that chemistry is important in their everyday lives and can inform struggles for justice in their communities" (Zaccor, 2014). Alejandra Frausto, Danny Morales-Doyle, and colleagues have engaged middle and high school students in youth participatory science related to heavy metal contamination on the South Side of Chicago (Frausto et al., 2019; Morales-Doyle et al., 2019). What does wielding science in the name of justice look like in elite communities?

Ironically, there are few examples of school science as/for justice and political empowerment in such communities. Brian Donavan, at the Biological Sciences Curriculum Study (BSCS), has developed a genetics unit to help counter racist ideologies that lead people to equate racial differences with having distinct skills or abilities. He is working with a group of biology teachers to test "the idea that the science classroom may be the best place to provide a buffer against the unfounded genetic rationales for human difference that often become the basis for racial intolerance" (Harmon, 2019). In our research and teaching (e.g., Tolbert et al., 2018), we are interested in exploring science and science education's potential for political consciousness-raising, or *conscientização* (Freire, 1971). For example, we developed an environmental justice investigation as part of a unit on sound. After identifying patterns related to how sounds are made, through a variety of inquiries (adapted from Gunckel, 2010), we introduced students to the concepts of noise pollution and environmental justice. Then we asked them, "Is noise pollution an equity/justice issue in [Tucson/Buffalo]?" After using a mobile app [Decibel X] to collect sound data at a variety of locations in their city, students came back to class the following week to analyze the data, looking for patterns in relation to the driving question.

One outcome of this work was when one of my (Sara's) students, a young white woman, experienced a moment of *conscientização* (what we refer to as "critical incidents"—see Tolbert et al., 2019) when she overlayed the noise pollution map she and her peers had constructed from the data with the income by ZIP code map and tree cover map I had provided to see how low-income residents of South Tucson were disproportionately vulnerable to both noise pollution (given their proximity to the airport and the military base) and the heat island effect (or at least increased exposure to ultraviolet [UV] radiation) due in part to the lack of tree cover. She then began to make other observations based on her own lived experiences about socioeconomic/political differences in the local environments by ZIP code. And then she looked up, visibly appalled, and exclaimed, "Oh my God! Everything is about money!" She more fully understood inequities around race/class/gender when the localized evidence intersected with her embodied experiences. We were able to have more organic conversations about who lives in South Tucson, move into complex discussions of intersectionality between race and class, and delve deeper into racism and environmental racism. A key challenge of the un-disciplining aspect of this work in practice is that students and parents may contend "that's not really science" or "isn't that social studies?" Part of the struggle here is learning how to respond to those very real-time, biopolitical forces that seek to discipline (in both senses of the word!) educators, and students, for daring to do science differently.

Another outcome for our teaching lies in students wielding the tools of science and school science as they practice the skills outlined in the Science and Engineering Practices of the Next Generation Science Standards. We want teachers and students to see the potential for supporting justice-oriented pedagogies within a standards-driven curriculum. In the example we describe earlier, students collect noise data, post their data on a Google map, then analyze and create a representation of the data in groups. Through this process, they also analyze the reliability of the data, as well as the rigor/quality of the scientific process they utilized to make sense of the data. We then ask students to plan and carry out an investigation of a new but related scientific question of their choosing. For example, student teachers have examined the relative noise levels of different study locations on campus and mapped their collective noise experiences at one point in time (a specific Saturday at noon). The preservice teachers also considered how they might use scientific data to examine noise production and location in their classrooms and schools; how noise affects students with hearing impairments, anxiety, and other learning differences; and how they and their students might enact change using the noise data they collected.

Wielding the power of science can also be employed in the name of decentering privilege, for example, heterosexual privilege. Per the

recommendation of a friend and colleague, Carol Brochin, whose scholarship focuses on bilingual and LGBTQ literature for youth (see Brochin,
2019), we read the book *And Tango Makes Three* (Richardson et al., 2005),
a children's book based on the true story of two male penguins in Central
Park who became partners and raised a chick together. We then read a short
article from *Yale Scientific*, titled "Do Animals Exhibit Homosexuality?"
(Fereydooni, 2012), which reports findings from a variety of scientific studies revealing the diversity of sexual behavior in nonhuman animals. The article also reports findings about how same-sex pairing is prevalent, reduces
competition, and increases evolutionary fitness (Bailey & Zuk, 2009). We
use the discourse and power of science as empirical evidence to combat the
discriminatory ideologies that homosexuality is "not natural" (or not "be-
stowed by God," as was the belief system of many of our preservice teachers
from evangelical Christian backgrounds).

These efforts, however, are not unproblematic. What are the implications of wielding science as power in the name of justice? We can look at
historical examples of tensions, for example, how the use of IQ tests in
scientific studies on the effects of lead contamination led to lead paint bans
(Needleman et al., 1979). It is well known, however, that IQ tests have also
been a tool of scientific racism and eugenics (Marks, 2017; Stern, 2016).[1]
We wonder if we are using the master's tools to dismantle the master's
house, only to "temporarily beat him at his own game" without bringing
about "genuine change" (Lorde, 1981). For example, do (should) you have
to test soils that are known to be contaminated with lead to provide evidence that the soils are making your family sick (when we know that lead is
a contaminant), whereas in white affluent communities, the NIMBY [Not In
My Backyard] phenomenon is powerful enough in its own right to insulate
those communities from hazardous toxins and other similar risks (Frausto
et al., 2019)? Does wielding science for justice not also contribute to the
idea that only science can "validate" one's experiences, dreams, and desires?

We do not have clear or straightforward answers to these questions,
but we see these as important ethical and political considerations that we
bring to bear when we engage in this work. This means educating students
who can critically appropriate and repurpose some aspects of scientific practice while transforming or rejecting others. We can turn to activists (e.g.,
those who transformed how clinical trials for AIDS are conducted) as inspiration for this sort of reimagination of science and education (see Steven
Epstein's *Impure Science* [1996] for more examples). What we ultimately
envision and aspire to is a project of both dismantling but also reclaiming
the "masters' tools" as our own. The sciences are unique knowledge systems
to which multiple diverse communities have contributed. What we strive
to maintain as central to our teaching and learning in science is cultivating
science(s) and science education(s) that bring about care, radical equality,
justice, and collective well-being.

CONCLUSION

When we engage in teaching and learning science in ways that may look different from how we were taught and in ways that align with our ethical commitments to justice and critical care, we need to know that we can turn to others for support, positive words, and critical thinking. There are many uncertainties in confronting ideas of science as politically neutral—the risk of school or parental backlash to justice teaching in science or alienating students. These risks are particularly poignant for teachers working with elite students as they confront their identities and positions regarding race, power, and privilege in science. How we negotiate these uncertainties and risks will determine the sustainability and continuity of the work—the heart-centered, community-focused, transformative work of teaching science for social justice.

For us as educators, one of the key sustaining forces has been developing a community or collective within schools or across distances. This need for a collective was one reason that Sara and Alexa began an online monthly meeting, which we call the Teaching Science for Social Justice Inquiry Group—now in its 5th year! Similarly, the Science Educators for Equity, Diversity, and Social Justice organization (http://seedsweb.org) was also founded to develop a community of teachers, researchers, and community members who are committed to the goals of justice in science and education. These groups provide support through the seemingly simple experience of hearing one's ideas or identity affirmed by others and by creating spaces where folks can co-construct ideas and activities relevant to justice-oriented science teaching. We invite the readers to join us in this work.

NOTE

1. See the mini-series *G* on RadioLab Presents for a more in-depth discussion of these cases: https://www.wnycstudios.org/podcasts/radiolab/projects/radiolab-presents-g

REFERENCES

Bailey, N., & Zuk, M. (2009). Same-sex sexual behavior and evolution. *Trends in Ecology and Evolution, 24*(8), 439–446.

Brochin, C. (2019). Queering bilingual teaching in elementary schools and in bilingual teacher education. *Theory Into Practice, 58*(1), 80–88.

Cajete, G. (2004). Philosophy of native science. In A. Waters (Ed.), *American Indian thought* (pp. 45–57). Blackwell.

Canipe, M., & Tolbert, S. (2016). Many ways of knowing: A multilogical science lesson on climate change. *The Science Teacher, 83*(4), 31–35.

Chambers, D. W. (1983). Stereotypic images of the scientist: The Draw-a-Scientist Test. *Science Education, 67*(2), 255–265.

Epstein, S. (1996). *Impure science: AIDS, activism, and the politics of knowledge.* University of California Press.

Farland-Smith, D., & McComas, W. (2009). Teaching the human dimension of science. *Science and Children, 46*(9), 48.

Fereydooni, A. (2012, March 14). Do animals exhibit homosexuality? *Yale Scientific.* http://www.yalescientific.org/2012/03/do-animals-exhibit-homosexuality/

Frausto, A., Morales-Doyle, D., Aguilera, A., Canales, K., Chappell, M., Clay, G., Herrera, E., Lopez, E., Rajski, T., Tolbert, S. (2019). *Youth participatory science.* Town Hall Presentation, Science Educators for Equity, Diversity, and Social Justice Conference. Norfolk, VA.

Freire, P. (1971). *Pedagogy of the oppressed.* Continuum.

Freire, P. (1985). *The politics of education: Culture, power, and liberation.* Greenwood Publishing Group.

Gunckel, K. L. (2010). Experiences, patterns, and explanations. *Science and Children, 48*(1), 46.

Harmon, A. (2019, December 7). Can biology class reduce racism? *New York Times.* https://www.nytimes.com/2019/12/07/us/race-biology-genetics.html

Kevles, D. (1985). *In the name of eugenics: Genetics and the uses of human heredity.* Harvard University Press.

Kirch, S. A., & Amoroso, M. (2016). *Being and becoming scientists today: Reconstructing assumptions about science and science education to reclaim a learner–scientist perspective.* Springer.

Larkin, D. B., Maloney, T., & Perry-Ryder, G. M. (2016). Reasoning about race and pedagogy in two preservice science teachers: A critical race theory analysis. *Cognition and Instruction, 34*(4), 285–322.

Lensmire, T., McManimon, S., Tierney, J. D., Lee-Nichols, M., Casey, Z., Lensmire, A., & Davis, B. (2013). McIntosh as synecdoche: How teacher education's focus on white privilege undermines antiracism. *Harvard Educational Review, 83*(3), 410–431.

Levine, P. (2017). *Eugenics: A very short introduction.* Oxford University Press.

Levine-Rasky, C. (2000). Framing whiteness: Working through the tensions in introducing whiteness to educators. *Race Ethnicity and Education, 3*(3), 271–292.

Lorde, A. (1981). The master's tools will never dismantle the master's house. In C. Morago and G. Anzaldua (Eds.), *This bridge called my back: Writings by radical women of color.* Persephone Press.

Marks, J. (2017). *Is science racist?* John Wiley & Sons.

McIntosh, P. (2008). White privilege: Unpacking the invisible knapsack. In P. Rothenberg (Ed.), *White privilege: Essential readings on the other side of racism* (pp. 123–127). Worth.

Morales-Doyle, D., Childress Price, T., & Chappell, M. J. (2019). Chemicals are contaminants too: Teaching appreciation and critique of science in the era of Next Generation Science Standards (NGSS). *Science Education, 103*(6), 1347–1366.

Needleman, H. L., Gunnoe, C., Leviton, A., Reed, R., Peresie, H., Maher, C., & Barrett, P. (1979). Deficits in psychologic and classroom performance of children with elevated dentine lead levels. *New England Journal of Medicine, 300*(13), 689–695.

Richardson, J., Parnell, P., & Cole, H. (Illustrator) (2005). *And Tango makes three.* Simon & Schuster.

Ross, S. (1962). Scientist: The story of a word. *Annals of Science, 18*(2), 65–85.

Rutherford, A. (2019). *Humanimal: How homo sapiens became nature's most paradoxical creature—A new evolutionary history.* The Experiment.

Saini, A. (2020). *Superior: The return of race science.* Beacon Press.

Schindel, A., & Tolbert, S. (2016). Ebola: Teaching science, race, and the media. *Rethinking Schools, 31*(1), 50–56.

Sheth, M. J. (2019). Grappling with racism as foundational practice of science teaching. *Science Education, 103*(1), 37–60.

Stern, A. (2016). *Eugenic nation.* University of California Press.

Tolbert, S., & Schindel, A. (2017). Altering the ideology of consumerism: Caring for land and people through school science. In G. Reis, M. Mueller, R. Lather, L. Silveres, & R. Oliveira, (Eds.), *Sociocultural perspectives on youth ethical consumerism* (pp. 115–129). Springer.

Tolbert, S., Schindel, A., Gray, S., Kenny, L., Rivera, M., Snook, S., & Widimaier, C. (2019). Empowerment. In D. Ford (Ed.), *Key words in radical philosophy and education* (pp. 191–209). Peter Lang Publishing.

Tuck, E., & Yang, E. W. (2012). Decolonization is not a metaphor. *Decolonization: Indigeneity, Education & Society, 1*(1), 1–40.

Washington, H. A. (2006). *Medical apartheid: The dark history of medical experimentation on Black Americans from colonial times to the present.* Harlem Moon.

Zacor, K. (2014). Lead poisoning: Bringing social justice to chemistry. *Rethinking Schools, 31*, 1.

CHAPTER 13

Opening the Proverbial Can O' Worms

Teaching Social Justice to Educated Elites in Suburban Detroit

Robin Moten

In 2012, our team of teachers began to develop curriculum for our Global Literature/Global Studies course, and I expressed an interest in teaching with "pillars" in mind, specifically social justice. To this day, I'm not sure exactly what another team member was trying to convey when he contributed the following: "You know, [pregnant pause] if you talk about social justice, you're stating there is an inequity that has to be dealt with." "Well, duh," I thought to myself, but I also wondered why this concept seemed to be controversial—or at least worthy of pause to him.

Before we go any further, let me give you some context. Nestled among large maple trees, a well-manicured public golf course, and an even more well-manicured private country club sits the high school where I've been teaching for over 20 years. Ernest W. Seaholm High School is in Birmingham, Michigan, a suburb located about 20 miles north of downtown Detroit. Birmingham was built up by the white-collar work force of Detroit's automotive industry—the engineers, the advertising folks, and the executives. The school district draws its students from not only Birmingham, but several other suburbs. The median income for a family in Birmingham is over $100,000 per year, and the school's population is over 98% white.

Our traditional language arts program featured many of the same novels that have been staples in English departments around the country: *The Odyssey*, *The Adventures of Huckleberry Finn*, *Catcher in the Rye*, and so forth. But ever so slowly, Birmingham's demographics started to shift, which prompted a decision from our central administration's office in 2014 to overhaul the curriculum. English teachers at both high schools came together to vote on which new courses would be offered. The final vote brought three new options for seniors: "Future Studies," based on a long-running, popular course at Seaholm's sister school that featured dystopian novels and short stories; "Heroes and Humanities," which had been a pilot course focusing on novels and plays illuminating Joseph Campbell's *The Hero's Journey;* and "Social Justice."

Now I am far too scared to ever watch the film *The Exorcist* in its entirety, but I do know the premise of the story, and I'm sure my head turned on a swivel like Linda Blair's when I heard we would be offering a class called "Social Justice." Hadn't I just been a part of a conversation when one of my colleagues sought to warn me about the dangers of talking about inequities in our privileged, predominately white school? One of my colleagues and I, both African American, signed up to work on the new Social Justice curriculum. Regardless of how prepared we were for the moment of change at our schools, the change had come. The Social Justice class was happening in our district. The journey was beginning.

YEAR 1

My colleague (we'll call him John) and I developed a social justice curriculum relatively quickly once our district decided to offer the course. At the time, both of us felt like we had a good grasp of the term "social justice" and had a vision of what a language arts social justice class could be. In hindsight, I wonder if we felt that way because we are both African American? Regardless, we ran headlong into the complexity of the term and our chosen pedagogical approach. John had taught a course at the other high school called "Minority Literature," so it seemed natural, at least to him, to have most of the material used in the new Social Justice class come from his course with a few new twists. That simplistic view bothered me, yet neither he nor I looked for pedagogical literature on social justice courses or had any other support to find the best way to teach the class.

John was quickly greeted with some criticism about the class from both students and parents who were looking for deeper insights into what we were covering and a chance to engage in meaningful conversations and student-led research about the chosen topics. At my high school, which has a different demographic than John's, I received no complaints. But I was terrified waiting for the inevitable shoe to drop. From my observations, many students and staff lean politically conservative. Every presidential election year, our school newspaper conducts a school-wide vote where students and staff cast their ballot to predict the next president of the United States. In 2016, Seaholm chose Donald Trump over Hillary Clinton. Many of my building colleagues thought 2016 would be the first year the survey results would be wrong. Turns out, we were wrong. In other words, I was teaching a class called "Social Justice" in Trumpland (Moten, 2018).

While I wasn't held to the same scrutiny as John, I began to internally doubt what I was doing with the class. I didn't have time for deep seminars, and I didn't believe in our "social justice person of the week" plan. It felt insufficient for high school seniors. And did we just revamp a "minority literature class" and paste it onto a social justice blank page? While we decided not to embark on longer novels such as *Invisible Man*, *Beloved*, or *Native Son*, we did decide to use short stories, poetry, and articles. For me, this approach promoted breadth over depth, and I was deeply dissatisfied and worried whether or not the class would survive. As I pondered all of this, John applied and got a position as an administrator, which gave me the chance to revamp our curriculum.

THE REDUX

The course revamp began by considering two things: (1) What scholarly literature was available about teaching social justice to high school students? (2) What was important to me, a veteran teacher with a background in curriculum and human development and a Black female teacher looking to be as authentic as possible for my students' (and my own) benefit? I started with researching social justice in secondary classrooms, looking for what others used as a framework for the course. Were there guidelines out there at a state or local level? What needed to be in every class calling itself a "social justice" class? *Teaching Tolerance* (now *Learning for Justice*) was helpful. I also tried contacting professors at nearby universities. One I spoke with was shocked that a social justice class could be/would be taught at the high school level and politely wished me luck.

I knew I wanted the class to be authentic, allow students to feel like they were a community of learners, offer diverse texts and service-learning opportunities, and, most importantly, promote depth over breadth. And I knew the class had to be seminar based. Seminar, in this context, meant deep, meaningful, student-led conversations, the goals of which would be student growth, the building of a community of learners, and the building of knowledge through fuller understanding of our texts. In other words, I wasn't going to consider the course a success if we held discussions the way too many teachers still do—completely teacher-led with one or two eager students participating and the others in a trance, or worse (Rush, 2017).

Seminars were also part of the strategy to establish trust and build community in our classroom. Was this even possible in a trimester (12-week) course, with 70-minute daily classes? I believed it was not only possible but *necessary* for a class exploring issues such as race and gender as "only when we are connected and care for the well-being of the whole that a civil and democratic society is created" (Block, 2018, p. 9). This may not be what is typically imagined when one is thinking about a public high school classroom with 25 or more students, all competing for the highest grade or the largest amount of attention. But if meaningful, impactful conversation is the ideal we're aiming for throughout the duration of the class, then seeking to establish community and building trust must be the preceding actions taken to reach that ideal.

The next important element in designing the course was giving students the space and time to define the term "social justice" for themselves. Considering the politically conservative environment that is our school, I knew better than to put a politically liberal definition of social justice in front of them and then assess whether they had learned that definition. Also, from a developmental perspective, having students define social justice for themselves is aligned with what "emerging adults" (Arnett, 2004) should be attempting to accomplish. Because I knew from a developmental perspective that my students needed to feel safe as they formed their definition of social justice, I was never concerned with whether or not their definition was in sync with mine. In fairness, I struggle with a pat and potentially static definition of a term that, to me, seems to be rooted in dynamism. That decision was also important for my own continual growth as an educator (Palmer, 1997). Allowing them to work throughout the trimester to answer the question posed during the first days of class ("What is social justice?"), the curriculum becomes more like a story/narrative they create for themselves (Nakkula &Toshalis, 2020). This is a more difficult task than it appears.

Another important concept of the revamped social justice class was to prevent it from becoming a political battleground. A contentious atmosphere wasn't going to help sustain the class, nor was it going to help students do the critical work of defining, reflecting, and then acting upon social justice (Freire, 1990). Often, students are looking for a political fight—which is acceptable to an extent. Educators know students in this age range (17 to 18 years old) are exploring and forming opinions about life's biggest questions, and politics are certainly part of that process. The second reason students think the social justice classroom discussions should look like a showdown at the OK Corral is because they are used to seminars becoming debates as opposed to discussions. Once we establish how seminars are framed as conversations with no winners or losers, the desire for that political battleground usually subsides (Hess, 2009).

ROUND 2: SO MUCH TO DO, SO LITTLE TIME, OR WHEN SEMINARS AREN'T ENOUGH

After deciding what was necessary for the class to succeed, it was time to implement. After revamping the curriculum, I decided to dedicate one section of the class to race and the African American experience, basing the decision to do that on student evaluations from the previous year's classes. I knew Ava DuVernay's (2014) documentary *13th* was something we had to watch. After viewing it, my class settled down to have a mini-seminar. A complete discussion wasn't scheduled until the next day, but the documentary had stirred a lot of emotions that I wasn't comfortable leaving unaddressed. Not even 5 minutes into our check-in, one of my African American students started to cry and yelled out in anger that her mostly white classmates had no feeling or emotions about the Black men the documentary highlighted. She abruptly left the room, with her African American friend following closely behind to make sure she was okay. The awkward silence after they left was palpable. What had I done? The curriculum was meant to be engaging and challenging. It included the documentary and a selection from Michelle Alexander's *The New Jim Crow*. It all fit together neatly. But what I had *not* done was allocate enough time for the unforeseen parts of the learning experience. I was unprepared for my student's reaction to have the ripple effects it did. The class was wholly afraid to react after she left the room. Was she calling them racists? Some of the white students believed this student herself was "racist" (they told me much later). The next day's seminar carried the weight of the previous day's interactions. Students could not fully engage with the text (the documentary) because they couldn't engage with each other on the same level they had before they viewed the documentary. I realized I had not taken the appropriate time to prepare them for the possible conversations following the documentary.

Why, if seminars were to be the central focus of the course, would I not prepare them adequately for that one? It had everything to do with time. As every teacher has experienced, I felt like I wouldn't have enough time and I would have to cut curriculum, which I was more than reluctant to do. It's a social justice class, after all—everything that is relevant is important, right? This outlook had to change—and my approach to designing a curriculum for the course along with it.

DELVING INTO THE DEEPER DIVE

After the incident with *13th*, I decided I was simply trying to do too much in one course, so I revamped the curriculum once again. Besides coming to terms with how the class should be taught, it was also time to come to terms with what the content of the class should be. In an attempt to change the focus of the class from a broad overview of several topics to depth of material, each section of English 12A-Social Justice would embark on a deep dive into a topic and then a deeper dive into that same topic before final projects/exams became due. The new format led me to choose four topics for the course: poverty, race, LGBTQ issues, and immigration. Each section had its own mandatory readings at the beginning of the unit, followed by section-specific material the rest of the way. It was a conscious decision to make poverty a separate section so students received the message that race and poverty *sometimes* have a corollary relationship, but not necessarily a causative one. Once poverty became its own section, texts such as *Hillbilly Elegy* and films like *American Winter* could be added to provide conversations around the concept of meritocracy. In addition, separating race from poverty allowed for myriad approaches to teaching the sections on race, such as focusing on one novel or homing in on specific issues like mass incarceration.

The LGBTQ section of the social justice course was designed to provide awareness about that community. This is the section that gave me the most anxiety, in part because of the small number of students who openly identified as LGBTQ, its nature as controversial for some of our parent community due to religious and political preferences, and my identity as a straight cisgender woman. Maybe because I'm African American, I don't feel as much fear teaching a section on race? Also, when I teach about race, I explicitly inform my students that I'm aware of the tension in the room when we're engaging in difficult conversations, but my job as their teacher is my number-one priority. They are also aware of my goal to hold that tension with both hands open, looking for the courage to embrace those moments—not run away from them (Palmer, 1997).

On the first day of class in the LGBTQ section, I tell students if they believe they truly cannot participate fully due to their religious or political beliefs, a transfer is possible. The fact that no one has ever done so is a point of pride, but I also wonder about whether or not there should even be an opt-out? I don't offer the option to white students who sign up to be in the race section. The decision to offer an opt-out in the LGBTQ section was not an easy one, and it came out of an acquiescence to the often small, but vocal community members who are not only personally religious but also desirous of their public school community to reflect their private values.

One of the visual texts we use in the LGBTQ section is the feature film *Milk* (2008) starring actor Sean Penn as Harvey Milk, the San Francisco elected official assassinated by his co-worker who wasn't on board with what he believed was Milk's "gay agenda." It is rated R, but there isn't a hyper-focus on Harvey Milk's sexual activities. However, the audience does see Milk being affectionate with his various partners. I had no idea how this was going to go over with my students the first time I taught it. With about 10 minutes left in class, I stopped the film and told students I wanted to check in with them. One of the boys, a popular, football-playing type, raised his hand. "Was it really like that back then?" he asked. "Like what?" I replied. "Did people, strangers really hook up like that?" "Well, I don't know. I didn't come of age until the 80s so I can't tell you what the 70s dating scene was like. Why is that significant for you?" I responded. Then came the mic drop. "I don't care that men love each other in this movie. I want to know if total strangers would hook up on the subway because these days I can't even talk to a girl, let alone take home a total stranger." I was standing when he shared his thoughts, and I thought I was going to topple over. The rest of the class was a little stunned by his honesty, but the friends he was sitting with nodded their heads in understanding. I was so grateful to him for his honesty and his trusting spirit. What I had feared the most (dismissal of the film or the curriculum due to homophobia) didn't occur.

Not only were my fears unfounded, but this student had made himself vulnerable to the class in what was a truly beautiful moment. He decided this was a space where he was safe enough to bring up his anxiety about approaching girls, knowing full well he appeared as the type who would never have that problem. Establishing the class as a safe space for open, meaningful dialogue was a goal from the beginning. Students are informed, on multiple occasions, about the role meaningful conversations have in the course. We evaluate ourselves on how well we did, or didn't do, in our seminars. In other words, our constant "talk about talk" seems to help students feel less pressure to perform and more at ease to say what needs to be said so our conversations measure up to our expectations.

YET ANOTHER CURRICULUM REWORK: THE LOST BATTLE OF THE SECTION ON IMMIGRATION

The end-of-trimester student evaluations told me the section on immigration wasn't going well. For 2 years, I tried to create a curriculum that would allow students to recognize the arguments within the current national debate surrounding immigration, empathize with the plight of immigrants through their stories, and make informed and compassionate decisions about the subject. That didn't happen. All the students in that section of Social Justice were white nonimmigrants who have little exposure to immigrants, particularly immigrants of color, beyond cafeteria workers in the school and domestic workers at their home. With that in mind, it's easy to assume they simply were not interested in immigration as a matter of urgency for our nation. But I also think this topic was where the Trump rubber met the road. There was apathy, but there was also a small, intense faction of students who considered themselves to be politically conservative (even though they had no clue who Edmund Burke or Jack Kemp were or what the John Birch Society stood for). They were strong Trump supporters, and they stayed mostly quiet throughout the class. Adding yet another layer of complexity, not enough students considered themselves liberal or progressive enough to interact with or contradict the conservative students' ideas. So, *no* ideas were brought to the table, and the silence was deafening.

The end-of-trimester evaluations told me what I already knew: The seminars were flat, and my students didn't feel a connection to each other or to the material. I made the decision to pull the plug on immigration as a section. There are very few nights when I turn on the news and don't see something associated with the topic of immigration; questions about the future of the DACA program or concerns about the boundaries of ICE officials, and I know by removing the section on immigration I lost an opportunity to give students the space to ponder one of our republic's deepest core questions: Who should be here and why? I'm still not sure my students would say there was any great loss as a result of the decision to cut the section. What I am sure of is that their resistance (shown through apathy or outright refusal to do the work) and the results produced are representative of the power of their voice. But should high school students' voices carry the kind of weight where they can change curriculum—especially when they represent communities of power and privilege with an investment in the status quo?

NEXT STEPS

The Social Justice class at Seaholm is still in an exploratory stage, even though it is 5 years old. Many lessons have been learned over the last 5 years, with many more to come. It is indeed an accomplishment that the class has not only survived but grown during that time—but there's more to do. We are barely 20 miles from the city of Detroit. Close proximity to an urban area gives us opportunities to form partnerships with other schools, nonprofits, or businesses. We could also participate in more meaningful and longer-term service-learning projects like traveling to Detroit to listen to current residents' stories of how gentrification is affecting their lives. Experiences like this would also allow us to study and discuss race in a less theoretical or abstract manner. While I love the novel *Invisible Man* or reading James Baldwin's works with my students, how much better would it be if we simply spent time in a location where there are more than a handful of Black people? I would also hope opportunities for relationships in Detroit would lead to more engaged, less politically charged conversations about topics such as Black Lives Matter or affirmative action and, perhaps, most importantly, to a more connected feeling to the city that surrounds our suburb (Kielsmeier, 2010). Immersion trips; dialogue sessions; and partnerships with Detroit schools, nonprofits, and businesses are just a few ways we can (and should) sustain and grow the class and turn it into a viable school program.

REIMAGINING AND TRANSFORMING THE CLASSROOM EXPERIENCE

Believe it or not, I originally did not want to teach Seaholm's social justice class. I talked to my principal and department chair about the "optics" of having one of only two Black teachers in the building teaching the course.

The perception that it was bound to be a "liberal" course would also label me as a liberal Black teacher—and I just don't like labels of any sort. Once I stopped focusing on all the things that could go wrong, however, I began to focus on all that could be accomplished, and I got excited. This class could create an environment where conversations around race, class, and gender weren't at the margins of the curriculum, but at the center. Instead of relegating the study of poverty, LGBTQ issues, or mass incarceration to a unit in Social Studies, this class could make them the focus of language arts where they would be brought to life through poetry, documentaries, and narrative nonfiction literature. It could weave in intergenerational dialogue sessions, service learning, and guest lectures from professors at our nearby universities. We could establish an advisory board so members of our community could observe and participate in the academic and social-emotional growth of Seaholm students. The Social Justice class could open the moral imagination of each student who takes it. Through seminars, the heart of the class, students would elevate inquiry, compromise, and reflection (Roth, 2019) and leave Seaholm more ready to participate in America's grand democratic experiment.

So, to my former colleague who asked if I knew what can of worms I was opening when I dared to start talking about social justice with our "elite" students, I would say yes—I knew then and I know now exactly what I'm trying to do. Hopefully, that can of worms will remain open as long as possible.

REFERENCES

Alexander, Michelle (2010). *The new Jim Crow: Mass incarceration in the age of colorblindness*. The New Press.

Arnett, J. J. (2004). *Emerging adulthood: The winding road from the late teens through the twenties*. Oxford University Press.

Averick, S., Barish, H., & DuVernay, A. (Producer) & DuVernay, A. (Director) (2014). *13th* (Documentary). Kandoo Films.

Block, P. (2018). *Community: The structure of belonging*. Berrett- Koehler Publishers.

Cohen, B., Jinks, D., & Schwartz, P. (Producers) & Van Sant, G. (Director) (2008). *Milk* (Motion Picture). Focus Features.

Freire, P. (1990). *Pedagogy of the oppressed*. (Myra Bergman Ramos, Trans.) The Continuum Publishing Company. (Original work published 1968.)

Hess, D. (2009). *Controversy in the classroom: The democratic power of discussion*. Routledge.

Kielsmeier, J. (2010). Build a bridge between service and learning. *The Phi Delta Kappan, 91*(5), 8–15.

Moten, R. (2018). Teaching social justice in the Trump Era. *Teachers College Record*. https://www.tcrecord.org/books/Content.asp?ContentID=22519

Nakkula, M. J., & Toshalis, E. (2020). *Understanding youth: Adolescent development for educators*. Harvard Education Press.

Palmer, P. (1997). *The courage to teach: Exploring the inner landscape of a teacher's life*. Josey-Bass.

Roth, M. S. (2019). *Safe enough spaces: A pragmatist's approach to inclusion, free speech, and political correctness on college campuses*. Yale University Press.

Rush, M. (2017). *Beat boredom: Engaging tuned-out teenagers*. Stenhouse Publishers.

CHAPTER 14

Intersectional Feminist and Political Education with Privileged Girls

Beth Cooper Benjamin, Amira Proweller, Beth Catlett,
Andrea Jacobs, and Sonya Crabtree-Nelson

As educators committed to the tradition of shining a spotlight on dynamics of power, privilege, and oppression to foster a more equitable and just world (Ayers et al., 2009; Case, 2013; Stoudt, 2009), our work uses critical participatory action research (CPAR) with youth as a tool of critical consciousness raising for young people with privilege. This chapter examines how Jewish teen girls with racial and class privilege developed an emerging critical consciousness through an extracurricular community-based program called the Research Training Internship (RTI).

YOUTH CRITICAL PARTICIPATORY ACTION RESEARCH

CPAR is collaborative inquiry enabling people to investigate social issues that affect their lives and to devise steps toward change. The word "critical" signifies a commitment to interrogating structures and dynamics of power, both in researchers' framing of the phenomena they study and in the research process itself. Youth participatory action research (YPAR) is a form of PAR developed for work with adolescents. As distinct strands of PAR methodology, both CPAR and YPAR are designed to enable those most immediately affected by structural injustices to give voice to their lived experiences and take action as agents of change (Torre & Fine, 2006). In this chapter, we use the acronym Y/CPAR to refer to our use of critical participatory action research with youth.

Y/CPAR engages youth directly in collaborative critical inquiry to probe the systemic bases of inequality and strategize actions toward social change (Bautista et al., 2013; Reason & Bradbury, 2006). Commonly, it has provided economically, socially, and politically marginalized youth with skills to challenge oppressive systems that undermine their daily lives (Ozer, 2016; Stoudt et al., 2016; Wright, 2015). Recently, however, Y/CPAR has been adapted as an approach for involving youth with race and class privilege in inquiry into how power and oppression function and the role that privilege plays in producing, sustaining, and normalizing injustice (Case, 2013; Stoudt, 2009; Stoudt et al., 2012). Through Y/CPAR, privileged youth have the opportunity to become more critically aware of how privilege operates systemically, both within and beyond their communities, and to wrestle with their accountability to actively participate in social change (Stoudt et al., 2012).

In addition to Y/CPAR, our work draws on a critical, intersectional feminist theoretical and pedagogical legacy focusing attention on the root causes of social problems and compelling examination of intersecting axes of privilege and oppression related to identities, experiences, and structures integral to the fabric of our lives (Crenshaw, 1994; Hill-Collins, 1990; Okun, 2010; Richie, 2012). Critical reflection on one's own social locations is part of a larger goal to cultivate a more active citizenry working to change current structures (Muzak, 2011, Russo, 2019; Stoudt et al., 2012). We've also drawn inspiration from social work grounded in a critical ecological systems model calling for an examination of one's unique position in a larger changing environment (Payne, 2014; Rothery, 2008) as the foundation for social change (Finn, 2016; Shulman, 2016) and the field of education's critical approaches studying systems of power, privilege, and oppression that limit education as the practice of freedom (Freire, 1972). Such perspectives are vital, particularly for engaging youth in close examination of social problems that affect their lives and identifying strategies to remedy these problems (Cammarota & Fine, 2008).

RESEARCH TRAINING INTERNSHIP PROGRAM

The RTI is a university- and community-based social justice leadership program for self-identified Jewish adolescent girls in grades 9 to 12. Recruited through parent and alumni networks, as well as outreach to youth programs, schools, and synagogues, the participants attended Jewish day schools, nonsectarian private schools, and public high schools. Many of them were involved in social justice programming or feminist clubs at their schools and were drawn to RTI as an opportunity to be part of innovative Jewish feminist programming diving deep into a topic in which they were already invested. While most were white Jews, some cohorts included Jews of color. Most were middle-to-owning class and spanned the continuum of sexual identities. They represented a range of Jewish identities and levels of engagement with Jewish communal life from secular-cultural to Orthodox.

The RTI was created by co-author Beth Cooper Benjamin and colleagues at Ma'yan, the Jewish feminist project of the Jewish Community Center (JCC) of Manhattan, New York. Launched in 2007, the RTI-NY ran for six cohorts over 10 years. In 2014, Ma'yan supported launching the RTI in Chicago, where it has run for 5 years as a partnership between the Jewish Federation of Metropolitan Chicago and co-authors Amira Proweller, Beth

Catlett, and Sonya Crabtree-Nelson (faculty at DePaul University).[1] Each cohort spends 10 to 14 months in bimonthly sessions held at the JCC in New York and the DePaul University campus in Chicago. Each two- to three-hour session includes facilitated discussions and activities. Participants also spend time developing an action research project and preparing a final presentation for parents, peers, and other stakeholders.

As the RTI evolved, the goals of the program became addressing oppression and privilege that shape girls' lives, using research to more credibly challenge systemic inequalities, and modeling a welcoming Jewish space that allows for multiple expressions of feminist and Jewish identities and engagement. To do so, we used the Y/CPAR component as a tool to support participants examining their own lives, beginning with their shared identities as Jewish girls. This led us to teaching explicitly and intersectionally about power, oppression, and privilege in order to cultivate their critical consciousness. For example, one session examined the ways participants' anger was *constrained* by discourses of niceness and meanness—cultural norms common among white, wealthy girls—and addressed the ways that anger is often *criminalized* for girls of color, resulting in school pushout and involvement in the criminal justice system (Brown, 2003; Morris, 2016).

Eventually, we established a permanent theme: "Secrets of the Perfect Girl," a framing developed in response to issues and questions raised by the girls in previous cohorts. Through this lens, facilitators supported participants to interrogate the messages they receive about who they are supposed to be and become, where those expectations come from, and what happens when girls try—or don't try—to live up to them. This framing allowed advisors to support participants in critically interrogating how the pressure to be "perfect" (in appearance, academics, social media, and so forth) shapes girls' choices and perceptions in ways both profound and subtle (Brown, 2003; Girls Incorporated, 2006; Simmons, 2018), a fundamental practice if adult women are to support girls in confronting injustice (Brown, 2016). Participants worked with advisors to design a unique research action project exploring these issues in depth, such as the impact of entertainment media messaging on girls or mapping experiences of "everyday sexism" in New York. In Chicago, each RTI cohort examined a wide range of youth-generated topics including anti-Semitism, the gendering of Jewish food spaces, the perpetuation of beauty myths, mental illness, and rape culture.

Interrogating ideals and myths of perfection through the lenses of race, class, gender, religion, and sexuality proved an effective doorway into examining the dynamics of power, privilege, and oppression as they manifested in the lives of the RTI participants. This process was facilitated through the power chart,[2] a pedagogical tool that was utilized in initial sessions to enable a shared language for discussions of power, oppression, and privilege (see Figure 14.1). It remained in use throughout the program as a touchstone for participants to locate and critically examine their own positionality/ies.

Figure 14.1. Power Chart

Identity	Group with power	Group denied power	Example: Internalized	Example: Interpersonal	Example: Institutional or cultural	System and manifestation
Race	White people	People of color	Colorism (preference for lighter skin)	Using a racial slur	Redlining, school funding, school-to-prison pipeline	White supremacy (racism)
Gender	Men, cisgender people	Women, transgender, gender nonconforming people	Internalized body hatred (women); internalized superiority (men)	"You throw like a girl"	Lack of access to reproductive health care, gender pay gap	Patriarchy (sexism, transphobia)
Religion	Christians	Jews, Muslims, Buddhists, Sikhs, Hindus, all non-Christian religions	Trying to "pass" or hiding visible religious symbols and appearance	Attacks on Jewish and Muslim holy sites, cemeteries, and businesses	Christmas and Easter are federal holidays, "War on Christmas" in the media	Christian hegemony (anti-Semitism, Islamophobia)
Sexual Orientation						
Class						
Nationality						
Ability/Learning Style						
Age						

FINDINGS: NO STRAIGHT LINES

Our findings, drawn from interviews with each applicant at the beginning and end of their RTI cohort, demonstrate that growth and learning in the program are uneven and nonlinear. In our data and experiences with the program, we see substantial evidence of what Monique Guishard (2009) has called "moments of critical consciousness" where new ways of thinking are evident, even if they are not fully integrated. We examine this uneven and somewhat sporadic learning through the following themes.

Thinking Intersectionally, But Not Systemically

The RTI participants typically leave the program able to articulate some understanding of intersectionality as a system in which it is possible to occupy both privileged and oppressed positions simultaneously. Said one participant:

> I would define intersectionality as . . . how different privileges and oppressions in one area can connect with privileges and oppressions or like another system. Like . . . if you're a woman and you're also Jewish, or if you're a woman and you are African American, everything's connected. And, like, if you have oppression . . . from one system, then you would maybe have privileges from another one or vice versa.

While our participants began to understand and embrace the concept of feminist intersectionality, we found that they more readily identified the ways they *experience oppression* rather than the ways they are *implicated in systems of privilege*. For example, several interviewees articulated the oppressive nature of idealized femininity:

> Girls are supposed to be super thin and super sexual and super straight and have boyfriends, but not too many boyfriends. And have perfect grades but also have a social life and be an extrovert and . . . girls should want both a family and a career. . . . If she only wants a career, that's "iffy."

Our experience as facilitators has shown us that increasing awareness of the impossible expectations to which girls and women are held can be simultaneously infuriating and liberating. For participants who arrive already attuned to gendered double-binds, the opportunity to air frustrations, commiserate, and strategize action builds a deep sense of connection and solidarity within the RTI group.

Coming into awareness of one's privilege and recognizing how one's systemic advantages are necessarily connected to others' systemic disadvantages, on the other hand, often generated experiences of discomfort, confusion, and guilt. Here, a participant wrestles with the idea that she might hold disproportionate power in the world:

> I felt a little bit guilty sometimes just because I know I am privileged in so many ways that people around me and then even people very far away from me, are not. . . . I think that's one of the things you have to kind of ask yourself about your power, like, is it too much? Do you have too little? Like where do you meet in the middle?

This self-interrogation of privilege is a practice of critical consciousness consistent with program goals: inviting youth to attend to the power they hold relative to others and pose challenging questions about fairness, justice, and equity. That said, her final question about "meet[ing] in the middle" between privilege and oppression can be read either as a vision of power that is equitably distributed or as a desire to be relieved of the burden of individual guilt and sense of responsibility that often result from the awareness of one's unearned advantage.

Defaulting to the Individual and Interpersonal/Difficulty Seeing the Structural

When participants considered strategies to create change, they often defaulted to individual, interpersonal frames of reference:

> I think there really is a big value in just making people informed. . . . [W]hen it's interpersonal . . . it's more personal. [Chuckles] Shocker. . . . Because that person is gonna . . . maybe go out and spread that more. And you kinda get this domino effect.

When participants default to locating racism or sexism in individual "racist" or "sexist" behavior and speech, rather than recognizing the systemic source, their orientation aligns with the dominant neoliberal discourse of individual liberty and personal responsibility. Systemic oppression functions, in part, by rendering privilege invisible to those who hold it, and that makes attending to structure both an imperative and an ongoing challenge with this population. In ways both planned and spontaneous, facilitators worked to draw participants' attention back to the systemic, structural, and ideological to help them recognize how it plays out in their lives. This example from an exit interview illustrates how *slippery* this grasp of systemic and ideological oppression tends to be:

> *RTI:* I think that (. . .) if feminism wants to continue, it needs to be rebranded. . . . I would make every organization call itself a 'humanist' organization, I guess. I don't know. . . . I really think

that now a lot of people see feminists as just, like, 'anti-male,' which is not what it is, but for some people it is. So, then they feel the need to start their own thing which is like pro-male/anti-women and then it starts [a] war between the sexes. . . .

Interviewer: I wonder whether . . . talking about feminism instead of humanism draws attention to a power imbalance . . . that there are systems in place . . . that perpetuate men having more power than women. And that . . . if you call it "feminism" then they're implicated . . .

RTI: [cuts off interviewer] No, I think that is what it is. Yeah, and that makes them really uncomfortable. Like then they feel blamed. They don't wanna help if they feel targeted.

Interviewer: And then they respond, finding ways that they're victimized.

RTI: Exactly, exactly. . . . The "male victim," which is ridiculous.

In this exchange, a participant asserts that feminism has a branding problem and maybe more people would join if it were called "humanism" instead. After hearing her out, the interviewer decides to draw the interviewee's attention to the systemic sexism in her story. Once the interviewer names it, the young woman can recognize how it infuses her thoughts: She cuts the interviewer off in order to affirm and elaborate what she was suggesting. But without the explicit signposts referring her back to systemic oppression, she is ready to call it a marketing problem rather than a deeper issue of power and privilege.

We did observe some moments when participants were able to employ a more structural or systemic understanding of inequality. In this exit interview, a participant explains how she has come to question what she had previously believed about affirmative action in college admissions:

We can have the same amount of money and go to the same school and get the same grades, and if the other person is Black . . . and they get in [to college], . . . I'd be like, "Well, they just want diversity," but actually it's like "no." . . . It's not like, "Oh, we had slavery back in the days." . . . There are still repercussions from that, and how people see them and how they have to work harder than I would have to work.

The participant tees up arguments she has heard against affirmative action and applies new insights about structural inequality in order to counter those arguments. Her critique is incomplete (e.g., she fails to recognize underlying issues like inequitable school funding), but she nonetheless articulates a profound shift in her own perspective.

The incompleteness of her critique illustrates how the relative homogeneity of the RTI is both necessary and insufficient for the development of critical consciousness. Homogeneous spaces enable privileged youth to interrogate privilege with less of a tendency to become paralyzed by guilt and shame or to revert to anger and rationalizing inequality (DiAngelo, 2018), but they are insufficient to enable privileged youth to recognize when their analyses perpetuate assumptions and stereotypes about people who don't share their advantages. For example, one participant had the opportunity to present the group's research at a conference attended primarily by girls of color. In her exit interview, she reflected on how this experience challenged the assumptions she'd held during the RTI:

> Because [the RTI was] all white girls . . . something that I never thought about is people of different races that weren't really represented [in the video we created] . . . I feel like I was making too many conclusions speaking just "for girls," and assuming that my experience and the experience of the girls in the room and those that I get at school were, like, *the* experience of girls.

Through sharing her cohort's research with a racially diverse group of girls, she comes to realize that what she had assumed was a universal norm had not included or accounted for the particular, distinct experiences of the girls of color she met at the conference. Although we had worked to illuminate the limits of the RTI participants' perspectives based on the homogeneity of their research group, their independent recognition of those limits remained inconsistent.

Another participant articulated how broad cultural norms and assumptions become internalized and subtly shape our individual attitudes toward ourselves and relationships with others:

> As people we're incredibly social animals. We're designed to . . . try to fit in . . . to try to make it so that other people like us. And I think that because of that, culture has a tremendous effect on how people view themselves and how they view others. . . . I think that it has a tremendous influence on my life, even in ways that I don't realize.

While participants typically depicted biased attitudes as an individual trait and a personal failing, this participant is actively wrestling with the concept that her own biases grow from the messages she absorbs from sociocultural institutions—media, school, family, religion. As she continues, she explains that these attitudes are not easy to eradicate, requiring a high degree of critical consciousness and self-interrogation:

> I'm much more forgiving of aggression in guys than I am in girls and I catch myself doing it and thinking, "Well, this is a problem, and this is 100% due to the standards that society sets for women and girls." But it's not really something I can prevent.

Even in the best-case scenario, in which one is aware of the "problem" of internalized bias and committed to challenging it, she acknowledges there is no easy solution, only the rigorous practice of critical self-interrogation.

Moving Toward Social Change

Most participants persisted in endorsing social change strategies that focused on interpersonal transformation grounded in the assumption that sharing enlightened attitudes and perspectives would naturally lead to dismantling oppression. Such strategies fail to grapple with the reality of systemic oppression and are, at best, partial solutions. Yet some did generate strategies that reflected a more systemic or structural analysis. One participant spoke of the value of working in solidarity with larger movements:

> It feels very daunting to have the pressure of trying to change other people's minds when you're just by yourself. And I think that the RTI helped build a sense of solidarity, . . . a fuller understanding of what it meant to be part of a movement. That it's not just me, it's not even just the RTI, but it's hundreds, thousands, millions of people working towards the same goals as us. . . . [E]ven if I can't make a huge impact on the world . . . every little step that I take is sort of one step in a giant movement that's constantly shifting forward.

Implicit in this emphasis on collective change-making is a critique of achievement culture: the notion that each person's value is determined by what they accomplish or earn. Rather than highlighting how long-term change is won through collective organizing, achievement culture can privilege the leadership or pivotal actions of individual "change makers" (what Brown [2016], in girl culture, calls "the myth of the special girl"). This participant explains that it's less "daunting" to recognize that no one has to (or ever does) change the world on their own, but rather by acting alongside "millions of people working towards the same goals."

Finally, understanding structural oppression requires holding the reality that, even as we recognize and resist it, we're still inside and unavoidably affected by it. Occasionally (typically late in the program) we hear participants deploying this critical consciousness. In her exit interview, this participant describes a dilemma: She wants to challenge her friends to see new possibilities for liberation from cultural ideals of femininity while recognizing that she herself is not immune to them and might alienate her friends through what looks like competitiveness or shaming.

> *RTI:* Like if [my friends say], "I didn't eat lunch today," I'll be like, "Haha! Eating forever!" Do you know what I mean? [Interviewer: Yeah] Or if they're like, "Oh, I just ran the race three times," I'll be like "Haha! Exercising never!" . . .

Interviewer: Well, that's another form of resistance, right? It's counter-narrative. "I'm gonna represent the opposite so you see the possibility [of a different] choice if you wanted."

RTI: Yeah, definitely. I just wanna always make sure . . . that [I don't make it seem like] I'm immune to it and [they're] not.

She demonstrates a key understanding for an emerging activist: that oppression is a systemic problem rather than an individual failing and that disrupting oppressive narratives/behaviors among peers requires acknowledging that critical awareness does not exempt one from being affected by those same oppressive forces. Her recognition that we have all internalized and compromised over oppression is key to cultivating intersectional solidarity. While in this example, she is promoting liberation interpersonally through her peer friendships, this same critical awareness is also fundamental to collective work for social change (Brown, 2016; DiAngelo, 2018).

CONCLUSIONS AND IMPLICATIONS FOR PRACTICE

Many common tools for critical consciousness raising turn out to be ill suited or inadequate to illuminate issues of privilege for youth who hold structural advantages—the knowledge they need often doesn't yet exist in the room. Social justice educators working with privileged youth must thus take into account the knowledge these youth bring and listen for the "gaps" pointing to what is more challenging for them to grasp. We have also come to believe that while it is necessary to do this work in homogeneous groups of privileged youth, this alone is insufficient. Through exposure and participation in a space in which differently situated individuals engage together in critical analysis across their differential power (Torre, 2005), awareness of one's privilege and the implications for disenfranchised communities becomes that much more apparent. We want to caution practitioners, however, that along with the opportunity for deep learning across differences, bringing privileged youth into these "contact zone" spaces can risk harm to marginalized peers if privileged youth are in the role of savior or spectator. Mitigating that risk requires educators to prepare privileged youth to participate thoughtfully, critically, and responsibly in such spaces.

The process of critical consciousness raising in the RTI is uneven, non-linear, and dynamic, taking shape in moments where individuals identify, perceive, and, in some instances, strategize actions they can take against unjust conditions in their own lives and the lives of youth around them. This is hard work. But adapting Y/CPAR as a methodology provides opportunities, whether in formal or informal educational settings, to engage youth in generative learning with guidance from adults based on issues of immediate relevance to their lives. This approach holds promise for preparing privileged youth to play a key role in pursuing a more socially just and equitable world.

NOTES

1. Both RTI sites were facilitated by teams that included at least one researcher and one youth educator. All facilitators identified as white and female; the majority were also Jewish. The facilitators were queer and straight-identified and ranged in age from 20s through 50s. All of the co-authors of this piece were involved in some aspects of the design and development of the program at each site, though not all worked directly with the participants.

2. Used as a curricular tool, this chart was presented in various stages of completion, often with a few rows left blank for participants to complete together during program sessions.

REFERENCES

Ayers, W., Quinn, T., & Stovall, D. (Eds.). (2009). *Handbook of social justice in education*. Routledge.

Bautista, M., Bertrand, M., Morrell, E., Scorza, D., & Matthews, C. (2013). Participatory action research and city youth: Methodological insights from the Council of Youth Research. *Teachers College Record, 115*(10), 1–23.

Brown, L. M. (2003). *Girlfighting: Betrayal and rejection among girls*. NYU Press.

Brown, L. M. (2016). *Powered by girl: A field guide to supporting youth activists*. Beacon Press.

Cammarota, J., & Fine, M. (Eds.). (2008). *Revolutionizing education: Youth participatory action research in motion*. Routledge.

Case, K. (Ed.). (2013). *Deconstructing privilege: Teaching and learning as allies in the classroom*. Routledge.

Crenshaw, K. (1994). Mapping the margins: Intersectionality, identity politics, and violence against women of color. In M. Fineman and R. Mykitiuk (Eds.), *The public nature of private violence* (pp. 93–118). Routledge.

DiAngelo, R. (2018) *White fragility: Why it's so hard for white people to talk about racism*. Beacon Press.

Finn, J. L. (2016). *Just practice: A social justice approach to social work* (3rd ed.). Oxford University Press.

Freire, P. (1972). *Pedagogy of the oppressed*. Herder & Herder.

Girls Incorporated. (2006). *The supergirl dilemma: Girls grapple with the mounting pressure of expectations (Summary findings)*. Girls Incorporated.

Guishard, M. (2009). The false paths, the endless labors, the turns now this way and now that: Participatory action research, mutual vulnerability, and the politics of inquiry. *Urban Review, 41*(1), 85–105.

Hill-Collins, P. (1990). *Black feminist thought: Knowledge, consciousness, and the politics of empowerment*. Routledge.

Morris, M. (2016). *Pushout: The criminalization of black girls in schools*. The New Press.

Muzak, J. (2011). Women's studies, community service-learning, and the dynamics of privilege. *Atlantis*, *35*(2), 96–106.

Okun, T. (2010). *The emperor has no clothes: Teaching about race and racism to people who don't want to know*. Information Age Publishing.

Ozer, E. (2016). Youth-led participatory action research: Developmental and equity perspectives. In S. Horn, M. D. Ruck, & L. S. Liben (Eds.), *Equity and justice in developmental science: Theoretical and methodological issues* (pp. 189–207). Elsevier.

Payne, M. (2014). *Modern social work theory* (4th ed.). Lyceum Books.

Reason, P., & Bradbury, H. (2006). *Handbook of action research*. Sage Publications.

Richie, B. E. (2012). *Arrested justice*. New York University Press.

Rothery, M. (2008). Critical ecological systems theory. In N. Coady & P. Lehmann (Eds.), *Theoretical perspectives for direct social work practice* (pp. 89–118). Springer.

Russo, A. (2019). *Feminist accountability: Disrupting violence and transforming power*. NYU Press.

Shulman, L. (2016). *The skills of helping individuals, families, groups, and communities* (8th ed.). Cengage Learning.

Simmons, R. (2018). *Enough as she is*. Harper Collins.

Stoudt, B., Fox, M., & Fine, M. (2012). Contesting privilege with critical participatory action research. *Journal of Social Issues*, *68*(1), 178–193.

Stoudt, B. G. (2009). The role of language & discourse in the investigation of privilege: Using participatory action research to discuss theory, develop methodology, & interrupt power. *Urban Review*, *41*(1), 7–28.

Stoudt, B. G., Cahill, C., X, D., Belmonte, K., Djokovic, S., Lopez, J., Matles, A., Pimentel, A., & Torre, M. E. (2016). Participatory action research as youth activism. In J. Conner & S. M. Rosen (Eds.), *Contemporary youth activism: Advancing social justice in the United States* (pp. 327–346). Praeger.

Torre, M., & Fine, M. (2006). Researching and resisting: Democratic policy research by and for youth. In P. Noguera, J. Cammarota, & S. Ginwright (Eds.), *Beyond resistance! Youth activism and community change: New democratic possibilities for practice and policy for America's youth* (pp. 269–285). Routledge.

Torre, M. E. (2005). The alchemy of integrated spaces: Youth participation in research collectives of difference. In L. Weis & M. Fine (Eds.), *Beyond silenced voices: Class, race, and gender in United States schools (rev. ed.)* (pp. 251–266). State University of New York Press.

Wright, D. E. (2015). *Active learning: Social justice education and participatory action research*. Routledge.

CHAPTER 15

"Not Me!"

Anticipating, Preventing, and Working with Pushback to Social Justice Education

Diane Goodman and Rebecca Drago

Social justice education asks students to consider their positions within unequal power hierarchies, examine how oppression operates on individual and structural levels, and develop visions and strategies for greater equity (Adams et al., 2016; Hackman, 2005; Sensoy & DiAngelo, 2012). For privileged students, this can be threatening to their senses of self and worldviews. Because of this, they may respond with the sentiment of "Not me!" (e.g., I'm not a bad person, I'm not prejudiced, my family earned everything we have, and so forth). The better we as educators can understand this resistance, the more effective we can be at minimizing pushback in ways that help students develop a critical consciousness. In this chapter, we draw on research and our experiences[1] to share a range of strategies educators can use to reduce and address resistance with affluent students.[2]

ELITES, SOCIAL JUSTICE EDUCATION, AND RESISTANCE

We define resistance as the unwillingness and/or inability to consider new information or perspectives that challenge one's views regarding social inequities and the refusal to engage in critical self-reflection (Goodman, 2011). Resistance can take many forms, including refusing to listen, rebutting every fact, discounting the experiences of people from marginalized groups, spouting what they think a teacher wants to hear, derailing the conversation, getting overly defensive, and withdrawing. Students may legitimately hold different beliefs or may question and argue, which can result in stimulating conversation that produces new learning for all. However, if a student is unwilling to entertain new thoughts or viewpoints, it veers into resistance.

The challenges of elites' resistance to social justice education are not new (Beeman, 2015; Bohmer & Briggs, 1991; Davis, 1992; Ouyang, 2014; Swalwell, 2013; Watt, 2015) but are critical to understand for several reasons. First and foremost, having a sense of why there is resistance can allow an educator to more effectively prevent and/or work with students' reactions. Additionally, appreciating why students from dominant groups push back may enable educators to feel greater empathy toward them, allowing for more meaningful relationships that, in turn, increase educational effectiveness.

Given dominant students' social locations, they are more likely to experience the world in ways that impede an openness to social justice perspectives. While we are all exposed to messages that perpetuate dominant ideologies maintaining oppression via media, schools, and other institutions,[3] being constructed as elite and living with class privilege can affect attitudes, beliefs, and behaviors in predictable ways (Dittmann, 2016; Piff, 2014). For example, relative to people of lower socioeconomic status, people who are upper class have more essentialist views of social groups and explanations for inequality (Kraus & Keltner, 2013; Kraus et al., 2009). They typically do not subscribe to a contextual explanation for inequalities; justify the social hierarchy and their elevated status as fair (Jost et al., 2004); and are more narcissistic with a greater sense of entitlement (Piff, 2014), less developed empathy, and less compassion leading to less prosocial behavior (Kraus et al., 2010; Oveis et al., 2010; Piff et al., 2010; Stellar et al., 2012). We are not suggesting that all people constructed as elite possess these qualities, nor that they are conscious or immutable—just that there is a relationship between social class and worldview. Knowing this, we can anticipate privileged students' pushback and plan for it.

EDUCATIONAL STRATEGIES TO ADDRESS RESISTANCE

Before discussing five interrelated strategies to address resistance, we want to highlight a few considerations. First, educators need to be intentional about how they build capacity for increasingly more challenging material and experiences. Creating a classroom learning community that is inclusive and respectful is an essential first step—and an ongoing process. Additionally, we try to identify the most effective place to meet students where they are with the goal of helping them handle more complex content that is, perhaps, more threatening to their worldview. Educators need to read the group to decide which approaches will work best in that moment.

Second, it is always challenging to try to meet the varying needs of students in a class, especially when it involves power dynamics associated with different social identities and social locations. To be clear, this is not to say that identity or location always predicts the level of awareness or readiness to deal with specific content, but societal power hierarchies are real. We find it helpful to ask ourselves: Is this activity serving all students? Whose needs are most being met and centered? For example, particular content may not be new to a student of lower wealth, but the way the content is framed might provide new insight. Or that student might benefit from watching how the teacher handles pushback, learning new skills and developing greater trust in the teacher. While in any given moment, all students may not be getting their needs met in the same ways, it is important that we not repeatedly privilege students from dominant groups. Assigning reflection papers where teachers can write comments, intentionally structuring small groups where students can process their learning, and providing choice in projects can help meet students' unique needs. Keeping these considerations in mind, we now outline the five strategies for preventing and minimizing privileged students' resistance.

Build Relationships and Environments That Allow Risk Taking

Elite students may anticipate that social justice education will be threatening or expect to be vilified for their privileged position(s), increasing their defensiveness from the start. Intentionally fostering positive relationships and creating an environment that supports intellectual and emotional risk taking are critical for establishing a supportive learning community.

Build a Safe-Enough Classroom Climate. In any kind of social justice education, creating a space that is "safe enough" is essential. By "safe enough," we mean an environment that strives to be respectful and inclusive, free from psychological and physical harm, where students can ask questions and grapple with new ideas. While we recognize that no one ever feels completely "safe," especially people from marginalized groups, it is important to explore the difference between safety and comfort. All students should feel safe from harassment and verbal violence, but this material often brings us out of our comfort zones—especially for dominant students, who might be exploring these issues for the first time. We can encourage students to explore this discomfort rather than run from it. A "safe-enough" environment can be co-created by establishing group norms, providing clear structures and expectations (to relieve anxiety about what they may be expected to do), and doing group-building activities like ice breakers and regular class meetings (Arnold, 2018; Schneidewind & Davidson, 2014).[4] These can be repeated throughout the class to maintain a positive environment, especially when the content gets more challenging.

Develop Rapport and Trust with Students. When teachers are perceived as compassionate and respectful, students see them as someone they can trust and with whom they can be vulnerable (Goodman, 2015). Chatting with them before and after class, showing interest in who they are, and sharing about your own life are ways to show you are someone who is caring and trustworthy. This rapport building (hopefully) comes naturally for teachers, but it can be more challenging if there is a large disparity between the students' and teachers' socioeconomic statuses. Nonetheless, teachers can find ways to look for shared interests or life experiences.

Model Appropriate Vulnerability. When teachers appropriately self-disclose, particularly about their own struggles with learning about oppression, it can foster connections with students and model openness to personal growth. For example, I (Diane) often share a story that reveals my own internalized privilege. I would go into supermarkets and open bags of snacks and taste them to see if my kids would like them. If I thought they would, I would buy several bags. If not, I would buy the bag I opened. The first time I told this story to a group of students, I watched the faces of some look at me with horror. It was only then that I realized that blithely engaging in this behavior without worrying I would be suspected of stealing was a reflection of my unconscious privilege. When I share this story, it humanizes me, models critical self-reflection, and gives students permission to share their own realizations without worrying that they will be judged.

Heighten Investment

When educators get students to care about the content, it provides a hook for engagement. This is especially important for "elite" students, since, as the research suggests, they may be particularly self-focused and not see the need to examine social inequities or the conditions that create them (Nurenberg, 2020).

Allow Students to Have Input into and Help Design and Lead the Class. Encourage students to contribute to how they will explore different topics. What questions or concerns do they have? How would they like to learn it and demonstrate their learning? How can they take responsibility for sharing their knowledge? Having students bring in real-life examples is another way to solicit their input and make the class feel meaningful. Incorporating current events and pop culture makes topics relevant and reinforces that oppression is not just a thing of the past, but very much a reality today—one they have the ability to critically analyze and potentially change.

Increase Empathy and Humanize the Issues. Facts, theories, and analyses are all essential aspects of social justice education. However, they are less likely to be as compelling as seeing the impact on real people's lives. For example, when doing teen-dating violence prevention workshops in "elite" classrooms outside New York City, I (Rebecca) regularly faced the belief from students that abusive relationships only happened in areas where poor people of color lived. I redesigned the curriculum starting with narratives from "elite" spaces, allowing the conversation to start at a place of greater personal connection to the issue. Readings, personal sharing, panels, media, and guest speakers are all ways to humanize an issue and increase empathy. In addition, critical service learning (Mitchell, 2008; Wang & Rodgers, 2006) can foster the development of empathy and relationships that shift assumptions, increase perspective taking, and motivate action for social justice.

Appeal to Shared Values, Principles, and Goals. Do students believe in equal opportunity, democratic values, or everyone being treated fairly? Do their religious or spiritual beliefs encourage them to relieve suffering or care for poor communities? If so, how does our current system live up to those ideals, and what would need to change in order for it to do so? Although upper-class individuals may have a more utilitarian moral orientation, look for elements of their values or goals to connect to the discussion of social justice and social change. Encourage students to think beyond just a "charity" perspective where the focus is on helping individuals in need to a "social change" perspective that addresses root causes of problems.

Explore Self-Interest in Social Justice and Alternatives to Systems of Domination. Often, social justice is framed as a win-lose situation, in which people with privilege simply lose. Yet many social justice leaders have recognized that people in the role of oppressor are also dehumanized by systems of oppression and that all of our liberation is intertwined. Have students explore both the personal and societal costs of classism, racism, heterosexism, and other forms of inequities (e.g., Luthar, 2013; Luthar & Becker, 2002; O'Neill, 1997). How could they personally benefit from living in a more just world? Stories of people who have used their privilege for social justice can offer positive, alternative role models (e.g., www.responsiblewealth.org or Mogil et al., 1992). On a societal level, provide examples of other ways of structuring societies that are more just and healthier for all and examine how more equitable societies benefit everyone (e.g., Pickett & Wilkinson, 2009; www.equalitytrust.org).

Affirm, Validate, and Convey Respect for Students

Within the context of a supportive educational environment, teachers structure activities so students feel they are valued members of the learning community, thus lowering their defensiveness. In general, if people don't feel seen, heard, and valued, they are less likely to listen to other people or perspectives.

Acknowledge Feelings, Experiences, and Viewpoints. If we want to create environments where students take emotional and intellectual risks, we need to ensure that students know that their feelings and perspectives matter.

Even if teachers do not agree with their views, it's useful to try and understand where students are coming from so we can develop effective responses. One strategy is to reflect back what you are hearing students say and ask more questions about their beliefs or experiences. "How have you come to think that? How might this be perceived differently by someone else?" These kinds of questions, asked in an open, curious, and respectful manner, will often allow the student to understand their own socialization while reinforcing the practice of critically examining internalized beliefs. Teachers need to use their discretion as to whether the student is genuinely open to reflection or just trying to challenge the teacher. A private conversation might be more appropriate. A simple "I appreciate you stretching yourself" or "It's not easy to talk about these issues, and I am always open to discussing more" helps build a meaningful relationship, communicating that you value their presence.

Often students bring up examples of how their lives are not free from challenges (e.g., divorce, physical illness). Acknowledge their pain and convey that just because a person comes from privileged identity groups does not mean they have had a painless life. It just means they don't face barriers *because* of their identity, and their privilege allows them access to resources to address those difficulties in ways that would not be available to others from less privileged groups. The point is not to equate the experiences of personal life challenges with generational, systemic oppression.

Recognize Current Knowledge and Allow Students to Discover Information Themselves. There are a few ways to avoid having students feel that they are being told that everything they believe is wrong or that they are being forced to accept particular viewpoints. Look for ways to recognize and build on what students already know about an issue. It is unlikely that all information students bring to class is accurate and without cultural biases, however. Students and educators can work through the content together, modeling the process of uncovering truths missing from the larger cultural narrative. Additionally, allow students to discover information themselves, tasking them with conducting observations, interviews, and more traditional research to find out how oppression operates. In one class I (Diane) taught, we were discussing sexism and I showed a slightly dated video about violence against women in advertisements. Several male students insisted that such images no longer existed. I asked the class to look at ads to analyze. In the following session, students were amazed that these violent images were still so prevalent and how often they didn't even register in their consciousness.

Discuss Common Reactions and Social Identity Development. Naming and foreshadowing some common responses to learning about social justice (e.g., feeling sad, angry, resentful, defensive, guilty, excited, confused, and so forth) can normalize students' feelings while staying engaged with the learning process. Consider asking students (often anonymously) at the beginning of a unit what their hopes and concerns are for this material. Hearing these fears named can validate their struggle with the content and allows teachers to address their concerns. Teachers can encourage students to identify up-front how they react when they feel defensive and help them develop tools to manage these feelings through mindfulness practices and self-reflection exercises. It can also be useful to introduce students to social identity development theories to have a sense of how their experience might change them (e.g., Hardiman & Jackson, 1997; Helms, 2020). These theories hold a positive vision for engaging in social justice education, even when it feels difficult emotionally and intellectually.

Ground the Personal in a Structural Analysis

"Elite" students are often challenged by thinking systemically. A systemic analysis allows students to see the historical legacies that shape our realities today, shift away from blaming the victim or assuming inherent superiority/inferiority, and notice patterns in what may appear to be isolated events.

Differentiate Between Personal and Social Identities. When asked to name identities that are important to who they are, "elite" students tend to name *personal* identities they have, for the most part, chosen for themselves (e.g., soccer player, artist) rather than *social* identities (e.g., white, straight, documented)—categories that society has constructed that affect people's access to resources and power. Students with marginalized identities, on the other hand, are more likely to name social identities first. It can be helpful to explore the difference between these identities while recognizing the significance of both. For example, Rebecca describes herself as a white, queer woman (social identities) who loves music and drinking coffee (personal identities). Acknowledging that we are all a combination of social and personal identities and exploring why we are more aware of some than others can be a useful way to mitigate resistance.

Expand Analysis Beyond Individual Effort and Qualities. Critiques of our current systems and social hierarchies can be heard as attacks against oneself or one's family and as discrediting hard work, talent, or smarts. When we encounter this from a student, we will often first recognize the personal characteristics and efforts that contributed to their success. Once the student has felt acknowledged, we can place these achievements in a larger social context, considering the ways there was "wind at your back" (Kimmel, 2003) (e.g., housing and banking policies that allowed their family to accrue wealth, not being targeted and incarcerated for possessing drugs, and so forth). For example, during one class, a middle-class, white male student was objecting to the idea that he got any benefits from his social identities and insisted that he worked hard for everything he had. After acknowledging his efforts, I (Diane) asked him and the other students to identify some of the factors that worked to his benefit, helping him achieve what he had. The class filled the board with examples of advantages (i.e., being a U.S. citizen, speaking English, having family he would utilize for work connections, being able-bodied, and so forth). I then asked what "headwinds" other people with his same personal qualities (smart and hard-working) might face who don't have these advantages, and we filled the board again. This activity helped students examine how our individual lives are shaped by larger systemic forces and how people with privilege often reap the rewards of their personal efforts, while people from marginalized groups may not. This activity could also be depersonalized, asking students to do this analysis with two hypothetical individuals.

Shift the Conversation Away from Guilt and Shame. Providing a structural and historical analysis of oppression helps students see that no individual (including themselves) is responsible for entire systems of inequality. Noting that the system is designed to keep itself invisible is important. It's also important to note that moving through guilt should not absolve students of their responsibility for enacting change, but serves the important purpose of shifting away from feelings that shut down thinking and acting. Instead, help students consider how they can use their privilege in the service of social justice and how to work in solidarity with people from marginalized groups to change the things they think are unfair. Examples of people with privileges who are working for social justice help students envision addressing issues without being mired in guilt.

Use Accessible Resources and Activities

As with any good educational practice, teachers should think about scaffolding to move toward more complex and challenging content and experiences.

Consider the Messenger. We are often most influenced by someone who seems like us (Farmer et al., 2013). Hearing about a social justice issue from someone students can easily relate to (e.g., a school alum, someone with a similar class background) might initially be a good choice—although teachers must at some point shift to centering the voices of people from the oppressed group. The goal is not to speak for or overshadow people from oppressed groups, but to create an openness to hear directly from those most affected by oppression. Moreover, when someone with a privileged identity speaks about a societal inequity, it reduces the burden on people with the marginalized identity and communicates to "elite" youth that these issues are important enough to care about and work on—even if not directly targeted with that form of oppression.

Utilize Less Direct Approaches. Sometimes when students' attitudes and beliefs are directly challenged, they are more likely to push back. We can create some distance for students to examine issues in ways that feel less personal and threatening. One way is through case studies or analogies. By first talking about a hypothetical situation, students can explore topics without feeling like they are being personally implicated. Simulations and experiential activities can be powerful because students are having actual experiences, not just reading or talking about an issue. In processing the case studies or other experiential activities, students can make connections to their own lives or to the social issue, allowing for further self-reflection and analysis.

CONCLUSION

Understanding "elite" students' worldviews, senses of self, and the larger sociopolitical contexts that shape them can aid educators in addressing social justice issues. Teachers can better anticipate and plan for dealing with resistance—that sense of "not me." When teachers support students in exploring content that challenges how they see themselves, others, and the world, they better engage them in social justice education and the process of social change.

NOTES

1. Diane is an upper-middle-class white woman who has over three decades' experience educating about social justice issues with elite students, while Rebecca is a middle/upper-middle-class white woman engaged in social justice education as an administrator at an elite independent school outside New York City.

2. We focus on students with class privilege while acknowledging the relationship between affluence and whiteness (Asante-Muhammad et al., 2017). Nevertheless, we do not assume that all elite students are white.

3. See Goodman (2011) for elaboration of these and other factors.

4. See www.icebreakers.ws/classroom-icebreakers for specific ideas.

REFERENCES

Adams, M., Bell, L. A., Goodman, D., & Joshi, K. (2016). *Teaching for diversity and social justice*. Routledge.

Arnold, S. (2018). 12 ways to create a safe and effective space for student learning. https://braveintheattempt.com/2018/02/17/12-ways-to-create-a-safe-and-effective-space-for-student-learning/

Asante-Muhammad, D., Collins, C., Hoxie, J., Nieves, E. (2017). The road to zero wealth: How the racial wealth divide is hollowing out America's middle class. *Institute for Policy Studies & Prosperity Now.* https://ips-dc.org/report-the-road-to -zero-wealth/

Beeman, A. (2015). Teaching to convince, teaching to empower: Reflections on student resistance and self-defeat at predominately white vs. racially diverse campuses. *Understanding and Dismantling Privilege, 5*(1), 13–30.

Bohmer, S., & Briggs, J. L. (1991). Teaching privileged students about gender, race, and class oppression. *Teaching Sociology, 19*(2), 154–163.

Davis, N. J. (1992). Teaching about inequality: Student resistance, paralysis, and rage. *Teaching Sociology, 20*(3), 232–238.

Dittmann, A. (2016). Understanding social class as culture. *The Psych Report.* http:// thepsychreport.com/science/understanding-social-class-as-culture/

Farmer, H., McKay, R., & Tsakiris, M. (2013). Trust in me: Trustworthy others are seen as more physically similar to the self. *Psychological Science, 25*(1), 290–292.

Goodman, D. (2011). *Promoting diversity and social justice: Educating people from privileged groups.* Routledge.

Goodman, D. (2015). Can you love them enough to help them learn? Reflections of a social justice educator on addressing resistance from white students to anti-racism education. *Understanding and Dismantling Privilege, 5*(1), 62–73.

Hackman, H. (2005). Five essential components for social justice education. *Equity & Excellence in Education, 38*(2), 103–109.

Hardiman, R., & Jackson, B. (1997). Conceptual foundations for social justice courses. In M. Adams, L. A. Bell, & P. Griffin (Eds.), *Teaching for diversity and social justice* (pp. 16–29). Routledge.

Helms, J. (2020). *A race is a nice thing to have: A guide to being a white person or understanding the white persons in your life* (3rd ed.). Cognella.

Jost, J. T., Banaji, M. R., & Nosek, B. A. (2004). A decade of system justification theory: Accumulated evidence of conscious and unconscious bolstering of the status quo. *Political Psychology, 25*(6), 881–919.

Kimmel, M. (2003). Toward a pedagogy of the oppressor. In M. Kimmel, and A. Ferber (Eds.), *Privilege: A reader* (1–12). Westview Press.

Kraus, M. W., Côté, S., & Keltner, D. (2010). Social class, contextualism, and empathic accuracy. *Psychological Sciences, 21*(11), 1716–1723.

Kraus, M. W., & Keltner, D. (2013). Social class rank, essentialism, and punitive judgment. *Journal of Personality and Social Psychology, 105*(2), 247.

Kraus, M. W., Piff, P. K., & Keltner, D. (2009). Social class, sense of control, and social explanation. *Journal of Personality and Social Psychology, 97*(6), 992–1004.

Luthar, S. (2013, November 5). The problem with rich kids. *Psychology Today, 87,* 62–69.

Luthar, S., & Becker, B. (2002). Privileged but pressured? A study of affluent youth. *Child Development, 73*(5), 1593–1610.

Mitchell, T. D. (2008). Traditional vs. critical service-learning: Engaging the literature to differentiate two models. *Michigan Journal of Community Service Learning, 14*(2), 50–65.

Mogil, C., Slepian, A., & Woodrow, P. (1992). *We gave away a fortune: Stories of people who have devoted themselves and their wealth to peace, justice and a healthy environment.* New Society Publishers.

Nurenberg, D. (2020). *What does injustice have to do with me? Engaging white privileged students with social justice.* Rowman & Littlefield.

O'Neill, J. H. (1997). *The golden ghetto: The psychology of affluence.* Hazelden Press.

Ouyang, H. (2014). Transforming resistance: Strategies for teaching race in the ethnic American literature classroom. *Understanding and Dismantling Privilege, 4*(2), 204–219.

Oveis, C., Horberg, E. J., & Keltner, D. (2010). Compassion, pride, and social intuitions of self-other similarity. *Journal of Personality and Social Psychology, 98,* 618–630.

Pickett, K., & Wilkinson, R. (2009). *The spirit level: Why greater equality makes societies stronger.* Bloomsburg Press.

Piff, P. K. (2014). Wealth and the inflated self: Class, entitlement, and narcissism. *Personality and Social Psychology Bulletin, 40*(1), 34–43.

Piff, P. K., Côté, S., Cheng, B. H., & Keltner, D. (2010). Having less, giving more: The influence of social class on prosocial behavior. *Journal of Personality and Social Psychology, 99*(5), 771–784.

Schneidewind, N., & Davidson, E. (2014). *Open minds to equality: A sourcebook of learning activities to affirm diversity and promote equity* (4th ed.). Rethinking Schools.

Sensoy, O., & DiAngelo, R. (2012). *Is everyone really equal?: An introduction to key concepts in social justice education.* Teachers College Press.

Stellar, J. E., Manzo, V. M., Kraus, M. W., & Keltner, D. (2012). Class and compassion: Socioeconomic factors predict responses to suffering. *Emotion, 12*(3), 449–459.

Swalwell, K. (2013). *Educating activist allies: Social justice pedagogy with the suburban and urban elite.* Routledge.

Wang, Y., & Rodgers, R. (2006). Impact of service-learning and social justice education on college students' cognitive development. *NASPA Journal, 43*(2), 316–337.

Watt, S. (2015). Privileged Identity Exploration (PIE) model revisited: Strengthening skills for engaging difference. In S. Watt (Ed.), *Designing transformational multicultural initiatives* (pp. 40–61). Stylus.

Part IV

CONVERSATIONS WITH COLLEAGUES

CHAPTER 16

Out of This Chaos, Beauty Comes

Democratic Schooling in a Progressive Independent Middle School

Allen Cross

In the service of learning, we practice responsive and progressive education and strive for equity. In service of the whole person, we embrace unique gifts, experiences, and relationships. In the service of social justice, we foster responsibility, advocacy, and compassion. In the service of democracy, we nurture individual and collective growth. In the service of the world, we cultivate curiosity, creativity, and innovation.

—Mission Statement, Wingra School, Madison, WI

"This is what democracy looks like!" was the chant that still occasionally rings in my ears from the protests against union-busting legislation in Madison, Wisconsin, in 2011. Sometimes, when I have recess duty, I honk out the rhythm of it on a bike horn to indicate when it is time to go in. While shouting the slogan seemed powerful and meaningful in that protest context, it is overly simplified and pretty ambiguous in its general meaning. What does democracy look like in the context of a learning environment like that of Wingra School, an independent school founded nearly 50 years ago for children ages 5 to 15? Even though we describe Wingra School as democratic and progressive, our student body is made up of predominantly white students with most of the few enrolled Black and Brown kids adopted by white parents. While one may call this community "elite," all of the students are different in personality and have their own histories—some very complex. Of course, all are deserving of our full attention and care. Unfortunately, our teaching staff is also predominantly white. How does this group of teachers educate this group of young adolescents to be critical of their privilege and to become co-conspirators with those less privileged to affect positive change in our democracy? How can our private institution be one that serves the public good?

My efforts toward answering these questions and engaging in social justice education are influenced by interrogating my identity as a middle-class, white, male, cisgendered, heterosexual, atheist, feminist; being an active and informed citizen involved in the broader community; and honing my craft as a democratic progressive educator for 11- to 15-year-olds. Working in a private progressive school like Wingra affords me and my teaching partners the advantage and responsibility of co-creating a meaningful and responsive curriculum that serves the students' needs and challenges in an open and democratic environment free from the mandates of top-down policymakers. The school is guided by the same principles of our country's founding: *popular sovereignty, equality, liberty/freedom, individual rights, representation, pursuit of happiness,* and *checks and balances.* Each of these concepts has either been the primary topic or highlighted within a unit of study. What is most important to us, however, is how *living* these concepts daily makes for a rich and vibrant social and academic environment—one that demonstrates connectedness with each other and the Earth. Living and learning in a democracy like this can be time-consuming, complex, and sometimes messy, but it is always beautiful and important.

DEMOCRACY IN OUR CLASSROOMS

An important part of democracy in our classrooms is *deciding how to decide*. There needs to be time and a flexible schedule for coming to consensus about goals, identifying and interpreting the problem at hand, agreeing on fair strategies for decisionmaking, and discussing possible ways to move forward. Our students are presented with a number of collaborative tasks at the outset of every year to establish their version of community and democracy. One of the first is to create plans for the layout of the room. They facilitate a process for deciding who will fairly get what desk, finding just methods for working out conflicts that may arise. Returning students have experienced these decisionmaking processes inherent in popular sovereignty before, and a number of them have become skilled facilitators, though we step in if it advantages certain individuals or groups. Even with a process for creating a fair way to select desks, justifications for privilege still arise. Older students might argue that seniority is a good reason for them to get what they want or that a former student has "willed" the desk to them. Some surreptitiously resort to bartering or buying what they want. In a small way, we connect this experience when we discuss issues of structural or institutional advantage in the broader community.

In terms of power and authority in school, we function in a very informal manner at Wingra. Vital to teaching democratically is getting to know the students well and for them to get to know us. Working with mixed-aged classrooms helps in terms of understanding the range and variations in people regardless of age. Our all-school activities and monthly community circle meetings add to the understanding of equality. We make use of dialogue journals to aid in getting to know the students and for them to get to know us via informal writing. We encourage students to challenge decisions, policies, and behaviors in constructive ways. We regularly encourage students to keep an open mind, maintain a big heart, be forgiving, and receptive to others' honest criticisms. We create a learning space that is safe for making mistakes so that all members of our learning community can be honest about their strengths and challenges. Students tell us that they think we know them well and that we listen to them. They view teachers as *facilitators* of their learning. I believe this leads us to have a sensitivity to social injustices and a disposition to want to take action for positive change.

We are not an institution for the sole purpose of guaranteeing advanced educational opportunities or preparing students for the capitalist economy, but more an institution for living a fulfilling life centered in being an active participant in our larger democracy. Our theme-based integrated curriculum allows room for individual choice and negotiation with an emphasis on learning how to participate positively in any group or community of which students are a part. The tension between individual rights and freedoms, and the challenges of helping make sense of the concepts of *fairness* and *the common good*, is a constant one working with 11- to 15-year-olds. We often make use of centers, a form of structured choice where students decide in what mode they will learn the required content or skill. The weekly schedule includes work times where students decide what learning task they will engage in, with whom, and where they would like to work. Students tell us where they are going and don't ask permission—in general they take more charge of their lives and learning. Students are encouraged to initiate and run projects, clubs, and activities as part of their schooling.

One of the features in our program that students cite as vital to our democratic functioning is having opportunities to practice speaking their minds in discussions on topics of their choosing—a free exchange of ideas. Topics for discussion are signed up on the open agenda sheet, and students usually facilitate these discussions or problem-solving sessions. Teachers need to wait to be called on like the rest of the class. Recently, some of the older students expressed concern that the younger students were not speaking up freely during discussion times, so they signed up to address the issue with the whole class. The next day, after one of the older students introduced the topic, a younger classmate volunteered to facilitate the discussion. While there was some hesitation in offering thoughts on the topic, it turned out that many of the younger students felt intimidated by the older students. With more sensitivity and self-awareness, things improved. We also have had many lively and informative discussions, including on cultural appropriation, the use of personal electronic devices, "guys" and "bro" as a referent for any gender, meme culture, national defense spending, and "VSCO girls."

RESOURCES FOR DEMOCRATIC EDUCATION

Since we are co-creators of the curriculum, each of the teaching staff needs to be engaged in our larger democracy and knowledgeable about the world and willing to be honest about mistakes, weaknesses, and challenges—to be well-informed but also rather egoless. No one teacher can serve the purposes of reading the world and reading the students. Our combined interests, skills, strengths, and areas of knowledge are vital to creating a rich, responsive, and meaningful integrated curriculum. Since we do not have the wide range of Madison's voices present on a daily basis (or the world's, past and present), we need to represent them in some way. We make use of critical pedagogy guided by resources developed by *Rethinking Schools*, *Teaching Tolerance*, *Teaching for Black Lives*, *The 1619 Project*, Wisconsin First Nations, PBS Wisconsin, the University of Wisconsin School of Education, and Educators for Social Responsibility. We also draw from local media, including our community-sponsored radio station WORT; publications like *Green Card Youth Voices: Immigration Stories from Madison and Milwaukee*; and periodicals like *UMOJA*, *Hues*, *Isthmus*, and *The Capital Times*.

The arts and literature are marvelous ways to bring in underrepresented perspectives and voices. Our knowledgeable librarian and the Cooperative Children's Book Center help us find quality literature that challenges dominant narratives to help students engage with stories as windows and mirrors (Sims Bishop, 1990). For example, we play music from around the world and protest music in the mornings during our 15-minute morning adjustment time. We study the painter Jacob Lawrence's *Migration Series*, learn about Zora Neale Hurston and other artists of the Harlem Renaissance, learn about Navajo country music, and watch the hip-hop artist Supaman. We make use of the story of Billie Holiday's recording of *Strange Fruit*, compare Big Mama Thornton's version of *Hound Dog* with Elvis Presley's later version, discuss Lynyrd Skynyrd's *Sweet Home Alabama* as a racist response to Neil Young's *Southern Man* and *Alabama*, and learn about Marion Anderson's *Concert that Shook the Establishment* (with a 10-year-old Martin Luther King in the audience). We juxtaposed Gill Scott-Heron's *Whitey on the Moon* with information celebrating the 50th anniversary of the moon landing. I think my interest in free jazz, experimental, and world music has aided with this. I have also conducted research around the sonic culture of the classroom that has helped me take up less air space and better understand what we sometimes dismiss as noise.

CRITICAL SELF-REFLECTION

Does our students' education politicize them in a way that inspires them to action, or does their understanding of democratic functioning further bolster their privilege? I can't say for sure, but I do know that many of our former students enter fields that are active in working toward social justice, including law, the arts, journalism, politics, and teacher education. As individual educators, and as an institution, we need to continue to be self-critical and receptive to others' criticism of us—comfortable with discomfort. We have struggled over many years to develop and sustain strong meaningful partnerships with local organizations. While our older students have identified issues on which they would like to take action (climate change, restorative justice, tiny house movement, the homeless, LGBTQIA issues, sustainable food production /food deserts), we also have struggled to develop a meaningful, sustainable service-learning program. It is important that we make sure that students understand that while none of them are guilty of the wrongs in the world, they can be agents of change.

The question of whether (and how) Wingra School—and progressive education, for that matter—is racist has given us pause and forced a closer examination. Even with the COVID crisis consuming much of our energies with trying to adapt to distance learning, we continue to address social justice and white privilege. Actually, much thought went into considering those issues in the way we went about reopening in the fall. It feels to me like we, as an institution, are taking more seriously the often uncomfortable but essential work to directly address the lack of diversity in the student body and teaching staff. Much speculation has been made about why we have remained such a white institution, even though we say we are advocates for social justice and a strong democracy. Maybe it has to do with never having a critical number of people of color, both on staff and in the student body, so as to be safe or inviting to others? Maybe the informality here doesn't sit well with some people? Maybe the tuition is too high? We know that democratic and/or progressive schooling has been successful in other places with a wide range of populations (e.g., Meier, 2002). That said, during my time here, there have been periodic efforts to increase diversity in our school community—efforts led primarily by white members of the community. This time, however, the white people are trying to step out of the way and people of color are taking the lead. This time, we seem more committed to *real* change across all aspects of our school functioning.

Thanks to the efforts of our outgoing board of trustees president, 3 of the 12 board members are now people of color, including the incoming president. With the aim of truly being able to call Wingra School an antiracist institution, the board of trustees is more public in its commitment to developing a long-term plan for achieving this goal with specific actions to address ongoing issues.[1] On a classroom level, we are examining educational catchphrases we have used to guide and describe our teaching methods that so often center whiteness: "child-centeredness," "individualized learning," "holistic education," "progressive," and "democratic pedagogies." Abolitionist education (Love, 2019), Black Lives Matter curriculum, hip-hop pedagogy (Akom, 2009), and other nonwhite-centered forms of education are being implemented within a grounding in the principles of the democratic project. It has also been suggested that we end our affiliation with the Independent Schools Association of Central States (ISACS) and replace their accreditation process with one that is more local and community-based, composed of critical friends from organizations within our community that we develop mutually beneficial bonds with to help us toward our goals. This will take a concerted amount of time and energy but is worth it.

To read an interview with Allen Cross and learn more about other contributors to this volume, visit www.onewaytomakechange.org.

ACKNOWLEDGMENTS

I want to thank the Wingra students, parents, and staff of color who have helped the white members of the staff look at ourselves more closely and tolerated, up to this point, our slow processes of change—especially Angela Baker, Elizabeth Garcia, Daniel Torres-Rangel, Chhoeub Chaam, and Eddie Smith. Thank you to Gabby Arca for her suggestions on this piece. Lastly, I want to thank Kathy Oker, my teaching partner, who is an incredible inspiration. She is vigilant in questioning and critiquing schooling, society, and herself in healthy and hopeful ways. She is a mighty advocate for young adolescents and our democratic way of schooling and the larger democratic project of our nation.

NOTE

1. For an overview of the actions the board of trustees has committed to taking in support of Black Lives Matter, see https://www.wingraschool.org/aboutus/#board

REFERENCES

Akom, A. A. (2009). Critical hip hop pedagogy as a form of liberatory praxis. *Equity & Excellence in Education, 42*(1), 52–66.

Love, B. L. (2019). *We want to do more than survive: Abolitionist teaching and the pursuit of educational freedom.* Beacon Press.

Meier, D. (2002). *The power of their ideas: Lessons for America from a small school in Harlem.* Beacon Press.

Sims Bishop, R. (1990). Mirrors, windows, and sliding glass doors. *Perspectives, 1*(3), ix–xi.

CHAPTER 17

We Are Afraid They Won't Feel Bad

Using Simulations to Teach for Social Justice at the Elementary Level

Gabby Arca and Nina Sethi

We are halfway through our presentation at a conference. Participants are buzzing about the simulation they just experienced and asking procedural questions, sharing their responses and reactions. Then the inevitable happens. Someone asks, "How do you handle your students feeling guilt or shame? I don't want to make my students feel bad." We freeze. We look at each other. Our response? "We're afraid they *won't* feel bad."

We need our students to feel *something* because students will not truly understand or even engage with the dynamics at play unless they have an emotional involvement—including discomfort. In fact, discomfort is often where learning begins. It is good for our students to wrestle with it, especially those who live with great privilege. Beyond that, our simulations are never about assigning *individual* blame. They are about recognizing and experiencing (briefly, temporarily, and minutely) the systemic effects of privilege. Without that realization, students will be allowed to think that oppression is disconnected from them or someone else's problem.

The simulation in question is our pom-pom activity. We created it to attempt to simulate the dynamics of cyclical wealth and power and disrupt students' belief that poor people just need to work harder in order to no longer be poor. As co-teachers at a progressive private school in Washington, DC, we tried to teach with a social justice lens in all of our curriculum. This means we continually questioned whose voice is/is not heard or who is advantaged/disadvantaged by institutions and systems. This means that when we taught economics, we explicitly addressed cyclical poverty, wealth, and oppression and investigated who is (and who is not) valued in economic systems. The simulation we created was one of the most dynamic learning experiences we have ever had with 5th-graders. Before we explain it, however, a few words of caution.

First, while we love when students have fun, that was not the intention of this activity. In fact, many of our students did not find this experience "fun," instead feeling a mixture of anger, guilt, and shame. Second, this simulation was woven within an explicit instructional framework and should not be taught in a "constructivist" way. Cyclical poverty is a *real* concept that we can define—we do not want students to leave this experience with fuzzy understandings of that. We did not just toss the simulation into our day, but planned meticulously for this experience with explicit pre- and post-reflections. Lastly, students' misconceptions and questions should never be left floating in the air after this simulation, as they need multiple ways throughout the curriculum to think through their experience, make connections, and receive feedback. Without these caveats, we fear (and know) that the simulation and others like it will be used as an "exciting" experience that students are left to sort out by themselves. This explicit instruction also helps make the information accessible for all of our students.

THE SIMULATION

There are three rounds to the pom-pom simulation. Round 1 consists of collecting as many differently sized and colored pom-poms as they can in two minutes. Pom-poms, of course, represent wealth and power. There is a catch, however. Students receive slips of paper with "assignments" on them with instructions for how they can gather pom-poms (e.g., you can use both of your hands, but you may not move your feet at all). Only two people are allowed to use their hands and move around as they typically would. We also caution all students that if you touch or bump another body, you lose pom-poms. This is a safety requirement but also makes it harder for those already limited by their instructions.

After setting up the simulation and answering questions, we start a timer and tell them to go. Once pom-pom collection is over, we put students into three groups based on the number of pom-poms they collected: Group 1 includes a few students (out of 26 total) who have "great wealth and power," Group 2 has another few students who have "some wealth and power," and Group 3 is everyone else with "little wealth and power." For debriefing, we ask students to move to different areas of the room for each group to discuss Round 1. Group 1 moves to the biggest, most comfortable area. Group 2 moves to a smaller but still comfortable area. Group 3 is corralled into an uncomfortable corner of the room. Students are typically very engaged in the debrief, animatedly talking about how the process was "not fair" and how they deserved another chance. Group 3 students often loudly complain about the instructions they had, saying things like, "I could only use my two pointer fingers behind my back!" or "This is not fair—why are we all smushed back here?" As they air their grievances, we say, "We hear you complaining that Round 1 was not fair, so we will give you another chance in Round 2."

Round 2 consists of making "baskets" of crumpled up balls of paper, with each group using different color paper. We tell the third group with little wealth and power that they will have an advantage in the next round due to their large number of members. Every time one member of the group makes a "basket," each member of the group will earn another pom-pom. There are cheers when this is announced, but the celebration is short lived as we show each group where they have to stand to shoot. Group 1 is in front and Group 2 is behind them, and Group 3 is in the back of the room. Naturally, Group 1 makes many baskets, while Group 2 and 3 rarely make any. During this round, we witness some very creative teamwork, as well as enterprising blocking tactics. After Round 2 ends, we tend to hear more frustration about how "unfair" the whole situation was and many requests for a new "fair" round. "We couldn't even *see* the baskets. And Group 1 blocked our shots! They already have so many pom-poms." "It was basically impossible. I don't even know why we tried."

We move onto Round 3 during which each group gets to decide what they think is a "fair" system to distribute *all* of the pom-poms. We give them five minutes to discuss with their group and come up with a system they support. Each group must choose a spokesperson to present their plan to the class, with one minute to make a pitch for their group's plan. What students do not know until voting happens is that voting is weighted (Group 1 members get five votes each, Group 2 gets two each, and Group 3 gets a half-vote each) to represent the influence that wealth confers. When students see the unequal voting power, Group 3 is livid. They planned on winning the vote by virtue of their large number of people. Group 1 is pleased, as they planned on retaining their "wealth and power" and now have the votes to do so. When we voted, Group 1's proposal got the most votes after calculating the weighting. The other students were *frustrated*. Group 1 was pleased— they had started out trying to think of a "fair" system, but soon realized "it doesn't say it has to be fair." They also were influenced by two members who repeatedly said, "Stay wealthy! We should keep our power!"

THE DEBRIEF

At this point, we stopped the simulation for a debrief. First, we asked students to verbally share their reactions and feelings, limiting them to one comment per person and giving them time to reflect.

> When I first saw the amounts each group got, it made me feel like the people in the third group were being treated like they aren't humans . . . ½ a vote. ½ human! Half not real. Not seen. When the people with more wealth get so many more votes, it feels like just because they have more, they also should get more of everything always. We are the people working the hardest, but we can't get the things they have that we want and need. (Student from Group 3)

> I do agree with [student's name] that it wasn't fair. But our group was try-
> ing to make it so that we would still be at the top of the ladder, so it wouldn't be
> as fair—you had to be strategic and life isn't always fair. (Student from Group 1)

Once everyone shared, we reminded students that this was a simulation
and therefore *not* the same as actually experiencing poverty, discrimination,
and so forth. We *do not* suddenly understand how others in these situations
feel because we did an activity about pom-poms. This reminder is essential
to avoid trivializing or minimizing oppression or injustice, as most people
(whether they are 5th-graders or adults) find having perspective difficult
when they are frustrated. After this, we asked them to make connections to
real life—both in the debrief discussion and later as a homework reflection.[1]
A sample of their responses is included here:

> [T]hough the law says everyone can vote, there are examples in history when
> our voting wasn't fair. Even now, some people can't vote because they don't
> have access to it.
>
> I think that was an accurate representation of those with more or less
> power because there are less super wealthy people then super unwealthy people
> but if someone super wealthy says they are doing something it might sway other
> people to do the same. I think an example is endorsements during the election.
>
> I used to think that if you work hard you can get wealth but now, I think
> there is more to it. I think this because If you are born without wealth you will
> have a disadvantage and you will be stuck behind someone who started with a
> lot of resources and wealth.

We wrote this simulation as an antidote to the idea that people experiencing poverty should just "work hard" and in hopes of simulating the
experiences and effects of privilege (or not having privilege), but students
have made connections to ableism, racism, sexism, classism, politics, and
more in their written reflections.

CONSIDERATIONS

For teachers considering using simulations like this as a strategy for social
justice education in "elite" settings, we recommend the following essential
elements:

- Simulations should be long enough for students to feel emotions/
  responses genuinely (e.g., guilty for watching friends in an "unfair"
  situation or frustrated and ready to give up). Even after an hour,
  students will report that a simulation was "endless," "unbearable,"
  and "went on forever."

- Simulations must have an explicit, real-world analog.[2] Our pom-pom simulation occurs in the midst of our economics unit, after we teach students about the distribution of wealth in the United States. They often think of other applications on their own, especially as we continue to learn more economic systems.
- Try to have multiple rounds so that students can feel and observe the cyclical, repetitive, and defeating nature of the experience. If it is too short, it will just be a funny or odd activity and easily shrugged off. Multiple rounds also give students the possibility of redemption or "fresh start," so they often react with frustration when they thought it was finally going to be fair but is the same dynamics all over again.
- Debrief is key. Start with feelings and observations, move to reflection and connections, and end with identifying how your thinking has changed and next steps. Without a debrief, the students simply played a game or did an activity, so the application must be explicit!
- We have students share out orally immediately after the simulation about how they felt and what choices they made. Every student is given a chance to speak. Students are allowed to pass, and we encourage them to add to the discussion instead of repeating. We have them journal immediately after this share to get out their thoughts and reactions and complete a question sheet for homework. The sharing out, discussing, and journaling take at least 30 minutes, and we usually have to cut the discussion short (or at least pause it until the next class).
- Make sure to add a disclaimer that it is a simulation that only lasted an hour or so and is NOT the same as the actual experience. If this is not our lived reality, we cannot fully understand how others who *are* actually in the situation feel.

Simulations are critical teaching tools to make learning relevant, personal, tangible, and felt. We become numb to stories of injustice or misfortune that happen to others and report sadness or outrage, but soon move on. When we experience an injustice, even in small ways, those emotions stay with us far longer. When students have an experience like this, they use these feelings as prior knowledge that can be activated when confronted with new vocabulary and complex content. In addition, everyone (including children) already has preconceived ideas: People are poor because they are lazy, racism was "fixed" by Martin Luther King, only bad people believe stereotypes, and so forth. Once we have established these "facts," it is very hard to change our minds about things we already "know." Experiencing something that disproves our preconceived notions is key because it forces us to acknowledge what we think we know *and* it shows how it is not necessarily true. It also demonstrates to our students the ways in which they can grapple with some of the more unequal or unjust aspects of our society.

Sometimes, understanding concepts in our world like this might feel bad—and we won't avoid that. Concepts like oppression and cyclical wealth *are* painful. It *does* feel bad. But this is teaching, and this is learning. And one thing the students consistently see in this experience is that their learning is vast and connected to the actual world around them—and that their learning and voices matter.

To read an interview with Gabby Arca and Nina Sethi and to learn more about other contributors to this volume, visit www.onewaytomakechange .org.

NOTES

1. The discussion prompts included the following questions: Why were some people given more votes than others? Was this an accurate representation of those with more or less power in the world? What examples can you think of where this might play out in the world? The homework was to respond to the following prompt: "I used to think ___, but now I think ___."

2. Editors' note: This point Gabby and Nina make about analogs with real-world applications is crucial. We do not recommend engaging students in simulations that directly replicate injustice (e.g., holding a mock slave auction). Also, be careful never to assign students roles because of their real-world identities so as not to retraumatize or tokenize them. See Stephanie Jones's (2020) work on curriculum violence for more on this.

REFERENCE

Jones, S. (2020). Ending curriculum violence. *Teaching Tolerance, 64.* https://www .tolerance.org/magazine/spring-2020/ending-curriculum-violence

CHAPTER 18

Harnessing the Curiosity of Rich People's Children

International Travel as a Tool of Anti-Oppressive Education

Alethea Tyner Paradis

I was an unlikely founder for a travel company servicing privileged American teenagers. I had no formal business education background. I grew up in 1970s post–Vietnam War–era poverty, the eldest daughter of a disabled, Caribbean immigrant who became stigmatized as a "welfare mom" following divorce. We were occasionally homeless, living out of our Volkswagen van. I learned a great deal about Reaganomics personal sufficiency myths and the importance of ethical living to survive misfortune. Smart, determined, and self-supporting, I excelled through college and law school, pivoted from a legal aid career, and fell in love with teaching teens at an exclusive private high school. As a mixed-race person "passing for white," I managed to imbue my courses with social justice themes that, a supportive celebrity dad once told me, "You can get away with teaching this 'radical stuff' because you don't look Black."

After 15 years as an inspirational history teacher in one of California's richest communities, I grew to understand the psychological aspirations of wealthy parents. Sending their kids on expensive, short-term, faculty-led educational trips would "open their minds," "show them how good they have it," and also "be great for college apps." As their teacher, my motivations were loftier: I wanted these privileged youth—future senators, C-level executives, investors, inheritors of fortune—to make a soulful connection to people living with the legacy of poverty and conflict. I wanted this radical empathy to inform their professional and financial decisions as influential adults. Firsthand experiences, adventuring with heart, heightened consciousness of the global "Other" acquired by an adolescent—these activities, I am still convinced, concretize radical empathy and can help save the world from industrialized violence.

SOCIALLY CONSCIOUS TRAVEL

I started an educational travel company, Peace Works Travel (peacework-stravel.com) to provide social justice–minded, experiential education through ethical adventure. Not merely a "trip," the program included remote predeparture learning to ensure students know the basic significant relevancies of our destinations. Our *People's History of the United States,* Howard Zinn–style curriculum continues throughout the travel experience and is designed to balance the standard inquiry of iconic places, elevating the voices often left out of the traditional narrative. Vietnam, Cambodia, Laos, Cuba, Rwanda, Guatemala, Washington, DC, Chicago, the American Southwest, and the U.S.-Mexico border are rich with lessons in the resiliency of the human spirit to resist unthinkable oppression. Itineraries are mindful, balancing the "darkness and light" of a place, always emphasizing how students have power as Americans to make positive change.[1]

Why take rich kids on socially conscious trips? Our premise: Wealthy teenagers can become ethically engaged global citizens through experiential learning. Critics on the Left and Right express contrary opinions about the merits. What kinds of criticisms? On the Right, vehement accusations of "socialist youth indoctrination" from influential parents once pressured client schools in Florida against booking our programs in Cuba. On the Left, righteous insistence that short-term travel to developing communities is in effect "poverty porn" that fosters "white saviorism and imperialist thinking." While it is true that not all motives for social justice travel may be authenticated as longitudinally altruistic, many socially conscious travel programs attract teachers and students who share that goal. Peace Works Travel's approach focused on critical understanding of, in the big picture, the military industrial complex. As American consumers, do we want to feed a system that profiteers on the Global South? How will fostering a true curiosity for the human impact of U.S foreign and domestic policy allow young people to be more effective in the world? Asked differently: What is a wealthy child to "acquire" upon a deep dive into the ugly underbelly of American exceptionalism, greed, and the will to power?

Through active engagement with people adversely affected by U.S. policies—current and contemporary—our travelers ultimately understood three distinct but related facts: (1) As people who suffer the negative impact of U.S. policy primarily lack the means to redress injustice, it is our responsibility to know and care about this; (2) young people can help create peace by taking action now and taking lessons to the future; and (3) privileged student travel provides sustainable support for ethical nongovernmental organizations (NGOs) around the world. Using the travel experience to create radical empathy in privileged young people is, of course, irrefutably fraught. Risky. Laborious. And not for the reasons one might think.

The traditional model of elite education is nakedly transactional. Students "do X for points." This, then, translates into systems of grade point averages (GPAs) and athletics and scores. The reward is access to institutions of higher learning and, eventually, prestigious employment. Over the long term, the purpose and expense of elite education thereby become less about skills mastery and applied intelligence than about social currency. Elective educational travel experiences disrupt the traditional dispensation of knowledge. A student actively *chooses* to travel and seek new empirical evidence for their worldview. Contrasted with the passive acceptance of a standard annual curriculum, the demand for *real-world* applied learning is student-driven. Along the K–12 trajectory, young people—born naturally compassionate—are open to experiences of the heart. Many are very aware of how lucky they are. Inspired by teachers who pursue adventurous modalities of learning, authentic student interest travel experiences create an opportunity. Teacher chaperones who want to experience transformative learning with the students together supply the labor. Authentic student curiosity thus fuels the market demand for socially conscious travel.

RISK MANAGEMENT AND RELATIONSHIP-BUILDING

At the intersection of risk management, "urban wilderness with handrails," we are walking the line between making the experience judiciously "safe" for the students and respecting local practices. While we navigate relationships that foster effective cross-cultural connection for mutual benefit, we must proceed with mindfulness of the supposed "gain" for others. Along the Mekong Delta, the bicycle ride with local students in a lively cultural exchange is extraordinarily heart opening. The connections transcend the moment, with Vietnamese and U.S. kids in joyful friendships that live on through social media across the Pacific Ocean. It's a connection unthinkable to the ancestors of these nations, those who once fought and killed one another in what they refer to as the "American War." At home, in parent meetings disclosing all of our traveling activities, questions arise: "How safe are those bicycles? Do all students wear helmets? What accommodations are there for students who cannot ride bicycles?" These kinds of questions force the navigation of balancing acts. Our partners may not want their communities littered with (what will become) nonrecyclable broken bicycle helmets. It is made politely clear to us that some of our Mekong Delta friends may resent bicycle helmet introduction. Why are the American teenagers more precious than the Vietnamese teens? On balance, we teachers choose safety over cultural offense: shipping 50 bicycle helmets to this community for imposition of our standards.

Cross-cultural engagement is a weighing of interests and concerns. It's a dynamic process: shifting the priorities throughout the travel experience.

I'm reminded of a poignant moment on our Crossing Borders program in Tijuana, attending to a student who was feeling "triggered" by serving people at a refugee soup kitchen. The teenager literally couldn't handle "smelling poverty" up close. She requested chaperone supervision elsewhere so she could take a break and process her emotional disequilibrium, though our shift serving food was nowhere near complete. Accommodating the American teen's emotional preferences in that moment would be an absurd allocation of resources. I said no: She needed to finish the 90 minutes. "Take a seat in the corner. Keep your mind open to what's happening here." Privately, our NGO partner remarked: "When we talk about marginalized communities, the purpose of these travel programs is to bring the people who exist on the sidelines into the center." She took my wrist, turned my hand upwards, and pressed into the center of my palm, my fingers instinctually cupping to create a vessel. She continued. "Learning from desperate people who live on the fringe, means being present to their pain. And, honestly? The upset the rich kids might feel in here is not my primary concern. I care about the hungry."

On balance, most social activists enjoy building relationships with elite students who—let's name it—can end the suffering of hundreds with the swift intersection of a caring heart and easy access to wealth. Could that positive community change occur between Laotian cluster bomb survivors and privileged teenagers on a spontaneous Mekong Delta bike ride? It can, and it has, and it will again. In this way, we've generated funding for professional landmine clearing from countless hectares, rendering agricultural land productive after decades of random, injurious detonations. The benefits, as all stakeholders can attest, outweigh the costs.

The challenge of experiencing beautiful places with eyes open to social inequities requires trust and fortitude. Our work is to harness the edge of elite travelers' culture shock for good. The lines here are delicate. To be clear: Students with demonstrated history of mental fragility ought not travel as such. But the elite students we serve have different issues: They have been emotionally insulated from the cost of their privilege. The human capital, resource acquisition supply chain, the U.S.-led militarism, and environmental degradation which have afforded their comfortable existence are primarily invisible to them. The kids who self-select to travel with us suspect this to be true. Regardless, they want to go and see the world—warts and all—for themselves.

SHIFTING CONSCIOUSNESS

As Jean Theoharis (2018) brilliantly articulates in *A More Beautiful and Terrible History: The Uses and Misuses of Civil Rights History*, we must, "encourage young people to identify with those who challenge the status quo to fight for justice, not simply to emulate and celebrate the rich and power-ful" (p. 17). Framing civil rights education and justice struggles as something of "the past" allows us to ignore a national reckoning with contemporary inequality requiring redress. Systematized injustice is outsourced globally, and the poor are compelled to bear a disproportionate burden. Socially conscious student travel that highlights inequity necessarily fosters an awareness of one's own opportunity to make change.

Upon connecting meaningfully with the people in a given place, students can shift consciousness. What happens when we show students sweatshop textile factories and acres of imported plastic garbage that the Cambodians recently stopped purchasing from U.S. waste management companies? The intersection of love for the Khmer people they've befriended and personal awareness of their role as consumers compels a change in behavior. Use less. Need less. Help more. Armies of student travelers taking immediate social action upon return home is not the lone metric of success. Rather, it's the opening of possibilities to perceive others still fighting for basic human dignity with more nuanced appreciation. These lessons evolve over time into the future as young people more readily perceive someone else's reality. In this way, students can establish a shared purpose with others who demand that the United States live up to its promise of liberty and justice for all.

To read an interview with Alethea Tyner Paradis and learn more about other contributors to this volume, visit www.onewaytomakechange.org.

NOTE

1. See https://www.youtube.com/watch?v=pwdzCQhWvy4&feature=emb_logo for a video highlighting a Peace Works trip to Vietnam.

REFERENCE

Theoharis, J. (2018). *A more beautiful and terrible history: The uses and misuses of civil rights history*. Beacon Press.

CHAPTER 19

Building a Class

The Role of Admissions in Anti-Oppressive Education

Sherry Smith

Growing up in Southern California in the 1960s, I had the privilege of being surrounded by many ethnic and religious communities. In my toddler years, I lived in a community that was filled with people of color who looked like me. When I started school, however, my parents moved me and my twin brother to a new district where my mom was an elementary school teacher and, later, a school and district administrator. On this side of town, we provided the "diversity" for our public elementary school. I was the only African American girl and my brother the only African American boy in the school until my four cousins joined us a few years later. I participated in programs through the YMCA and Camp Fire Girls, joined by a few "others"— a Jewish family, a Mexican family, and a peer being raised by a single mom. Starting college, I was again the "only one"—the only African American female participating in Division 1 athletics. Four years later, I was one of only nine African American students to graduate in a class of over 800 students. In fact, for my first professional decade, I was often the "only one." From day one, I had to be better than everyone else, I had to be smarter than everyone else, *and* I had to embrace everyone.

Spending a large majority of my professional career in admissions and college counseling, I have often felt alone, wondering if I really belonged or would ever feel as if I did. And what would I do when I felt I couldn't do it anymore? Even when colleagues challenged my talent, my worth, my ideas, I just kept going and fighting to do better. Even when my peers questioned my ability to do the work—to attract, find, and select the "right" students— I kept going with a smile on my face during the day, frustration in my mind during the afternoon, and a mix of anger and sadness in the evening. I was giving so much to "other people's children" and rarely got to see and spend time with my own two kids. Still, I kept pushing and believing that I could make a difference to be the change I wanted to see in this world.

THE WORK OF ADMISSIONS

While working in independent schools, I created communities and spaces that I hoped looked, felt, and operated in a more inclusive and vibrant manner. My office was a place of honesty, warmth, patience, and reality checking. I helped students and peers put on their "armor" as they went back in the outer world—holding their heads high and their hearts full, asking them to recognize their strengths and challenges—their wide-eyed wonder and blind spots. Each fall, I would meet with the faculty and share the characteristics of their new class in terms of gender, ethnicity, family size, birth order, faith, caregivers, health issues, financial assistance, and parents' occupations. I would invite them to think about their biases as they learned this information and asked them to reflect on how those biases and feelings showed up in their class. And then asked them to think about how these characteristics presented in their own lives. These discussions helped highlight that we all see the world through our own lens.

As the leaders of the team who put these classes together, we tried to recognize all of these characteristics and consider how they might affect the group individually and collectively. How would our school feel to someone who lived these varied lives? It is why we rarely put a kid who could have been an "only" like me by themselves in a class if we could help it. It is why we tried to ensure the curriculum offered every child rich opportunities to see themselves. It is why we made sure that our meals and trips and activities were a part of our tuition so that no family would be singled out. And invariably, it was why, each year, I grew and learned that I would never get it all right—but would keep trying.

As I moved to deepen my professional work, I am reminded that, every day, I have to be better and more aware for those students and peers who work tirelessly to change the systemic "-isms" for those who have been born on or received the "short end of the stick." My hope is that if I stay "in the game" and on the pathway, I can help those that come after me to continue to make environments that serve all students well. And that we can then realize the talents, dreams, and possibilities of all in our care.

SUSTAINING THE WORK

I will never forget how I trembled with fear and utter sadness when the election of 2016 was over. Both of our daughters, now living in other states, called with deep guttural cries wondering how they were going to live in a world that we only imagined might be coming our way. We had no idea that some of our worst fears would come true. But when I called my mother who is in her 80s, sobbing and wondering how I could go to work and provide the service to students and staff, she said, "Get out of bed, put clothes on, and go to work. You need that and they need you. And, believe me, we have seen much worse." Again, I was reminded that through all my anxiety and trepidation, I forget to look at all our history and all the journeys that many ancestors had lived and walked. I continue to have perspective and make room for the growth mind-set that we all need to move forward.

And we are now asking the educational system to be the place where we initiate the awareness, change, acceptance, and celebration of so many issues that were ignored, buried, or taken for granted: race and ethnicity, economic class, religion, gender/fluidity/sexuality, mental health—and the list continues to grow. What generation will be able to truly see each precious human life as magical, proud, and important? I say to students often: "It's not about you, it's about the folks coming behind you," those you might have to put your arm back to lift and those who will finally understand that we all have something to get and give from being our best selves.

INTERVIEW WITH SHERRY SMITH

June 5, 2020

Katy: How did you get interested in admissions and college counseling?
Sherry: I went to work where I had gone to college trying to get more
   people like me to come to that institution. At some point, I was like,
   "Why?" I was raised as the only African American female child in my
   elementary school. It's in my blood system—it's just what you do. You
   go in and make the best of a situation. You don't just blend in, but you
   make it better for who is coming behind you. Admissions people get
   to create a community—you get to create a class. If you're there long
   enough, you get to create an entire community over time. I was really
   excited about that. But recognizing all of the injustices and inequities
   made it really, really challenging and trying to educate both the people
   going through the process for the first time—the families and the kids
   and then helping teachers understand their students in the classroom—
   it was just *constant*. It's an ongoing, necessary element. As I went
   through my career I kept saying, "I've come as far as I can go. The
   only way I can create deeper change is to walk away. If I walk away,
   then they will ask, 'Why did we lose that person when we didn't want
   to lose her, but she chose to leave?'" I was always able to say to the
   people who came behind me, the large majority of whom were white,
   "Demand these things before you take the job because I couldn't get
   them." Ironically, all the people who came behind me got all of the
   things I never had—not that they used the tools or systems in the ways
   that I would have, but small changes become bigger changes. I left the

schools feeling very torn. It was as simple as needing a database that worked. We "couldn't afford it," but the new person got it. I needed to get people to agree to some protocols. Couldn't get it. The new person came in, and because they were new, people wanted to please them, they got it.

Katy: I would imagine there is a lot of lip service paid to wanting a more diverse student body and then pushback, whether intentional or not, that makes it a lot harder than it has to be.

Sherry: First and foremost is getting people to define what they mean by "diversity," which I had to do *every* year. People would say "I'm diverse—I wear glasses!" I had to find out how people defined it, how they felt about that, and, then, how did that impact action and behavior. If diversity just means "I want people to look different than me, but I want them to act the same," then that becomes the struggle. I need to give people safe space. I'm going to do an admissions day for LGBTQ families so they can ask the questions they want to ask— and they can choose not to come, but I'm giving people space. I did admissions days for single moms who might need to talk about issues that concerned them. Neither of those were my current spaces—they aren't who I am, but I understand that they represented diversity that mattered in the school. Admissions in private school kindergartens? Some of these parents were 40 to 50-year-old white women, with six-year-olds, and they stood next to a 23-year-old Black mother with a five-year-old. Navigating the feelings and conversations with two groups of women could be challenging. The young mother says, "I can't relate to these women. I'm just starting my degree." What did that mean for her and for the others? How was she seen as a room parent since she was not there during the day and showed up in the evenings or on weekends? Again, getting people to understand that there are all these different levels and it's not about making a beautiful rainbow where everyone is the same in terms of how they act. That, for me, became a lifelong question: "How do you build a class?" Beyond appreciating difference, can you accept it and enjoy somebody else's way of being as long as it doesn't hurt and maim you? It may not make you feel good, but it doesn't mean that it's wrong. Because I've been the "only one" so many times in my life, I feel this incredible burden to be a spokesperson and understand the privilege I have, as a light-skinned Black woman with a Harvard degree. You just do the work. If you want to do this kind of work, you do the work and crumble when you crumble. You try to find your allies. Because my immediate family is multiethnic, I still believe in allies. I use my family a lot so that I'm not outing anybody else. I try to give examples from my life and talk about my context to have a conversation so that people can walk out feeling whole, like I wasn't mad at them. I'm just trying to get them to understand. It's about asking what people mean when they say they want "diversity" for their kid. Is it that they want their kid to have a Black friend or someone who speaks Chinese around their kid? For a teacher, it's the conversation about who is in your class and understanding what might trigger you. Can you see a whole child for who they are and what the context is? For the board member, do you understand power dynamics and do you have the capacity to take off your "parent hat" to think about equity for all? Do you know what that means? What are you willing to give up? Because, yes—the pie is as big as we want to make it, but it's still a pie. Do you think about the privileges you've had? Whether all your senses work, or you have food, or that you've never been followed in a store?

Katy: Can you talk about some of the other challenges you faced and how you navigated them?

Sherry: What I had to know when enough was enough. I worked for someone who told me, "You're going to sit on a phone, even if takes you 24 hours, to get this kid into 'this' university." But I said, "I will make one phone call just like I would for any other kid. It's not 24–7." And he said, "Yes, it is." And then I said, "Then I don't need to be here." You have to know yourself and know who you are and if you're willing to walk away. And you have to know when to speak up. We had students of color on financial aid at a very "elite" school I worked at. It was a three-hour commute for them every day. Kids were getting into college, they were applying to 15 different schools to get financial aid, but they couldn't visit a campus to determine the best fit. Their classmates were flying all over the place for months. I went to the head of school and said, "Can we get these kids the opportunity to visit some colleges?" and he said, "Yeah, but we're not paying for that." I said, "But you brought them here and you said they're part of our community!" So, I went home to my husband and said, "I'm going to take out $500 and get these kids on some campuses. I'm not sending kids who I encouraged to apply to a variety of campuses for growth and change to select a college campus they've never set foot on." I remember doing that and it was awful. I know how important it is to feel and taste and breathe a place. It's asking people how far are they willing to do the work for other people's children? If you need to read something, try Lisa Delpit. And there are so many others I could include here. We don't have to reinvent the wheel—there are things out there if someone wants to learn and grow.

Katy: So, you have a head of school that wants the photo op of a diverse school, but when it comes to actually meeting those kids' needs, abdicating any responsibility. You're saying, "If we're bringing in kids who, for whatever reason, can't afford to do campus visits, then we cover that." That feels like a tangible, concrete way to show up. Are there other examples, especially for schools having a reckoning with themselves and recognizing that they're *not* living up to the rhetoric or the mission of the school? Not silver bullets that get rid of racism or homophobia, but what are concrete action steps that people can take?

Sherry: It's about the policies and practices. How do you dismantle inequity? It's about systems and understanding how they were set up—banks and housing and schools. All of it was set up to do exactly what it's doing today. When I worked at one private school, everyone and their mother—college representatives and leaders in the community—wanted to talk to me because that was where the wealth was. They could get the rich white kid *and* the smart Black kid on financial aid—the power dynamics there were absolutely fascinating. Depending on what school you're at, you have different access. While working at another private school with lesser means, fewer folks called and wanted to spend time with our students. And when I went to public charter, *no one* wanted to take the time out of the precious school day to meet with our students—if anything, they would set up a time to come in late afternoon or Saturday. The "charity" happened outside of the school day. It made me feel that the vast majority of my relationships were transactional and that colleges did not actually want to change. I had to make people feel guilty and tell them to put their money where their mouth is. "Don't come into this college fair with Black and Brown children and tell an 11th-grade boy in Algebra 1 that he would be a great candidate for Engineering." Instead, be up-front about the things he needs to do to be ready. I'm trying to give kids opportunities and teach them how to navigate a system that was not set up for them. I had to find a way into people's hearts and minds to feel what so many of our marginalized students feel today. I remember saying to them at the "pre-talk" before a workshop or meeting with students, "If you're not working with Black and Brown students, then you're going to close. They are the future of your student bodies." And now with the pandemic? This is going to close a good 10% of our private colleges. And this was before we had the economic crisis and the racial inequity crisis—and, in California, the wildfire crisis. It's not hard to say and recognize things that lie before us that make our systems inequitable. But many of us have a hard time actually doing the work and making the necessary changes for all, and I mean *all*, students. And that is truly the hard work.

To read more interviews with other contributors to this volume, visit www .onewaytomakechange.org.

CHAPTER 20

"It Shouldn't Be that Hard"

Student Activists' Frustrations and Demands

Julia Chen, Haley Hamilton, Vidya Iyer, Alfreda Jarue,
Catalina Samaniego, Catreena Wang, and Jenna Woodsmall

In the summer of 2020, student activists met online for a Zoom call about their experiences in two wealthy, predominantly white suburban public schools in central Iowa. Affiliated with the Community of Racial Equity (CORE) for Advancement, a student-led organization pushing for anti-racist education, these high schoolers had a lot to say about how they experienced oppression within the schools, their perspectives of the schools' efforts to address inequities relative to the schools' rhetoric, and their advice for how to meaningfully center racial justice in "elite" schools like theirs.

WHAT ARE THE MOST PRESSING ISSUES IN YOUR SCHOOL?

Vidya: A lot of minoritized students at school—BIPOC or LGBTQ—we receive a lot of microaggressions on a daily basis, not only from students but teachers as well. If you try to report those, it is "Oh, I'm sorry" or they sweep it under the rug. You sort of expect that to happen—and that's not healthy to expect that.

Haley: The principal wasn't prepared for a lot of the questions that [we] were asking him [at our meeting about how to support the Black girls who were targeted by white boys calling them the n-word]. He has to love and respect all of his students but coddling the student who attacked these girls isn't respecting and loving his students of color.

Alfreda: Our principal is saying that a lot this year—that he "has to take care of every student" and I agree with that, but, at the same time, I don't, because that's not fair to the victim. One thing I notice a lot is when an act of racial hate is done, they try to sweep it under the rug.

Catreena: There was an incident at a basketball game where a group of white students had Trump masks and were holding signs that were derogatory toward the opposing team. The next couple weeks when they were supposed to be disciplined, there was no action that could be seen toward the students.

Jenna: I remember at a protest we had, one student said that he had been called the "n" word in the hallway and told a teacher and nothing happened and went to another teacher and nothing happened—and that happened *multiple* times. Someone asked what the punishment was for things like that and our administration hesitated because I don't think they knew and eventually someone said suspension, but I don't think that has ever happened. It's a struggle for students to share what happens because they don't think teachers are going to do anything about it because of how they've complacently responded in the past.

Julia: A derogatory term was written on a teacher's whiteboard and it was up for a couple of days, but the teacher didn't do anything about it. People think it's okay to do these types of things because they know the teachers are going to be hesitant to report it. Our school has a problem with establishing that acts of aggression will be punished in some way. I know there is a policy where student discipline has to be private, but even if they don't share *how* they are punished, they could at least share that this kind of behavior is unacceptable. But they don't, so kids continue to think it is okay and these things go unchecked.

Alfreda: It has become so normalized to the point that it's okay for a white kid to go through an "insensitive racist phase" where they think saying the "n" word is okay or say insensitive things to the LGBTQ+ community, but some of them don't grow out of that phase. It makes me angry.

Haley: There's a lack of diversity in advanced classes and extracurriculars. When I'm in an AP class, I feel like I have to be the smartest person in the room to debunk some sort of stereotype. It seems like teachers or coaches don't really understand that all Black students aren't the same.

Catalina: A teacher who runs a team a lot of us CORE students were on champions how woke and liberal he is and that's how our school is portrayed—as a wealthy, "woke" public school, but our real impacts don't seem to be at the forefront of our school's thoughts. Our coaches were blatant about pointing out our diversity in the name of "anti-racism." But when I and two other students are constantly being name dropped, used as props in photos, or the subject of many "jokes," it isn't anti-racism—it's tokenism.

Jenna: Show choir is really bad. It's definitely majority white kids and when they have their outfits and hair and makeup and all of them have to look alike—I'm just so frustrated for the students of color, the few that [there] are. I remember one had to wear the same tights as the other girls and she is Black—it was just so frustrating for her because you had to look "uniform." It's just a very whitewashed activity. It's really telling that one of the things we pride ourselves on a lot is something that is not diverse.

Vidya: I know that there's a lot of tokenism and racism in athletics. Our new coach kept passing students of color that had gone to a lot of meets before and replaced our spots with other white students. We all had similar experiences of asking the coach if we could go to meets and she would make up excuses that were false. I didn't diffuse the situations because I was young, and I wasn't in CORE yet. I didn't know my voice and I didn't want to speak up about something and get in trouble.

WHAT IS WRONG WITH CURRENT EQUITY WORK?

Catreena: Our school has been saying they're open to conversations with students of color. In theory, the plan is good but when you bring up concerns, a lot of the administration get really defensive and say what they've been doing in the past, which is not helpful because we're trying to give critique on what could be done better.

Jenna: It's like they're putting Band-Aids on stuff and they get really defensive about everything. When we do try to offer things, they just get really confused. Our leaders tell us that they need our voices, but we offer things and then they don't do anything.

Vidya: Seeing all the teachers in the library during professional development for this "deep equity" thing—I don't know much about what they learn, but I do know that a lot of the teachers I have would openly make fun of it or express their boredom and frustration with having to do it, which I think is really harmful. If I'm in the classroom and a teacher is like, "Oh, I have an equity meeting today" [in a sarcastic voice] I feel invalidated because this stuff is made for students of color so that microaggressions don't happen. When they hear teachers say "Ugh, equity," a lot of white students internalize that, and it ends up perpetuating what we see in our school. So, that's counterproductive.

Haley: It seems like at our school, the things they're doing are baby steps. Everyone in that building is an adult above the age of 14 and they should be treated that way. If a kid yells at girls and calls them monkeys and other racial slurs, he's an adult. [Some of the equity work is] a step in the right direction, but we need to be *10,000* steps in the right direction right now. It shouldn't be that hard.

Alfreda: One time [in the principal advisory group for which the principal actively recruited BIPOC students], we were talking about safety and all the white kids were like, "Oh, I feel safe," and I was like, "Well, I don't." And then they tried blaming it on the people I hung around and I was like, "That's not even it right there. I don't feel safe because there are white supremacist kids at our school. You guys don't see that, but I do." [The principal] tries to make it "diversity" more than "equity." That's not really helping—you want equity, you want us to be there so it looks like students of color are being heard, but we're actually being silenced.

Vidya: I remember that meeting where we talked about safety and I was the only person of color in my small group and I was like, "Yeah, I don't feel safe at this school because there are white supremacists here" and the people writing down my answers were like, "Oh, okay," but they didn't write it down and then they would write stuff down about vaping or something stupid. Sometimes I feel so invalidated because I'm talking to these people and I want them to understand so badly, but they choose not to.

HOW DO YOU KNOW WHEN YOU CAN TRUST ADULTS TO SUPPORT ANTI-RACISM?

Haley: Even before [our advisor] talked about how she was into all the work she does, you can just tell. On the first day, she made everybody feel comfortable when she made everyone use their pronouns so nobody felt on the spot for that. I've had teachers ask me if I like [the TV show] *Blackish*. No, I don't. [Our advisor] was more helpful than that. It was a comforting space. There was a lot of representation in her room. If there were kids saying sexist things, she would shut it down immediately: "No, you're not going to talk like that in my classroom."

Julia: There's this one teacher—I think it is her transparency that makes me feel so comfortable in her class. She teaches World History so naturally we talk about race and culture quite frequently. However, she acknowledges that her being white is going to affect her views and she makes it clear that she's never going to truly understand certain aspects because of her identity. Despite this, I know she's always willing to try to learn more.

Catreena: My relationships with teachers depend on their personal beliefs. I like it when teachers share their viewpoints even though I know admin doesn't want them to have a bias, but it's nice knowing what teachers think so you know to go to them if you have a problem.

Catalina: The teachers I feel safe with are all very productive people and members of society. [One] is a city council member. He consistently goes out of his way to teach about Black, Chicano, Indigenous, queer history. [Our advisor] goes out of her way to welcome students. She creates spaces that showcase authors or students or people of color who are women and that's a signal to me that I'm welcome in that space. They all go out of their way to include me in conversations, to include my history, to be intersectional. Especially for students of color who are queer and overachieving students— we don't get peace throughout our day or breaks so, while I'm in school, to see that I am wanted and showcased in that space is super helpful.

Vidya: Last year, when I was taking my European history class— Europe is majority white, but Europe kind of screwed over a lot of countries in its history and we didn't cover that in its entirety. We talked about it a little bit, but it was all from a white perspective. We talked about the British Raj for like one minute during the French and Indian War. I definitely didn't feel like I was represented in that curriculum, but I *did* feel represented in [my other history teacher's] curriculum, which was really great. And being a queer student—I'm not out to a lot of teachers because I don't feel comfortable being out to them. It's difficult to judge whether a teacher will be receptive, but there are signs when they have an inclusive curriculum, or they go out of their way to make you feel welcome.

Alfreda: When students of color go to them with a complaint, their job isn't the first thing on their mind or how the principal is going to react. The student and how they can help is what they're thinking about. I remember one time we were so frustrated, and we were telling [our history teacher] about it. He used his city councilman privilege and he sent this email to the principal. [Our advisor] went out of her way to make [the girls who were attacked] feel safe and that if they wanted to have a protest that CORE would support them. It's just making sure that they know they have a support system and not caring about everything else.

Jenna: The same teacher Julia was talking about—I really value her honesty and openness. I feel like she has a physically open room that is comforting. I remember when they announced that AP World was going to be cut, she talked about how frustrated she was about it. Even though it was cut, she still taught us stuff. It showed me that no matter what the college board decides to do, she's going to make sure history is not going to be whitewashed.

WHAT IS YOUR IDEAL SCHOOL?

Vidya: My ideal school? There would be some sort of protocol that would happen if a student was hateful. It doesn't have to be a huge punishment—I just want them to know it was wrong and never do it again.

Haley: I would say less things being reactionary. We all knew that kid was going to do something racist [who attacked the girls]. He's literally a white supremacist. We should have been able to stop four girls from being traumatized by this scary, weird dude. There should have been a punishment for him way before.

Alfreda: I agree with making sure there are set guidelines. I think of the school handbook where it talks about dress code—the fact that they have these rules and punishments if you disobey the dress code, then they should have something dealing with racial hate and microaggressions. The white coddling thing? That needs to stop.

Julia: I would love to see more people of color as teachers and administration because there aren't any teachers of color—on the school board, there might be one and she's working really hard to fight with us, but I think that if we were able to get more POC onto the school board, it would hold the school more accountable for doing these things they might not realize they're doing because of their white identity. Having representation is *so* important for young people growing up. Not only does this positively affect students of color, but it also can be beneficial for the general population of students because it would expose them to a new level of diversity in a field that has been predominantly white.

Catreena: The biggest for me would be, instead of fixing these racial problems in high school, is teaching about this in elementary. Now we're trying to fix problems people grew up thinking, so just prevent them from even starting.

WHAT LESSONS HAVE YOU LEARNED FROM YOUR ACTIVISM?

Jenna: [We just issued a] list of demands that was actually created by an alum who goes to Stanford. It was a big collaboration of sharing resources and [figuring out] when to release it to the school. It was based on our school's response to Black Lives Matter. They wrote a one-page thing and it was really generic and then two days later, they posted a picture of graduates with police officers and called them "Heroes in Blue." It was so hypocritical and that sparked it. The beginning was us asking them to apologize and condemn the police officers.

Julia: After that statement came out, they were like "Okay, we hear you and we're going to listen to you" but they never released any type of apology. It took multiple people sending multiple emails that they should acknowledge their mistakes until they would actually do it. It's not until we have angry emails that they actually acknowledge their mistakes.

Catreena: Another thing we did that made them reply was that we did it so publicly. All the other students at our school who weren't involved with CORE were saying things to them online so everyone could see what was happening rather than sending a private email that no one could see.

Jenna: Another big problem with us is a Twitter account that basically talks about [school] sports, but they have done a lot of really bad stuff. It's run by students, but they had to put it in their bio that they're not affiliated with the school. There are so many stories about them harassing people. One of our demands was that the admin condemns those actions, but that hasn't happened. They just keep saying they're not affiliated, but that's not doing anything for anyone.

Catalina: Alfreda was the mastermind behind this—getting the equity cords at graduation. It validates equity work, you know? And then having our presence around the Des Moines area and having organized state meetings and having merch is incredible. Our CORE students are frequently talking to teachers, admin, or staff whether it be on the business of CORE or a personal issue with some injustice in school. It's so many small things, but they all work to validate CORE and show how organized, how professional, how productive we are as an organization.

Vidya: We're not going to rest until this is fixed. The school board and superintendent at our district wrote up a six-point plan of stuff they want to do to make our schools more equitable. As CORE, we're working with the superintendent and we're talking about hiring an equity director. They had written up a job description before and we had suggestions—it was amazing because the superintendent was super receptive and added in our input. It was super refreshing to see her responding to us without being defensive or vague. By the end she was like, "Okay, so you want us to use stronger language and not be too careful" and we're like, "Yeah, you get it. Great."

Catreena: Reaching out to your community as a resource—we are trying to write a new proposal with parents of color, so it's nice to know that you're not the child trying to do stuff, but you have adults. It's frustrating to be a student and not having your voice heard in a room of adults—but if you have another adult with you, they'll take you seriously.

Catalina: You have to come in with a plan and you have to come in with students who are ready to be organized. I am not the most organized person in the world, but when I work with Vidya, we make probably the best team. You need the passion, the organization, and the resources for it. I'm very proud of us and our entire CORE chapter because, to put it simply, we don't care how many hours it takes. Vidya is always ready to pull me back when I get too angry and I'm always ready to make a plan and say, "This is entirely feasible" or "How can I help you?" You need to make sure that your guys are safe and that anyone who is in opposition is handled and called out. You're building a family that's prepared and wants to protect each other from racism, homophobia, misogyny, and so forth. When any organization starts like GSA or CORE, you have those kids who started it and were passionate about it, but if you don't get enough younger kids to pick it up to continue the organization, then your "family" dies, and you lose your foundation. You have to be super strategic in who you're recruiting.

Vidya: A good example is the protest at our school after a student called a group of Black girls "monkeys" and other really awful racial slurs. They came to our advisor and she helped them make a plan for a protest where we were all going to come wearing shirts that say "Racial Justice Now." A ton of teachers participated, so many students. I think it's a really great example of CORE helping other students—to lift them up and create a super successful event through organization, people coming together to create change. We didn't take over the event. It was *their* event, they were leading, and it was their struggle that we were trying to show. You need to have the passion, but you also have to be able to make that change with really good organization. There are so many students who want to take the baton and go on next year.

Katy: So, here's a tough question. Something that happens in high-status schools is that leadership opportunities can easily become social capital things that students do to leverage access to more privilege. This just sounds like such a deep part of who you are and the hours and energy you pour into it are totally worth it. How do you keep a group like CORE from becoming something for a student to write a really good college essay?

Alfreda: Something that our CORE chapter did really well was that we made sure to call out whoever we thought wasn't respecting what we did. We all call each other out on our BS.

Catalina: Making it personal is the biggest thing. CORE is mostly in-person activities and a lot of it is social [to build family] so when you do that, it's really, really hard to commodify people who you care for. When it's about how people are being marginalized, oppressed, and invalidated and you know people who feel like that or you are a person who feels like that, it's impossible to continue that commodification or objectification in your head. People who are able to commodify other human beings are not going to last more than three meetings.

To read more interviews with other contributors to this volume, visit www. onewaytomakechange.org.

Afterword

Paul Gorski

Full of curiosity and tempered hope, I watched educational leaders very closely during the months following the murder of George Floyd. As the protests grew, I wondered how school and district leaders would respond to growing pressure to at least perform new concern about racism and to show solidarity with Black communities. The performances weren't disappointing as performances. I read dozens of letters written by white principals and superintendents extolling the virtues of unity and inclusion, insisting they and their institutions were anti-racist. Some, knowing the backlash that would come, even insisted in these letters that Black Lives Matter. (Not surprisingly, I know of several schools and districts where there were fierce battles over whether to change "Black" to "All.") I especially noted how many of these letters came from suburban public school districts and prestigious independent schools, where leaders might feel especially pressed to present themselves and their institutions in carefully crafted do-gooder terms.

Here's what I never saw during that time: any such letter to which school leaders appended either a list of ways racism persisted in their own institutions or a list of ways they were determined to eliminate that racism. All of these leaders were committed to the idea of anti-racism, it appeared, everywhere but their own spheres of influence. Sometimes it seems as though educational gatekeepers, especially the liberal-ish ones, feel tremendous pressure to appear "woke" while trying to navigate competing pressure to not act "woke."

This is one clear and troubling way Derrick Bell's (1980) interest convergence theory operates in education. Bell's assertion is that, in the end, progress toward racial justice is won only when it benefits white people. Once the interests of racial justice start to crowd too far up against the interests of white people, most white people and white-dominated institutions will divest their resources and energies from anti-racism. School and district leaders—white school and district leaders in particular—know how important it is to cultivate the illusion of a commitment to equity and justice. It's the *illusion* of equity and justice that is rewarded.

That's why so much of the equity and justice work in predominantly white and wealthy schools is high on visibility and low on institutional impact. Sure, we have a neat restorative justice initiative and some cool student diversity programming. But as soon as the equity and justice work might infringe upon the racial, economic, or other systems of advantage and disadvantage—as soon as we move our diversity, equity, and inclusion (DEI) efforts from the D and the I to the E—we risk hitting a point of interest *divergence* (Johnson & Caraballo, 2019). If we're in a private school we might risk alienating donors, whose disproportionate whiteness and distaste for anti-racism may be attributable in part to the racist history of the institutions that produced them. If we're in a public school, perhaps we risk the wrath of an equity-skittish board or community members. As Ayo Magwood explained in Chapter 6 of this book, if we're feeling more vulnerable to white parents than to students who are racially marginalized in our classrooms and schools, we might be performing racial equity but we are practicing racial oppression.

In equity literacy terms, we call this the "pacing for privilege" racial equity detour (Gorski, 2019). We create the illusion of movement toward anti-racism, toward equity and justice more broadly, but we move only in carefully choreographed baby steps, embracing equity and justice commitments in ways that are more responsive to the interests of the people with the least amount of interest in equity and justice while sacrificing the well-being, access, and opportunity of the people most desperate for equity and justice. Of course, against a tidal wave of white supremacy, taking baby steps means, in essence, that we're moving backward or, at best, stuck in the wet heavy sand of oppression. As a diversion to our inaction, we point vigorously at the diversity celebrations and micro-bits of neat-sounding curricular inclusion. This happens in bigger institutional work around equity and justice, and, more relevant to this book, it happens in the equity, justice, and anti-oppressive educational efforts in schools.

This is why I was thrilled when the editors of this volume, Katy Swalwell and Daniel Spikes, took a critical turn in their introduction, redefining "elite schools" as those that are genuinely anti-oppressive and that strive in serious, uncompromising ways toward justice. It's also why I felt energized by the ways the chapter authors collectively refused to settle for the illusion. That's what this book felt like to me: a collective insistence that we leap out of our baby steps and take more seriously the moral imperative to educate ourselves and all students—including, if not especially, those attending predominantly white and wealthy schools—not just about oppression but also about the work of anti-oppression.

Broadly speaking, my most important takeaway from this book was the sophistication with which the contributors collectively constructed a framework—philosophical, theoretical, practical, applicable—for what this can and ought to look like on the ground, in practice. In that spirit, rather than identify core points from each chapter, I offer in this afterword my humble synthesis of the collective knowledge, nudging, and framing the authors, with guidance from the co-editors, gifted me in this book.

I MUST BE VIGILANT AGAINST THE DANGERS OF WHITE LIBERALISM

Primary among the barriers to creating and sustaining elite-ly anti-oppressive schools might be the sort of white liberalism (Matias, 2016) so clearly demonstrated in the aforementioned "solidarity" letters from school and district leaders. When I gather with colleagues who have spent much of their professional lives doing equity and justice work in schools, this is something we often discuss: In many cases the hardest contexts in which to achieve real racial justice traction are those with the highest percentages of liberal-ish white educators or those where the gatekeepers embrace a white liberal-ish approach to equity and justice.

In his "Letter from a Birmingham Jail," the Reverend Dr. Martin Luther King Jr. lamented white moderates' tendency to "prefer a negative peace, which is the absence of tension to a positive peace which is the presence of justice." If we're being honest, we have to acknowledge that a vast majority of the DEI teaching and initiatives to which white and wealthy children are exposed is rooted firmly in that negative peace. Their comfort and the false sense of their "innocence" are prioritized over the truth or the anti-oppressive needs of students of color, students experiencing poverty, and students marginalized in other ways. And those more marginalized classmates so often are forced to sit and smile through that, another layer of marginalization.

Sure, I might be celebrated for helping students appreciate diversity, learn about cultures, and maybe even participate in service learning, but say the words "white supremacy" and I might find myself in trouble at work. Although few of the authors named white liberalism of this type explicitly, many alluded to it. Liberalism, with its multicultural arts fairs and Diversity Days, can be alluring, especially to white educators. But we can't multicultural arts fair our way to justice. I need to be vigilant about that reality by prioritizing equity and justice over diversity education, over kindness, over vague notions of niceness, over all the edgeless and fluffy reimaginings of anti-oppressive education.

I MUST REMEMBER THAT, NO, EVERY PERSPECTIVE IS NOT VALID

Yes, part of educating for social justice is helping students with privileged positionalities understand how those positionalities inform their worldviews and perspectives. This requires me to have the patience needed to help them work through cognitive dissonance, especially in those moments when I feel as though I'm teaching against every other influence in students' lives. It does little good to wag my fingers at what, for some students who are white or wealthy or otherwise privileged, is the only socialization to which they've had access at home or perhaps even at school prior to walking into my classroom.

However, I must be careful not to bow to the pressure to see myself merely as an objective facilitator. I must reject the notion that every perspective is equally credible and worthy of validation in anti-oppressive learning. If I allow white supremacist views or deficit-oriented bootstrap ideologies to go unaddressed in my classroom, seeing them simply as additional viewpoints, then in essence I reproduce in my classroom or school the same oppressive conditions that exist everywhere else. That's anti-anti-oppressive.

The best-case scenario pedagogically has students comfortable and prepared to speak up and push back against oppressive views shared by one another. But if that doesn't happen, I *must* speak up. I *must* push back. I must never, under any circumstance, allow oppressive views to float in the air unchecked.

I MUST TAKE HONEST STOCK OF MY
ANTI-OPPRESSIVE PACING AND INTENTIONS

Part of the contextual trickiness of emphasizing social justice and anti-oppressive teaching in white and wealthy schools—and, by extension, for white and wealthy students—is that white and wealthy students are not the only types of students attending white and wealthy schools. As important as implementing authentically anti-oppressive education in these schools is, we risk re-privileging privilege even in the context of anti-oppression education when we focus too intensely on how to implement it effectively for white and wealthy students if we set aside the pedagogical and well-being interests of their less racially, economically, or otherwise privileged classmates. Those students—the ones experiencing the oppression—need us to embrace an approach that prioritizes *their* interests, that moves at *their* intellectual, experiential, and political pace.

What this means for me, as an educator, is that under no circumstances should students or participants of color in my classes or professional development workshops be forced to sit through a debate about, for example, whether systemic racism exists or whether "white supremacy" is too harsh a term to describe white supremacy. It does and it's not.

They should not have to sit through conversations about appreciating diversity or lessons about cultural competence while we step gingerly around any real conversations about racism. This is what I was thinking about as, in Chapter 1, Quentin Wheeler-Bell described the "pathology of privilege"—a sort of privilege-infested class consciousness in which people embrace their privilege as earned and justifiable. I thought, I wonder how I might unintentionally reproduce this dynamic even in the context of social justice teaching or institutional change efforts by pacing and framing conversations with the intention of helping white people "get" racism, cisgender people "get" transphobia and other forms of gender identity oppression, and so on. When I imagine good pedagogy as "meeting people where they are," to which people am I referring? If I cater to the learning needs of wealthy and white students at the expense of real learning experiences for students who are racially or economically marginalized, am I supporting the former's sense of educational entitlement? I think so.

I must be careful not to embrace an approach to anti-oppressive education for which my primary intention is to nudge along the most resistant students. I especially should not use the emotional labor (or any sort of labor) of people who are targeted with oppression to do the nudging. (Please check that privilege walk.) They, too, deserve a pedagogy and pace crafted around their learning needs and desires, around their well-being. I also must avoid classroom ground rules or community norms that, whatever their intention, protect the feelings of privileged students while policing the emotions of students who are marginalized. Students who experience racism have the right to be pissed off about that. I must encode that right into my pedagogy.

I MUST CULTIVATE STRUCTURAL UNDERSTANDING AND ACTION, NOT JUST INTERPERSONAL AWARENESS

Racially, economically, and otherwise privileged people need to understand our own positionalities, how advantage operates in our lives, and our individual biases, as well as how to work toward deeper anti-oppressive consciousness and action. The trouble is, too often this inward-facing learning is seen as the end goal. Perhaps we hope to encourage white educators to consider the implications of their white privilege knapsacks or help white students explore how their implicit biases cause them to stereotype classmates. These are worthy formative goals, but insufficient summative goals.

All of that inward-facing or even interpersonal learning ought to be in service to, in preparation for, the work of understanding deep structural oppression and what transformative structural change looks like. It's important to grasp individual positionalities, presumptions, and privileges, but I have to be careful not to emphasize that process at the expense of grasping how racism operates structurally or institutionally. I must recognize that white privilege is a symptom of white supremacy, not its cause, so exploring individual white privilege (I can do *this* because I am white) while not connecting it to white supremacy and structural racism (*this* is how racial disadvantage is built into policies, practices, and institutional culture) severely understates the severity of racial injustice (Leonardo, 2004). Whether I'm leading professional learning with educators or teaching a roomful of youth, I must ensure that individual identity work is what prepares us to work toward that structural destination and is not mistaken for the destination itself.

Similarly, I must realize that awareness or consciousness raising is what prepares us to work toward justice; it is not justice itself. So, as many of this book's contributors argued one way or another, the measure of social justice learning isn't just awareness or consciousness, but action. I must educate toward action. Otherwise, social justice learning for privileged-identity people and privilege-propping institutions is more about helping those people and institutions gain knowledge and build their own intellectual capital—the knowledge and skills to perform wokeness—than about actual anti-oppressive change.

ACKNOWLEDGMENTS

I'd like to end this afterword by thanking Katy Swalwell, Daniel Spikes, and the contributors to *Anti-Oppressive Education in "Elite" Schools: Promising Practices and Cautionary Tales from the Field* for their humility, wisdom, and truth telling. I am a better educator for having read it. I aspire to the book's integrity.

REFERENCES

Bell, D. (1980). Brown v. Board of Education and the interest-convergence dilemma. *Harvard Law Review, 93*(3), 518–533.

Gorski, P. (2019). Avoiding racial equity detours. *Educational Leadership, 76*(7), 56–61.

Johnson, L., & Caraballo, L. (2019). Multicultural education in the US and UK in the 1980s and beyond: The role of interest convergence-divergence. *Multicultural Education Review, 11*(3), 155–171.

Leonardo, Z. (2004). The color of supremacy: Beyond the discourse of 'white privilege.' *Educational Philosophy and Theory, 36*(2), 137–152.

Matias, C. (2016). 'Why do you make me hate myself?': Re-teaching Whiteness, abuse, and love in urban teacher education. *Teaching Education, 27*(2), 194–211.

About the Editors and Contributors

Katy Swalwell, PhD, is a former classroom teacher and professor specializing in anti-oppressive education, especially in "elite" contexts. As lead equity specialist for the Equity Literacy Institute, she conducts professional development for schools and districts across the United States and beyond. Her scholarship, podcast (*Our Dirty Laundry*), curriculum projects like the Amazing Iowa children's books series, and teacher guides like *Social Studies for a Better World* (written with Noreen Naseem Rodríguez) all stress the importance of anti-oppressive histories in developing a critical consciousness. www.katyswalwell.com

Daniel Spikes, PhD, is a former classroom teacher and assistant professor whose research focused on racial disparities in educational outcomes and the policies and practices of school districts, schools, and school leaders that serve to perpetuate and/or ameliorate these disparities. He also focused on the professional development of adult learners on critical consciousness and how this development contributes to the improvement of educational experiences and outcomes for all students. He is currently an assistant superintendent in the state of Texas.

Ashley Akerberg is an educator, facilitator, emotional intelligence coach, community organizer, and human resources professional. She has facilitated anti-racism workshops and program development for schools and was a pioneering member of the CENTER Coalition in Portland, Oregon, which empowers children and youth to lead positive change in their communities.

Gabby Arca is currently the Special Education teacher at a bilingual public elementary school in Oregon. She's passionate about supporting all kids in being their best selves and in honing their voice for themselves and others.

Beth Catlett, PhD, is an associate professor in the Department of Women's and Gender Studies and the director of the Faculty Scholarship Collaborative in DePaul's College of Liberal Arts & Social Sciences. Beth also co-founded and directs the Beck Research Initiative for Women, Gender, and Community that specializes in community-based research involving gendered violence and social movements to create community change.

Julia Chen (she/her/hers) is a senior at Johnston High School in Johnston, Iowa. Julia joined CORE her sophomore year to learn more about the different people and cultures that make up the student body at Johnston. She also wanted to actively engage in CORE discussions and events to promote inclusion, diversity, and equity in her school and community. Julia is grateful to have been given the opportunity to work with such motivated students in the CORE community.

Christiane M. Connors, EdD, served as director of civic engagement at Edmund Burke School in Washington, DC, from 2012 to 2020.

Beth Cooper Benjamin, EdD, is a researcher, educator, consultant, and writer with expertise in girls' leadership development and civic and social justice education, with a particular focus on "elite" and privileged youth. Most recently, she served as founding associate director of the Joseph Stern Center for Social Responsibility at JCC Manhattan, and prior to that she spent a decade on the staff of Ma'yan.

Sonya Crabtree-Nelson, PhD, LCSW, is an associate professor in the Department of Social Work at DePaul University in Chicago. Her research focuses on domestic violence, trauma, and resiliency.

Allen Cross has taught at Wingra School since 1988, co-creating and implementing a theme-based integrated curriculum with his teaching team and multiage groups of 11- to 14-year-olds. He and his partner, Mary Klehr, facilitate local teacher research groups, are among the Founders of Troy Gardens (now Community Groundworks), and have each served as president of the Friends of the Cooperative Children's Book Center.

Rebecca Drago is the director of public purpose at a K–12 independent school outside New York City. She has her master's in social justice education from UMass Amherst, with a focus on dialogue work across race and gender. Prior to this position she has worked in the domestic violence prevention field and has been involved with several radical anti-racist community organizing collectives.

Diane Goodman, EdD, has been teaching and training about diversity and social justice issues for over 30 years. She is the author of the book *Promoting Diversity and Social Justice: Educating People from Privileged Groups* (2nd ed.) and co-editor and contributor to *Teaching for Diversity and Social Justice* (3rd ed.) and other publications. www.dianegoodman .com

Paul Gorski, PhD, is the founder of the Equity Literacy Institute and EdChange. He has more than 20 years of experience helping educators, nonprofit workers, and others strengthen their equity efforts. He has worked with educators in 48 states and a dozen countries. Paul has published more than 70 articles and has written, co-written, or co-edited 12 books on various aspects of education. www.equityliteracy.org

Brandon Grossman is a doctoral student in education at University of Colorado Boulder and an adjunct faculty member at University of Northern Colorado's Center for Urban Education.

Haley Hamilton (she/her/hers) is a 2020 graduate of Valley High School in West Des Moines, Iowa. She joined CORE last year and made great connections with the other students. CORE was a safe place for her to share her struggles as a student of color. CORE helped Haley find her voice and make change possible.

Adam Howard, PhD, is professor of education at Colby College. He is author of *Learning Privilege: Lessons of Power and Identity in Affluent Schooling,* co-author (with 23 of his undergraduate students) of *Negotiating Privilege and Identity in Educational Contexts,* and co-editor (with Rubén Gaztambide-Fernández) of *Educating Elites: Class Privilege and Educational Advantage.*

Vidya Iyer (she/her/hers) is a senior at Valley High School in West Des Moines, Iowa. She joined CORE last year, and it has completely changed her worldview. She has discovered her voice, and she has worked with many people to change their community. She no longer feels afraid to speak up because she knows how important it is for her to speak on these issues, and she loves spending time with all these amazing young activists.

Andrea Jacobs, PhD, is an educator, researcher, and organizational consultant with over 25 years of experience. She is co-founder and partner at Rally Point for Collaborative Change LLC, a consulting practice focused on working across difference to facilitate transformative change.

Cori Jakubiak, PhD, is an associate professor of education at Grinnell College, where she teaches courses in educational foundations, the cultural politics of language teaching, dis/ability studies in education, and ESL and World Language methods.

Alfreda Jarue (she/her/hers) is a 2020 graduate at Valley High School in West Des Moines, Iowa. She was one of the founding members of the first CORE chapter at her school during her junior year and went on to be a facilitator her senior year. CORE not only helped Alfreda decide on a career she sees herself enjoying, but CORE also provided her with many opportunities and the best of friends she could share her experiences with.

Damian R. Jones has been serving as the head of Edmund Burke School in Washington, DC, since the fall of 2014. Prior to his appointment at Burke, Damian spent 11 years as the assistant head of school at the Francis W. Parker School in Chicago, Illinois.

Callie Kane is a language arts teacher at Valley High School in West Des Moines, Iowa. She is the co-sponsor of her school's CORE (Community of Racial Equity) program.

Marc Kruse is a criminal defense lawyer at Rees Dyck Rogala law firm and an instructor in the politics department at the University of Winnipeg.

Petra Lange is one of the founders of CORE for Advancement and the Anti-Racist Collaborative in Des Moines and is a language arts teacher at Valley High School in West Des Moines, Iowa.

Steven Lee currently serves as director of equity, inclusion, and civic engagement at Edmund Burke School in Washington, DC.

Ayo Magwood is an educational consultant specializing in anti-racist education with a decade of classroom experience in both majority low-income Black/Latino charter schools and majority high-income white private schools. Her areas of expertise include teaching about race and social justice through history, root causes, statistical data, and "A Perspectives Consciousness Approach" to discussing race and current issues. www.uprootinginequity.com

Tania D. Mitchell, EdD, is an associate professor of higher education in the College of Education and Human Development at the University of Minnesota. Her scholarship has been published in a number of books and journals, and she is the editor (with Krista Soria) of *Educating for Citizenship and Social Justice: Practices for Community Engagement at Research Universities* (Palgrave Macmillan, 2018) and *Civic Engagement and Community Service at Research Universities: Engaging Undergraduates for Social Justice, Social Change, and Responsible Citizenship* (Palgrave Macmillan, 2016). She is also the editor (with Corey Dolgon and Tim Eatman) of the *Cambridge Handbook of Service Learning and Community Engagement* (Cambridge University Press, 2017) and (with Stephanie

Y. Evans and Andrea D. Domingue) of *Black Women and Social Justice Education: Legacies and Lessons* (SUNY Press, 2019).

Robin Moten has been a member of the English Department at Seaholm High School in Birmingham, Michigan, for over 20 years. Her areas of expertise include curriculum development, researching and practicing deliberative dialogue in the high school classroom, and coordinating service learning and civic engagement pathways for students.

Alethea Tyner Paradis is a history professor at Santa Barbara City College and founder of Peace Works Travel.

Amira Proweller, PhD, is an associate professor of educational policy studies at DePaul University and is the author of *Constructing Female Identities: Meaning Making in an Upper-Middle Class Youth Culture* (SUNY Press, 1998). Her publications have focused on the youth culture and identity formation, community-based service learning, and youth participatory action research and social change.

Tomas Rocha, PhD, is an assistant professor in the Social and Cultural Foundations program at the University of Washington's College of Education.

Gabriel Rodriguez, PhD, is an assistant professor in the School of Education at Iowa State University. His interdisciplinary research explores the relationship between educational inequality and race, specifically the interplay between the academic achievement, equality of opportunity, and identities of Latinx youth and other youth of color in the context of demographically changing schools and communities.

Catalina Samaniego (she/they) is a senior at Valley High School in West Des Moines, Iowa. After joining CORE as a sophomore, Catalina has found a place in her community and new opportunities that have helped her realize her calling to community building. Working with so many talented and productive activists has only stoked her passions and dedication to equity work; she will carry the education she has received from her job and collaboration in CORE in every future circumstance.

Alexa Schindel, PhD, is an associate professor of science education at the University at Buffalo, SUNY and a former middle school science teacher.

Nina Sethi is currently a 3rd-grade teacher, the co-teaching facilitator, and a faculty facilitator of a students of color affinity group at an independent school. Learn more about Nina and Gabby's work at teachpluralism.square space.com and @teachpluralism.

Lisa Sibbett, PhD, is a lecturer in teacher education at the University of Washington, Bothell. Her research explores how teachers can enact social justice pedagogy in classrooms where students with widely divergent levels of power and privilege are asked to reason about the social world together.

Kristin Sinclair, PhD, is an assistant teaching professor in the Masters of Educational Transformation program at Georgetown University. Her research agenda examines the pedagogical and emancipatory potential of the relationships between young people and their places.

Sherry Smith is an educational professional with nearly 40 years' experience in school and college admission, financial aid, recruitment, organizational management, organizational change, and school to college selection and matriculation.

Stacy Smith served as director of leadership until 2020 at Edmund Burke School in Washington, DC. She is a faculty member in the Department of Health, Values and Ethics at Burke.

Nicolas Tanchuk, PhD, is an assistant professor of social and cultural studies in education at Iowa State University.

Sara Tolbert, PhD, is an associate professor of science and environmental education at Te Whare Wānanga o Waitaha University of Canterbury in Aotearoa New Zealand and a former science, ESOL, and environmental educator in New York City, Atlanta, Latin America, and Aotearoa New Zealand.

Catreena Wang (she/her/hers) is a senior at Johnston High School in Johnston, Iowa. She joined CORE last year to share her experiences with discrimination and race after moving from Canada to the Midwest. Not only has CORE inspired her to speak out within her own school district, but she has since discovered a community within the Des Moines metro area of passionate teens working toward social justice. Though she has made meager steps in pushing her community in the right direction, Catreena hopes that no matter where life takes her, she will continue to fight for social change.

Brady Wheatley is the head of Upper School at Rocky Hill Country Day School in East Greenwich, Rhode Island. Brady's teaching expertise is in U.S. history with a focus on race and racism and social justice curriculum development.

Quentin Wheeler-Bell, PhD, is an assistant professor at Indiana University. His research interests are critical theory, critical pedagogy, and radical approaches to democratic education.

Jenna Woodsmall (she/her/hers) is a junior at Johnston High School in Johnston, Iowa. She joined CORE last year as a sophomore with a desire to meet new people and to learn about others' experiences. Joining CORE has been a significant stepping-stone in gaining a better understanding of the experiences those around her face and how to best work toward change.

Index